THE COMPLETE
COSORI AIR FRYER
COOKBOOK

1001 Vibrant, Fast& Easy and Delicious Recipes For The New

COSORI Premium Air Fryer

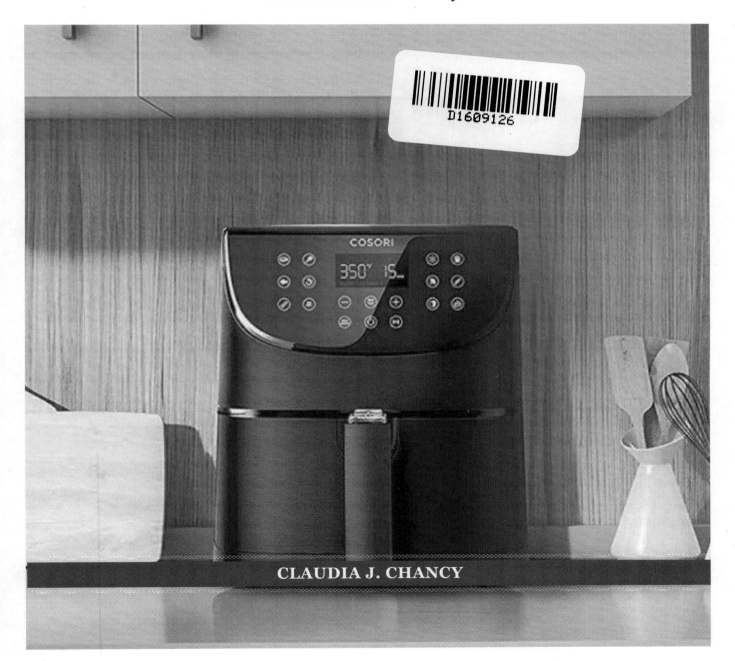

CLAUDIA J. CHANCY

Table of Contents

Introduction   8

Chapter 1
Basics of Cosori Air Fryer   2
Why Get an Air Fryer?   3
What is a Cosori Air Fryer?   3
How Cosori Air Fryer Works   4
Why Should you Get the Cosori Air Fryer?   4

Chapter 2
Start Your Cosori Air Fryer Journey   5
Basic Features of Cosori Air Fryer   6
Functions of Cosori Air Fryer   6
Cosori Air Fryer Safety   7
Tips to Use Cosori Air Fryer   8

Chapter 3
Sauces, Dips, and Dressings   9
Cauliflower Alfredo Sauce   10
Marinara Sauce   10
Red Enchilada Sauce   10
Spicy Southwest Seasoning   10
Dijon and Balsamic Vinaigrette   10
Lemony Tahini   10
Creamy Ranch Dressing   11
Creamy Coconut Lime Dressing 10   11
Hemp Dressing   11
Garlic Lime Tahini Dressing   11
Avocado Dressing   11
Fresh Mixed Berry Vinaigrette   11
Lemon Dijon Vinaigrette   12
Kale and Almond Pesto   12
Shawarma Spice Blend   12

Chapter 4
Breakfast   13
Spinach with Scrambled Eggs   14
Buttermilk Biscuits   14
Bacon and Egg Stuffed Peppers   14
Lush Vegetable Omelet   14
Syrupy Apple Oatmeal   14
Banana Churros with Oatmeal   15
English Pumpkin Egg Bake   15
Honey-Lime Glazed Grilled Fruit Salad   15
Mushroom and Squash Toast   15
Mushroom and Onion Frittata   16
Egg and Sausage Stuffed Breakfast Pockets   16
Bacon and Broccoli Bread Pudding   16
Creamy Raisins Bread Pudding   17
Almond Honey Bread Pudding   17
Doughnut Bread Pudding   17
Grit and Ham Fritters   17
Ham and Corn Muffins   18
Nut and Seed Muffins   18
Buttery Banana Muffins   18
Chocolate Chips Honey Muffins   18
Apple and Walnut Muffins   19
Potato Bread Rolls   19

Creamy Cinnamon Rolls   19
Posh Orange Rolls   20
Avocado Quesadillas   20
Banana Bread   20
Rye and Quinoa Porridge   20

Chapter 5
Poultry   21
Teriyaki Chicken and Bell Pepper Kebabs   22
Lemony Chicken and Veggie Kebabs   22
Spicy Chicken Kebabs   22
Tempero Baiano Brazilian Chicken   22
Sriracha-Honey Glazed Chicken Thighs   23
Lime-Garlic Grilled Chicken   23
Herbed Grilled Chicken Thighs   23
Piri-Piri Chicken Thighs   23
Ginger Chicken Thighs   24
Spicy BBQ Chicken Drumsticks   24
Air Fryer Naked Chicken Tenders   24
Maple-Teriyaki Chicken Wings   24
Crispy Dill Pickle Chicken Wings   25
Chicken Fried Steak   25
Roasted Chicken and Vegetable Salad   25
Lemon Chicken and Spinach Salad   26
Almond-Crusted Chicken Nuggets   26
Easy Tandoori Chicken   26
Roasted Chicken Tenders with Veggies   26
Dill Chicken Strips   27
Blackened Chicken Breasts   27
Israeli Chicken Schnitzel   27
Mayonnaise-Mustard Chicken   27

Chapter 6
Fish and Seafood   28
Honey-Lemon Snapper with Grapes   29
Miso-Glazed Cod with Bok Choy   29
Ginger Swordfish Steaks with Jalapeño   29
Fried Cod Fillets in Beer   29
Parmesan Fish Fillets with Tarragon   30
Cornmeal-Crusted Trout Fingers   30
Southwest Shrimp and Cabbage Tacos   30
Tandoori-Spiced Salmon and Potatoes   31
Baked Salmon in Wine   31
Garlicky Shrimp Caesar Salad   31
Lime-Chili Shrimp Bowl   31
Seasoned Breaded Shrimp   32
Country Shrimp   32
Spicy Orange Shrimp   32
Air Fried Spring Rolls   32
Cajun-Style Fish Tacos   33
Homemade Fish Sticks   33
Crispy Catfish Strips   33
Garlic-Lemon Tilapia   33
Tuna and Cucumber Salad   34
Tuna Patty Sliders   34
Marinated Salmon Fillets   34
Cajun-Style Salmon Burgers   34

Chapter 7
Pork, Beef, and Lamb   **35**
Air Fried Vegetables and Chorizo   36
Air Fried Pork Tenderloins with Apple   36
Air Fried Pork Escalops   36
Five Spice Pork Belly   36
Bbq Pork Empanadas   37
Pork Liver and Buns Soufflé   37
Bacon and Potato Roast   37
Balsamic Steaks   37
Ham and Pear Bake   38
Crispy Sausage Balls   38
Air Fried Steaks with Pesto   38
Bacon-wrapped Filets Mignons   38
Air Fried Lamb and Asparagus   38
Lamb Koftas   39
Air Fried Lamb Steaks and Red Potatoes   39
Herbed Lamb Chops with Roasted Garlic   39
Red Curry Staek   39
Air Fried Pork Tenderloin with Godlen Apples   40
Beef Eggs   40
Classic Beef Sliders   40
Godlen Scotch Eggs   40
Air Fried Baby Back Ribs   41
Ham and Apple Panini   41
Bratwurst Curry   41

Chapter 8
Vegan and Vegetarian   **42**
Black Bean and Tomato Chili   43
Corn and Potato Chowder   43
Grilled Vegetable Pizza   43
Arugula and Broccoli Salad   44
Summer Squash and Zucchini Salad   44
Bean and Corn Stuffed Peppers   44
Cauliflower Steaks with Ranch Dressing   45
Balsamic Mushroom Sliders with Pesto   45
Potatoes with Zucchinis   45
Chermoula Beet Roast   45
Mozzarella Broccoli Calzones   46
Sweet Potatoes with Zucchini   46
Lush Vegetables Roast   46
Potato and Broccoli with Tofu Scramble   47
Cauliflower Tater Tots   47
Lemony Falafel   47
Super Veg Rolls   47
Air Fried Potatoes with Olives   48
Grilled Mozzarella Eggplant Stacks   48
Potato Croquettes   48
Lush Vegetable Salad   48
Golden Pickles   49
Air Fried Asparagus   49
Fig, Chickpea, and Arugula Salad   49

Chapter 9
Rice and Grains   **50**
Polenta Rounds   51
Air Fried Millet Patties   51
Quinoa Cheese Patties   51
Mushroom and Rice Bake   51
Juicy Quinoa Porridge   51
Corn Kernels Koftas   51

Raisins Buttermilk Scones   52
Mini Cornbread Loaves   52
Banana Oatmeal   52
Pecans Oatmeal Cups   52
Almonds Oatmeal   52
Juicy Milk Oatmeal   53
Cranberry Granola   53
Mixed Berry Muffins   53
Apple Oat Muffins   53
Cocoa Muffins   54
Scallion Rice Pilaf   54
Curry Basmati Rice   54
Quinoa and Broccoli Cheese Patties   54
Creamy Butter Corn Fritters   54
Honey Prunes Bread Pudding   55
Cherry Cranberry Bread Pudding   55
Almonds Bread Pudding   55
Figs Bread Pudding   55
Cheesy Macaroni   55
Air Fried Butter Toast   56
Chocolate Chips Granola   56
Rice with Scallions   56
Carrot and Green Peas Rice   56
Pumpkin Porridge with Chocolate   56
Chawal ke Pakore with Cheese   57
Rice Cheese Casserole   57
Millet Porridge with Sultanas   57
Creamy Cornbread Casserole   57
Cheesy Carbonara with Pancetta   57

Chapter 10
Pizza   **58**
Pro Dough   59
Simple Pizza Dough   59
Pizza Margherita   59
Garlic Tomato Pizza Sauce   60
Pepperoni Pizza with Mozzarella   60
Mushroom and Spinach Pizza   60
Ham and Pineapple Pizza   61
Mozzarella Meatball Pizza   61
Arugula and Prosciutto Pizza   61
Spinach, Egg and Pancetta Pizza   62
Chicken and Butternut Squash Pizza   62
Pear Pizza with Basil   62
Prosciutto and Fig Pizza   63
Cheese Tomato Pizza with Basil   63
Black Bean Pizza with Chipotle   63
Spring Pea Pizza with Ramps   64
Zucchini Pizza with Pistachios   64
Zucchini and Summer Squash Pizza   64
Butternut Squash and Arugula Pizza   65
Double-Cheese Clam Pizza   65
Zucchini and Onion Pizza   66
Grilled Egg and Arugula Pizza   66

Chapter 11
Wraps and Sandwiches   **67**
Bulgogi Burgers   68
Nugget and Veggie Taco Wraps   68
Lamb and Feta Hamburgers   68
Veggie Salsa Wraps   68
Tuna and Lettuce Wraps   69

Lettuce Fajita Meatball Wraps	69
Chicken-Lettuce Wraps	69
Cheesy Chicken Sandwich	69
Smoky Chicken Sandwich	70
Cheesy Potato Taquitos	70
Chicken and Yogurt Taquitos	70
Pork Momos	70
Eggplant Hoagies	71
Air Fried Cream Cheese Wontons	71
Crispy Crab and Cream Cheese Wontons	71
Cabbage and Pork Gyoza	71
Pea and Potato Samosas with Chutney	72

Chapter 12
Appetizers and Snacks — 73

Sweet Potato Chips	74
Golden Onion Rings	74
Tortilla Chips with Paprika	74
Jalapeño Poppers with Bacon	74
Chicken Wings with Mustard	74
Chili Cauliflower Florets	74
Brussels Sprouts with Syrup	75
Carrot with Honey	75
Air Fried Potato Chips	75
Broccoli Florets with Butter	75
Apple Chips with Cinnamon	75
Sweet Potato with Herb	75
Pork Ribs with Honey and Butter	76
Panko Cheese Green Beans	76
Lemon Eggplant Chips	76
Green Tomato with Cayenne	76
Cheesy Zucchini Chips	76
Tomato Chips with Basil	76
Potato Chips with Paprika	77
Air Fried Mixed Nuts	77
Tomato Chips with Cheese	77
Ham and Cheese Stuffed Peppers	77
Cinnamon Mixed Nuts	77
Paprika Beet Chips	77
Cheese Stuffed Mushrooms	78
Kale Chips with Garlic	78
Bacon-Wrapped Sausages	78
Hot Dogs Rolls	78
Butter Cheese Cauliflower Bites	78
Pancetta-Wrapped Shrimp	78
Apple Cheese Rolls	79
Garlicky Kale Crisps	79
Beet Chips with Rosemary	79
Beer Onion Rings	79
Tortilla Chips with Lime	79
Bacon and Cheese Stuffed Peppers	79
Paprika Carrot Bites	80
Potato Wedges with Paprika	80
Glazed Pork Ribs	80
Vinegary Chicken Drumettes	80
Eggplant Cheese Chips	80
Zucchini with Cheese	80
Red Beet Chips with Cayenne	81
Honey Chicken Wings	81
Blueberry Cheese Rolls	81

Chapter 13
Desserts — 82

Biryani with Butter	83
Cinnamon S'mores	83
Sour Cream Biscuits	83
Cheesy Cornbread Muffins	83
Methi and Ragi Fritters	83
Apple Pie Cheese Rolls	83
Rum Grilled Pineapple Sundaes	84
Grilled Peaches with Bourbon Butter Sauce	84
Pound Cake with Mixed Berries	84
Strawberry Pizza	84
Lemon Cheesecake With Cracker Base	85
Walnut and Raisin Stuffed Apples	85
Cherry Pie	85
Brown Bananas	85
Blueberry Muffins	85
Coconut Cupcakes	86
Easy Lemon Curd	86
Honey and Peanut Butter Banana Toast	86
Chocolate Fondants with Easy Praline	86
Simple Blueberry Turnovers	87

Chapter 14
Fast and Easy Everyday Favorites — 88

Beet Salad with Lemon Vinaigrette	89
French Toast	89
Cheesy Butter Macaroni	89
Colby Potato Patties	89
Old Bay Shrimp with Lemon	90
Cheesy Cauliflower Risotto	90
Broccoli and Eggs	90
Salmon and Carrot Croquettes	90
Parsnip Fries with Garlic-Yogurt Dip	90
Apple Fritters with Vanilla Glaze	91
Hot Chicken Wings	91
Honey Bartlett Pears with Lemony Ricotta	91
Baked Rolls with Cheese	91
Lemony and Garlicky Asparagus	92
South Carolina Shrimp and Corn Bake	92
Spanakopita	92
Green Tomatoes with Almonds	92

Chapter 15
Holiday Specials — 93

Hasselback Potatoes	94
Spicy Black Olives	94
Hearty Honey Yeast Rolls	94
Bourbon Monkey Bread	95
Simple Butter Cake	95
Kale Salad Sushi Rolls with Sriracha Mayonnaise	95
Pão de Queijo	96
Eggnog Bread	96
Shrimp with Sriracha and Worcestershire Sauce	96
Supplì al Telefono (Risotto Croquettes)	97
Teriyaki Shrimp Skewers	97
Whole Chicken Roast	98
Lush Snack Mix	98
Holiday Spicy Beef Roast	98

Chapter 16
Rotisserie Recipes   **99**
Paprika Pulled Pork Butt   100
Orange Honey Glazed Ham   100
Smoked Paprika Lamb Leg   101
Sirloin Roast with Porcini-Wine Baste   101
Pulled Pork with Paprika   102
Ham with Honey-Orange Glaze   102
Bourbon Ham with Apple Butter   103
Spareribs with Ketchup-Garlic Sauce   103
Mutton Roast with Barbecue Dip   104
Whiskey-Basted Prime Rib Roast   104
Spareribs with Paprika Rub   105
Baby Back Ribs with Paprika Rub   105
Chipotle Chuck Roast with Garlic   106
BBQ Chicken with Mustard Rub   106
Porchetta with Lemony Sage Rub   107
Lamb Leg with Brown Sugar Rub   107
Barbecued Whole Chicken   108
Ham with Dijon Bourbon Baste   108
Sirloin Roast with Porcini Baste   109
Rosemary Prime Rib Roast in Red Wine   109
Balsamic Chuck Roast   110
Port-Marinated Chuck Roast   110

Appendix 1 Measurement Conversion Chart   **111**
Appendix 2 The Dirty Dozen and Clean Fifteen   **112**
Appendix 3 Index   **113**

Introduction

D o you enjoy eating fried food? Do you frequently worry that eating fried foods will make you fat since they are fatty? Have you ever considered eating something tasty and crispy without much oil? It's all happening right now. Simply purchase an air fryer, that's all. One of those excellent air fryers is COSORI.

Air fryers have grown in popularity in recent years, as their benefits for busy individuals become more evident. When you get home from a long, tiring day and don't feel like cooking, you no longer have to settle for takeout or fast food as your only options.

This cookbook will provide you with a basic understanding of how your air fryer functions and what it can do for you. One of the biggest misconceptions about the air fryer is that it can only cook fried dishes. But the truth is that it offers so much more. You will learn how to use your air fryer's features in this cookbook, including grilling, baking, roasting, frying, and steaming. Additionally, you'll discover essential advice for using an air fryer successfully along with safety and cleaning instructions. Let's start now.

Air frying is a new, quicker, and healthier method of cooking. It uses convection heat to cook dishes that would often be deep-fried, roasted, grilled, or baked while using less fat. As a result, the wonderful food is lower in calories and oil and therefore healthier.

Why Get an Air Fryer?

- **360° Air Circulation Technology:** When compared to deep-fat frying, air frying can produce food with an 85 percent lower fat content. It does this by air-cooking your food as it moves around the air fryer. You can often cook food in an air fryer with no oil at all.
- **It cooks food faster:** Using frozen food in the air fryer is a good example of this. Air fryer cooking reduces cooking time by half.
- **It is similar to baking food, except the food comes out crispier:** I discover that when I bake food in the oven, the food comes out with a mushy crust. You will be astounded by the outcomes, but the air fryer is your best buddy when it comes to crispy foods.
- **Perfect for diets:** As a long-time air fryer blogger, I've seen that the readership is concerned with their diets. Many of our readers follow the keto, paleo, Weight Watchers, and Slimming World diets.
- **Money-saver:** Because the air fryer is Ideal for fast food imitation recipes, you can save on takeout and supermarket rotisserie chicken.

What is a Cosori Air Fryer?

The best-selling Cosori air fryer has 13 cooking modes that cook your food at the optimal temperature and timing for maximum crispiness and crunch. Do you need to feed more than one or two people? The brand claims that the 5.8-quart basket can hold a five-pound chicken. The dishwasher-safe nonstick air fryer basket is removable. The quality air fryer comes in three colors: black, red, and white.

HOW DO AIR FRYERS WORK?

How Cosori Air Fryer Works

Air frying elevates traditional convection cooking to new heights. Superheated air is circulated around the cooking chamber by a convection fan to cook air-fried food. As a result, the food has a delicious, crispy, golden-brown crust that tastes just like deep-fried food. The flavor is locked in, but because the food cooks with little oil.

Although air frying requires slightly longer cook times than deep frying, you'll feel better about the foods you eat when you realize you're consuming less fat, fewer calories, and healthier ingredients. Air frying allows you to use fresher ingredients that would otherwise be destroyed by the high temperatures of a deep fryer.

Why Should you Get the Cosori Air Fryer?

You may be thinking that while an air fryer sounds great and another air fryer sounds impressive, why should you get the Cosori Air Fryer?

Here are a few reasons why you should choose the Cosori Air Fryer over other brands:

- Shiny Button Syndrome - If you like the Instant Pot Pressure Cooker for all its great preset buttons, you'll love the Cosori Air Fryer. There are presets for steak, seafood, chicken, shrimp, frozen foods, bacon, fries, bread, vegetables, and desserts. You simply press the button and return to your food!
- Air Fryer Temperature - The Cosori air fryer can cook food at temperatures ranging from 75°C/170°F to 200°C/400°F.
- Air Fryer Cooking Time: You can cook for 1 to 60 minutes at a time. Add more time later if necessary for longer cooking recipes, such as roast dinners.
- Air Fryer Shape: I adore the design of the Cosori Air Fryer. It looks like a smaller air fryer but has a much larger capacity because of the shape of the appliance. Ideal for individuals traveling in an RV or a kitchen with limited room.
- Food Warmer: Additionally, it will keep your food warm for up to an hour. You could leave your prepared food and return to it later knowing that it will still be warm in the Cosori Air Fryer.
- One-Year Guarantee - Because Cosori is so confident in their air fryer, they are offering a one-year buyers' guarantee.
- Nonstick Air Fryer Basket - Your Cosori air fryer comes with a fantastic large square basket. Dishwasher safe and simple to maintain.
- Price: I love the Cosori air fryer range's value for money. When purchasing an air fryer, you have two options: go super cheap and have a short-lived air fryer or spend a significant amount of money. The Cosori is your meeting point.

Basic Features of Cosori Air Fryer

Knowing the basic functions of an air fryer will help you succeed. Even though every brand and model varies slightly—some have pre-programmed cooking options, some may have manual temperatures and timer dials, and still others have a digital control panel—they still have a lot in common. You can see an overview of the essential elements of your air fryer in the diagram and explanations below.

Air Fryer Basket
Place your meal in this section of the air fryer to cook it. The two most crucial things to keep in mind when using the air fryer basket are (1) to spray it with olive oil before you load it up to help prevent the food from sticking, and (2) to avoid overloading it because your food won't brown and cook evenly, especially if it's anything that's been cooked in pieces (chicken wings, French fries, steak tips, asparagus, etc.).

Air Fryer Drawer
The air fryer drawer contains the basket. After you pull the air fryer drawer from the air fryer, press a button on top of the drawer handle to separate these two sections, which snap together while cooking. Before turning out (or removing) the contents of the basket, you should unlatch the basket from the drawer. Also, separate the drawer and the basket for cleaning.

Heating Element And Fan
The heating element resembles a burner coil on an electric stove and is located directly above the air fryer basket. A motorized fan found above the heating element circulates hot air all over the air fryer. Cooking is accelerated by the top-down heat, hot air circulation, and limited cooking area.

Air Inlet
As a result of the air entering the air fryer at this point, it will stay cool during cooking. The air fryer may overheat if the air input is blocked. Ensure that you leave this space clear.

Air Outlet Openings
As the air fryer cooks, the air departs at this location. Steam may occasionally be seen coming from this vent. Keep in mind that hot air and steam will be emitted through this outlet. Because of this, avoid placing your air fryer too close to a wall or behind cabinets as the heat may damage nearby paint and other surfaces. Do not have direct contact with the top of your air fryer.

Temperature Control
This could be a digital setting on a control panel or a manual dial, depending on the brand and model of your device. The temperature for your food is set here. The typical temperature range is 200°F to 400°F.

Timer
You may set the cooking time for your food here. It might be a manual dial or a component of an electronic control panel.

Bright Power
Your air fryer turns on when the power light illuminates.

Light Heating
The air fryer's heating up light lets you know when it's ready. (Only certain models come with this feature).

Functions of Cosori Air Fryer

The Cosori Air Fryer is capable of frying, grilling, baking, roasting, steaming, and toasting. It will save you not only time but also a lot of counters and cabinet space. So much so that you may soon be giving your oven-size pans away! Some air fryer models include presets for specific functions or foods. If your model lacks presets, the function is determined by the temperature, type of food, and method of preparation. I roast chicken breasts at 370°F, grill a whole steak at 400°F, and bake cookies at 320°F, for example.

Fry
Traditionally, frying entails cooking in extremely hot oil. Deep-frying (when you cook food by immersing it in a large amount of hot oil) and sautéing (when you cook food in a frying pan with one or more tablespoons of hot oil or melted butter) are two of the most common examples. The outside of the food becomes brown and crispy while the inside remains tender and moist because of the high temperature of the oil or butter.
Fried food absorbs a lot of fat during the cooking process, making it one of the least healthy ways to cook. So,

even if you start with healthy food, such as chicken breast, by the end of the frying process, your chicken will be high in calories and fat.

Similar to traditional frying, air frying also uses high heat to cook food, but instead of using hot oil, hot air is continuously cycled in a compact chamber. By doing this, you can get the same result as cooking with oil without all the fat and mess. Oil is typically just sprayed on top of the majority of fried items prepared in an air fryer (or another appliance that uses oil with a high smoke point) if any is used at all.

Fried eggs, onion rings, Sweet potato, French fries, and Buffalo chicken wings are just a few of the numerous items you can fry in an air fryer that are healthier. Another excellent method for reheating frozen foods is to use the fry setting.

Grill

Grilling is the process of cooking food by applying heat from below to quickly sear the outside while preserving the majority of the food's fluids. Given that it uses no oil or fat, grilling is typically seen as a healthy method of preparing meat.

High heat is also used while grilling in an air fryer; typically using temperatures between 370°F and 400°F. You can produce a slice of juicy meat with only a few teaspoons of olive oil, much like when grilled on the barbecue. The meat I've cooked in the air fryer has always been on par with, if not superior to, grilled foods. Air fryer hamburgers and hot dogs are amazingly tasty, juicy, and flavorful.

Bake

The air fryer's baking function is its most unexpected feature. Indirect dry heat is used in baking. The heat begins to cook the food on the surface and at the edges, heating it evenly from the outside to the middle. Anything that you could bake in a conventional oven can be baked in an air fryer, but the temperature is typically roughly 30% lower.

Air fryers' baking time may differ slightly from model to model. I advise you to closely monitor the cooking time for your first few air fryer baking projects and to take brief notes to learn the precise baking times for your specific machine. Keep some aluminum foil available as well in case the top of your baked products browns before the middle is done.

Roast

Roasting is similar to baking. Both techniques cook food utilizing indirect dry heat. When using this method to prepare meat and vegetables, the recommended term is roasting; however, when preparing items using a batter or dough, the ideal term is baking. It depends on what is being cooked, but roasting temperatures are often a little higher than baking temperatures.

Steam

When food is steamed, it signifies that it has been heated by the steam created by boiling water. In traditional cooking, this is typically accomplished by placing a double boiler or steaming rack over boiling water. Broccoli and spinach, among other veggies, steam beautifully in air fryers.

Toast

The air fryer's ability to toast bread, English muffins, or bagels is another surprising feature. The air fryer can be used for any task that your toaster currently does. As opposed to baking, toasting uses radiant heat to brown the bread. Because the heating source is typically located immediately above the basket where the food is placed, this is a task that the air fryer excels at.

Cosori Air Fryer Safety

Before using your air fryer, be sure to read the manual for crucial safety instructions. It's critical to be familiar with the safety features of your specific air fryer because every model is unique.

The position of your air fryer is the most vital component of utilizing it. Because the bottom of the air fryer might occasionally get hot, I strongly advise setting it on a heat-resistant mat rather than directly on a tabletop. Although some types cannot have anything underneath as it may obstruct the airflow and cause the air fryer to overheat, check your manual first to see what the manufacturer advises.

Avoid cleaning the air fryer while it is plugged in or still hot!

The area around and above your air fryer should be spacious. It is not recommended that you use an air fryer directly beneath a cabinet.

The air fryer could catch fire if it is placed on a stove or another surface that could accidentally switch on the power. Keep in mind that since your air fryer is connected to an electrical cord, neither heat nor water should be present.

After every use, don't forget to disconnect your air fryer.

Tips to Use Cosori Air Fryer

One of the best aspects of air frying is how simple it is to cook all your favorite foods. However, knowing a few tips and tricks will ensure that your air-fried food is perfect every time.

To make cleanup easier, use parchment paper.
For simpler cleanup, line the bottom of the air fryer baking pan or fryer basket with parchment paper. The parchment paper won't catch fire, but it will absorb much of the extra grease that may drip from fatty dishes.

To extend the life of your air fryer, keep it clean.
After each usage, clean the fryer basket and baking pan with a slightly moist paper towel or cloth for optimal results. For greasier things like meats or fish, as well as recipes with batter or breading, cleaning your air fryer may call for a little extra work. Your accessories can be soaked in warm, soapy water in these situations.

To minimize smoke, drain excess fat.
There is a risk of smoke escaping from the air fryer when fat drips and burns from meals like steak and chicken wings. If this happens, turn off the air fryer, gently drain the fat from the fryer basket, or pat any oily fat off the food with a paper towel, then quickly put the basket back in the air fryer and go on cooking.

Before cooking, preheat the air fryer.
When you insert the food into the air fryer, the temperature and airflow will already be at their ideal settings from the air fryer's preheating, which will help the food cook more evenly. This procedure may take 3 minutes (or less).

For breaded foods, use a baking pan.
Food fragments and small particles of breading may come loose and fly throughout the chamber because of the air fryer's air circulation. Cook food within the baking pan to avoid breading from coming undone. Using a baking pan can also stop food from falling apart and keep the air fryer clean.

To prevent uneven frying, shake the basket.
If you're having problems with uneven frying, the fryer basket is probably too crowded. During the cooking process, pause the air fryer once or twice (or as directed) and give the fryer basket a gentle shake for more equal frying. By redistributing the food, it will cook more uniformly and brown on all sides.

If used properly, the Cosori air fryer may produce surprisingly excellent food that is cooked in a way that is healthier than using a deep fryer or a conventional oven. To learn the basics of air frying, hopefully, this Cosori Air Fryer Cookbook will be the most useful to you. Thank you.

Chapter 3
Sauces, Dips, and Dressings

Cauliflower Alfredo Sauce

Prep time: 2 minutes | Cook time: 0 minutes | Makes 4 cups

- 2 tablespoons olive oil
- 6 garlic cloves, minced
- 3 cups unsweetened almond milk
- 1 (1-pound / 454-g) head cauliflower, cut into florets
- 1 teaspoon salt
- ¼ teaspoon freshly ground black pepper
- Juice of 1 lemon
- 4 tablespoons nutritional yeast

1. In a medium saucepan, heat the olive oil over medium-high heat. Add the garlic and sauté for 1 minute or until fragrant. Add the almond milk, stir, and bring to a boil.
2. Gently add the cauliflower. Stir in the salt and pepper and return to a boil. Continue cooking over medium-high heat for 5 minutes or until the cauliflower is soft. Stir frequently and reduce heat if needed to prevent the liquid from boiling over.
3. Carefully transfer the cauliflower and cooking liquid to a food processor, using a slotted spoon to scoop out the larger pieces of cauliflower before pouring in the liquid. Add the lemon and nutritional yeast and blend for 1 to 2 minutes until smooth.
4. Serve immediately.

Marinara Sauce

Prep time: 15 minutes | Cook time: 30 minutes | Makes about 3 cups

- ¼ cup extra-virgin olive oil
- 3 garlic cloves, minced
- 1 small onion, chopped (about ½ cup)
- 2 tablespoons minced or puréed sun-dried tomatoes (optional)
- 1 (28-ounce / 794-g) can crushed tomatoes
- ½ teaspoon dried basil
- ½ teaspoon dried oregano
- ¼ teaspoon red pepper flakes
- 1 teaspoon kosher salt or ½ teaspoon fine salt, plus more as needed

1. Heat the oil in a medium saucepan over medium heat.
2. Add the garlic and onion and sauté for 2 to 3 minutes, or until the onion is softened. Add the sun-dried tomatoes (if desired) and cook for 1 minute until fragrant. Stir in the crushed tomatoes, scraping any brown bits from the bottom of the pot. Fold in the basil, oregano, red pepper flakes, and salt. Stir well.
3. Bring to a simmer. Cook covered for about 30 minutes, stirring occasionally.
4. Turn off the heat and allow the sauce to cool for about 10 minutes.
5. Taste and adjust the seasoning, adding more salt if needed.
6. Use immediately.

Red Enchilada Sauce

Prep time: 15 minutes | Cook time: 0 minutes | Makes 2 cups

- 3 large ancho chiles, stems and seeds removed, torn into pieces
- 1½ cups very hot water
- 2 garlic cloves, peeled and lightly smashed
- 2 tablespoons wine vinegar
- 2 teaspoons kosher salt or 1 teaspoon fine salt
- 1½ teaspoons sugar
- ½ teaspoon dried oregano
- ½ teaspoon ground cumin

1. Mix together the chile pieces and hot water in a bowl and let stand for 10 to 15 minutes.
2. Pour the chiles and water into a blender jar. Fold in the garlic, vinegar, salt, sugar, oregano, and cumin, and salt and blend until smooth.
3. Use immediately.

Spicy Southwest Seasoning

Prep time: 5 minutes | Cook time: 0 minutes | Makes about ¾ cups

- 1 tablespoon granulated onion
- 1 tablespoon granulated garlic
- 2 tablespoons dried oregano
- 2 tablespoons freshly ground black pepper
- 3 tablespoons ancho chile powder
- 2 teaspoons cayenne
- 2 teaspoons cumin

1. Stir together all the ingredients in a small bowl.
2. Use immediately or place in an airtight container in the pantry.

Dijon and Balsamic Vinaigrette

Prep time: 5 minutes | Cook time: 0 minutes | Makes 12 tablespoons

- 6 tablespoons water
- 4 tablespoons Dijon mustard
- 4 tablespoons balsamic vinegar
- 1 teaspoon maple syrup
- ½ teaspoon pink Himalayan salt
- ¼ teaspoon freshly ground black pepper

1. In a bowl, whisk together all the ingredients.

Lemony Tahini

Prep time: 5 minutes | Cook time: 0 minutes | Serves 4

- ¾ cup water
- ½ cup tahini
- 3 garlic cloves, minced
- Juice of 3 lemons
- ½ teaspoon pink Himalayan salt

1. In a bowl, whisk together all the ingredients until mixed well.

Creamy Ranch Dressing

Prep time: 5 minutes | Cook time: 0 minutes | Serves 8

- 1 cup plain Greek yogurt
- ¼ cup chopped fresh dill
- 2 tablespoons chopped fresh chives
- Zest of 1 lemon
- 1 garlic clove, minced
- ½ teaspoon sea salt
- ⅛ teaspoon freshly cracked black pepper

1. Mix together the yogurt, dill, chives, lemon zest, garlic, sea salt, and pepper in a small bowl and whisk to combine.
2. Serve chilled.

Creamy Coconut Lime Dressing 10

Prep time: 5 minutes | Cook time: 0 minutes | Makes about 1 cup

- 8 ounces (227 g) plain coconut yogurt
- 2 tablespoons chopped fresh parsley
- 2 tablespoons freshly squeezed lemon juice
- 1 tablespoon snipped fresh chives
- ½ teaspoon salt
- Pinch freshly ground black pepper

1. Stir together the coconut yogurt, parsley, lemon juice, chives, salt, and pepper in a medium bowl until completely mixed.
2. Transfer to an airtight container and refrigerate until ready to use.
3. This dressing perfectly pairs with spring mix greens, grilled chicken or even your favorite salad.

Hemp Dressing

Prep time: 5 minutes | Cook time: 0 minutes | Makes 12 tablespoons

- ½ cup white wine vinegar
- ¼ cup tahini
- ¼ cup water
- 1 tablespoon hemp seeds
- ½ tablespoon freshly squeezed lemon juice
- 1 teaspoon garlic powder
- 1 teaspoon dried oregano
- 1 teaspoon dried basil
- 1 teaspoon red pepper flakes
- ½ teaspoon onion powder
- ½ teaspoon pink Himalayan salt
- ½ teaspoon freshly ground black pepper

1. In a bowl, combine all the ingredients and whisk until mixed well.

Garlic Lime Tahini Dressing

Prep time: 5 minutes | Cook time: 0 minutes | Makes about ¾ cup

- ⅓ cup tahini
- 3 tablespoons filtered water
- 2 tablespoons freshly squeezed lime juice
- 1 tablespoon apple cider vinegar
- 1 teaspoon lime zest
- 1½ teaspoons raw honey
- ¼ teaspoon garlic powder
- ¼ teaspoon salt

1. Whisk together the tahini, water, vinegar, lime juice, lime zest, honey, salt, and garlic powder in a small bowl until well emulsified.
2. Serve immediately, or refrigerate in an airtight container for to 1 week.

Avocado Dressing

Prep time: 5 minutes | Cook time: 0 minutes | Makes 12 tablespoons

- 1 large avocado, pitted and peeled
- ½ cup water
- 2 tablespoons tahini
- 2 tablespoons freshly squeezed lemon juice
- 1 teaspoon dried basil
- 1 teaspoon white wine vinegar
- 1 garlic clove
- ¼ teaspoon pink Himalayan salt
- ¼ teaspoon freshly ground black pepper

1. Combine all the ingredients in a food processor and blend until smooth.

Fresh Mixed Berry Vinaigrette

Prep time: 15 minutes | Cook time: 0 minutes | Makes about 1½ cups

- 1 cup mixed berries, thawed if frozen
- ½ cup balsamic vinegar
- ⅓ cup extra-virgin olive oil
- 2 tablespoons freshly squeezed lemon or lime juice
- 1 tablespoon lemon or lime zest
- 1 tablespoon Dijon mustard
- 1 tablespoon raw honey or maple syrup
- 1 teaspoon salt
- ½ teaspoon freshly ground black pepper

1. Place all the ingredients in a blender and purée until thoroughly mixed and smooth.
2. You can serve it over a bed of greens, grilled meat, or fresh fruit salad.

Lemon Dijon Vinaigrette

Prep time: 5 minutes | Cook time: 0 minutes | Makes about 6 tablespoons

- ¼ cup extra-virgin olive oil
- 1 garlic clove, minced
- 2 tablespoons freshly squeezed lemon juice
- 1 teaspoon Dijon mustard
- ½ teaspoon raw honey
- ¼ teaspoon salt
- ¼ teaspoon dried basil

1. Place all the ingredients in a mason jar. Cover and shake vigorously until thoroughly mixed and well emulsified.
2. Serve chilled.

Kale and Almond Pesto

Prep time: 15 minutes | Cook time: 0 minutes | Makes about 1 cup

- 2 cups chopped kale leaves, rinsed well and stemmed
- ½ cup toasted almonds
- 2 garlic cloves
- 3 tablespoons extra-virgin olive oil
- 3 tablespoons freshly squeezed lemon juice
- 2 teaspoons lemon zest
- 1 teaspoon salt
- ½ teaspoon freshly ground black pepper
- ¼ teaspoon red pepper flakes

1. Place all the ingredients in a food processor and pulse until smoothly puréed.
2. It tastes great with the eggs, salads, soup, pasta, cracker, and sandwiches.

Shawarma Spice Blend

Prep time: 5 minutes | Cook time: 0 minutes | Makes about 1 tablespoon

- 1 teaspoon smoked paprika
- 1 teaspoon cumin
- ¼ teaspoon turmeric
- ¼ teaspoon cinnamon
- ¼ teaspoon allspice
- ¼ teaspoon red pepper flakes
- ¼ teaspoon kosher salt or ⅛ teaspoon fine salt
- ¼ teaspoon freshly ground black pepper

1. Stir together all the ingredients in a small bowl.
2. Use immediately or place in an airtight container in the pantry.

Chapter 4
Breakfast

Spinach with Scrambled Eggs

Prep time: 10 minutes | Cook time: 10 minutes | Serves 2

- 2 tablespoons olive oil
- 4 eggs, whisked
- 5 ounces (142 g) fresh spinach, chopped
- 1 medium tomato, chopped
- 1 teaspoon fresh lemon juice
- ½ teaspoon coarse salt
- ½ teaspoon ground black pepper
- ½ cup of fresh basil, roughly chopped

1. Grease a baking pan with the oil, tilting it to spread the oil around. Preheat the air fryer to 280°F (138°C).
2. Mix the remaining ingredients, apart from the basil leaves, whisking well until everything is completely combined.
3. Bake in the air fryer for 10 minutes.
4. Top with fresh basil leaves before serving.

Buttermilk Biscuits

Prep time: 5 minutes | Cook time: 5 minutes | Makes 12 biscuits

- 2 cups all-purpose flour, plus more for dusting the work surface
- 1 tablespoon baking powder
- ¼ teaspoon baking soda
- 2 teaspoons sugar
- 1 teaspoon salt
- 6 tablespoons cold unsalted butter, cut into 1-tablespoon slices
- ¾ cup buttermilk

1. Preheat the air fryer to 360°F (182°C). Spray the air fryer basket with olive oil.
2. In a large mixing bowl, combine the flour, baking powder, baking soda, sugar, and salt and mix well.
3. Using a fork, cut in the butter until the mixture resembles coarse meal.
4. Add the buttermilk and mix until smooth.
5. Dust more flour on a clean work surface. Turn the dough out onto the work surface and roll it out until it is about ½ inch thick.
6. Using a 2-inch biscuit cutter, cut out the biscuits. Put the uncooked biscuits in the greased air fryer basket in a single layer.
7. Bake for 5 minutes. Transfer the cooked biscuits from the air fryer to a platter.
8. Cut the remaining biscuits. Bake the remaining biscuits.
9. Serve warm.

Bacon and Egg Stuffed Peppers

Prep time: 10 minutes | Cook time: 15 minutes | Serves 4

- 1 cup shredded Cheddar cheese
- 4 slices bacon, cooked and chopped
- 4 bell peppers, seeded and tops removed
- 4 large eggs
- Sea salt, to taste
- Freshly ground black pepper, to taste
- Chopped fresh parsley, for garnish

1. Place the crisper tray on the air fry position. Select Air Fry, set the temperature to 390°F (199°C), and set the time to 15 minutes.
2. Meanwhile, divide the cheese and bacon between the bell peppers. Crack one of the eggs into each bell pepper, and season with salt and pepper.
3. Place each bell pepper in the crisper tray. Air fry for 10 to 15 minutes, until the egg whites are cooked and the yolks are slightly runny.
4. Remove the peppers from the crisper tray, garnish with parsley, and serve.

Lush Vegetable Omelet

Prep time: 10 minutes | Cook time: 13 minutes | Serves 2

2 teaspoons canola oil
4 eggs, whisked
3 tablespoons plain milk
1 teaspoon melted butter
1 red bell pepper, seeded and chopped
1 green bell pepper, seeded and chopped
1 white onion, finely chopped
½ cup baby spinach leaves, roughly chopped
½ cup Halloumi cheese, shaved
Kosher salt and freshly ground black pepper, to taste

1. Preheat the air fryer to 350°F (177°C).
2. Grease a baking pan with canola oil.
3. Put the remaining ingredients in the baking pan and stir well.
4. Transfer to the air fryer and bake for 13 minutes.
5. Serve warm.

Syrupy Apple Oatmeal

Prep time: 5 minutes | Cook time: 12 minutes | Serves 4

- 1 cup old-fashioned oats
- ¼ cup agave syrup
- 1 cup milk
- 1 egg, whisked
- 1 cup chopped apple
- ½ teaspoon baking powder
- ½ teaspoon ground cinnamon
- A pinch of grated nutmeg
- A pinch of salt

1. Thoroughly combine all ingredients in a mixing bowl. Spoon the mixture into four lightly greased ramekins.
2. Place the ramekins in the baking dish.
3. Place the baking dish in the air fryer basket. Put the air fryer lid on and bake in the preheated instant pot at 380°F (193°C) for 12 minutes.
4. Bon appétit!

Banana Churros with Oatmeal
Prep time: 15 minutes | Cook time: 15 minutes | Serves 2

For the Churros:
1 large yellow banana, peeled, cut in half lengthwise, then cut in half widthwise
2 tablespoons whole-wheat pastry flour
⅛ teaspoon sea salt
2 teaspoons oil (sunflower or melted coconut)
Cooking spray
1 tablespoon coconut sugar
½ teaspoon cinnamon
For the Oatmeal:
¾ cup rolled oats
1½ cups water

To make the churros
1. Put the 4 banana pieces in a medium-size bowl and add the flour and salt. Stir gently. Add the oil and water. Stir gently until evenly mixed. You may need to press some coating onto the banana pieces.
2. Spray the air fryer basket with the oil spray. Put the banana pieces in the air fryer basket and air fry for 5 minutes. Remove, gently turn over, and air fry for another 5 minutes or until browned.
3. In a medium bowl, add the coconut sugar and cinnamon and stir to combine. When the banana pieces are nicely browned, spray with the oil and place in the cinnamon-sugar bowl. Toss gently with a spatula to coat the banana pieces with the mixture.

To make the oatmeal
4. While the bananas are cooking, make the oatmeal. In a medium pot, bring the oats and water to a boil, then reduce to low heat. Simmer, stirring often, until all the water is absorbed, about 5 minutes. Put the oatmeal into two bowls.
5. Top the oatmeal with the coated banana pieces and serve immediately.

English Pumpkin Egg Bake
Prep time: 10 minutes | Cook time: 10 minutes | Serves 2

2 eggs
½ cup milk
2 tablespoons cider vinegar
2 teaspoons baking powder
1 tablespoon sugar
1 cup pumpkin purée
1 teaspoon cinnamon powder
1 teaspoon baking soda
1 tablespoon olive oil

1. Preheat the air fryer to 300°F (149°C).
2. Crack the eggs into a bowl and beat with a whisk. Combine with the milk, flour, cider vinegar, baking powder, sugar, pumpkin purée, cinnamon powder, and baking soda, mixing well.
3. Grease a baking tray with oil. Add the mixture and transfer into the air fryer. Bake for 10 minutes.
4. Serve warm.

Honey-Lime Glazed Grilled Fruit Salad
Prep time: 10 minutes | Cook time: 4 minutes | Serves 4

½ pound (227 g) strawberries, washed, hulled and halved
1 (9-ounce / 255-g) can pineapple chunks, drained, juice reserved
2 peaches, pitted and sliced
6 tablespoons honey, divided
1 tablespoon freshly squeezed lime juice

1. Place the grill plate on the grill position. Select Grill, set the temperature to 450°F (232°C), and set the time to 4 minutes.
2. Combine the strawberries, pineapple, and peaches in a large bowl with 3 tablespoons of honey. Toss to coat evenly.
3. Place the fruit on the grill plate. Gently press the fruit down to maximize grill marks. Grill for 4 minutes without flipping.
4. Meanwhile, in a small bowl, combine the remaining 3 tablespoons of honey, lime juice, and 1 tablespoon of reserved pineapple juice.
5. When cooking is complete, place the fruit in a large bowl and toss with the honey mixture. Serve immediately.

Mushroom and Squash Toast
Prep time: 10 minutes | Cook time: 10 minutes | Serves 4

- 1 tablespoon olive oil
- 1 red bell pepper, cut into strips
- 2 green onions, sliced
- 1 cup sliced button or cremini mushrooms
- 1 small yellow squash, sliced
- 2 tablespoons softened butter
- 4 slices bread
- ½ cup soft goat cheese

1. Brush the air fryer basket with the olive oil and preheat the air fryer to 350°F (177°C).
2. Put the red pepper, green onions, mushrooms, and squash inside the air fryer, give them a stir and air fry for 7 minutes or the vegetables are tender, shaking the basket once throughout the cooking time.
3. Remove the vegetables and set them aside.
4. Spread the butter on the slices of bread and transfer to the air fryer, butter-side up. Brown for 3 minutes.
5. Remove the toast from the air fryer and top with goat cheese and vegetables. Serve warm.

Mushroom and Onion Frittata

Prep time: 10 minutes | Cook time: 10 minutes | Serves 4

- 4 large eggs
- ¼ cup whole milk
- Sea salt, to taste
- Freshly ground black pepper, to taste
- ½ bell pepper, seeded and diced
- ½ onion, chopped
- 4 cremini mushrooms, sliced
- ½ cup shredded Cheddar cheese

1. In a medium bowl, whisk together the eggs and milk. Season with the salt and pepper. Add the bell pepper, onion, mushrooms, and cheese. Mix until well combined.
2. Place the baking pan on the bake position. Select Bake, set the temperature to 400°F (204°C), and set the time to 10 minutes.
3. Pour the egg mixture into the baking pan, spreading evenly.
4. Bake for 10 minutes, or until lightly golden.

Egg and Sausage Stuffed Breakfast Pockets

Prep time: 15 minutes | Cook time: 23 minutes | Serves 4

1 (6-ounce / 170-g) package ground breakfast sausage, crumbled
3 large eggs, lightly beaten
⅓ cup diced red bell pepper
⅓ cup thinly sliced scallions (green part only)
Sea salt, to taste
Freshly ground black pepper, to taste
1 (16-ounce / 454-g) package pizza dough
All-purpose flour, for dusting
1 cup shredded Cheddar cheese
2 tablespoons canola oil

1. Place the baking pan on the roast position. Select Roast, set the temperature to 375°F (191°C), and set the time to 15 minutes.
2. Place the sausage directly in the pan. Roast for 10 minutes, checking the sausage every 2 to 3 minutes, breaking apart larger pieces with a wooden spoon.
3. After 10 minutes, pour the eggs, bell pepper, and scallions into the pan. Stir to evenly incorporate with the sausage. Let the eggs roast for the remaining 5 minutes, stirring occasionally. Transfer the sausage and egg mixture to a medium bowl to cool slightly. Season with salt and pepper.
4. Place the crisper tray on the air fry position. Select Air Fry, set the temperature to 350°F (177°C), and set the time to 8 minutes.
5. Meanwhile, divide the dough into four equal pieces. Lightly dust a clean work surface with flour. Roll each piece of dough into a 5-inch round of even thickness. Divide the sausage-egg mixture and cheese evenly among each round. Brush the outside edge of the dough with water. Fold the dough over the filling, forming a half circle. Pinch the edges of the dough together to seal in the filling. Brush both sides of each pocket with the oil.
6. Place the breakfast pockets in the crisper tray. Air fry for 6 to 8 minutes, or until golden brown.

Bacon and Broccoli Bread Pudding

Prep time: 15 minutes | Cook time: 48 minutes | Serves 2 to 4

- ½ pound (227 g) thick cut bacon, cut into ¼-inch pieces
- 3 cups brioche bread, cut into ½-inch cubes
- 2 tablespoons butter, melted
- 3 eggs
- 1 cup milk
- ½ teaspoon salt
- Freshly ground black pepper, to taste
- 1 cup frozen broccoli florets, thawed and chopped
- 1½ cups grated Swiss cheese

1. Preheat the air fryer to 400°F (204°C).
2. Air fry the bacon for 8 minutes until crispy, shaking the basket a few times to help it air fry evenly. Remove the bacon and set it aside on a paper towel.
3. Air fry the brioche bread cubes for 2 minutes to dry and toast lightly.
4. Butter a cake pan. Combine all the ingredients in a large bowl and toss well. Transfer the mixture to the buttered cake pan, cover with aluminum foil and refrigerate the bread pudding overnight, or for at least 8 hours.
5. Remove the cake pan from the refrigerator an hour before you plan to bake and let it sit on the countertop to come to room temperature.
6. Preheat the air fryer to 330°F (166°C). Transfer the covered cake pan to the basket of the air fryer, lowering the pan into the basket. Fold the ends of the aluminum foil over the top of the pan before returning the basket to the air fryer.
7. Air fry for 20 minutes. Remove the foil and air fry for an additional 20 minutes. If the top browns a little too much before the custard has set, simply return the foil to the pan. The bread pudding has cooked through when a skewer inserted into the center comes out clean.
8. Serve warm.

Creamy Raisins Bread Pudding
Prep time: 6 minutes | Cook time: 20 minutes | Serves 5

- 1½ cups cubed ciabatta bread
- 2 eggs, whisked
- ½ cup double cream
- ½ cup milk
- ½ teaspoon vanilla extract
- 1 tablespoon bourbon
- ¼ cup honey
- ½ cup golden raisins

1. Place the ciabatta bread in a lightly greased baking dish.
2. In a mixing bowl, thoroughly combine the eggs, double cream, milk, vanilla, bourbon, and honey.
3. Pour the egg mixture over the bread cubes. Fold in the raisins and set aside for 15 minutes to soak.
4. Place the baking dish in the air fryer basket. Put the air fryer lid on and bake in the preheated instant pot at 350°F (180°C) for 20 minutes or until the custard is set but still a little wobbly.
5. Serve at room temperature. Bon appétit!

Almond Honey Bread Pudding
Prep time: 10 minutes | Cook time: 20 minutes | Serves 6

- 2 cups cubed brioche bread
- 1 cup almond milk
- 2 eggs, whisked
- ¼ teaspoon ground cinnamon
- ¼ teaspoon ground cardamom
- ½ teaspoon vanilla extract
- ¼ cup honey
- ½ cup chopped almonds

1. Place the bread cubes in a lightly greased baking dish.
2. In a mixing bowl, thoroughly combine the remaining ingredients.
3. Pour the custard mixture over the bread cubes; set aside for 15 minutes to soak.
4. Place the baking dish in the air fryer basket. Put the air fryer lid on and bake in the preheated instant pot at 350°F (180°C) for 20 minutes or until the custard is set but still a little wobbly.
5. Serve at room temperature. Bon appétit!

Doughnut Bread Pudding
Prep time: 8 minutes | Cook time: 20 minutes | Serves 6

- 2 cups diced doughnuts
- 2 eggs, whisked
- 1 cup milk
- 1 cup half-and-half
- 4 tablespoons honey
- 1 teaspoon vanilla extract
- A pinch of salt
- A pinch of grated nutmeg

1. Place the doughnuts in a lightly greased baking dish.
2. In a mixing bowl, thoroughly combine the remaining ingredients.
3. Pour the custard mixture over the doughnuts. Set aside for 15 minutes to soak.
4. Place the baking dish in the air fryer basket. Put the air fryer lid on and bake in the preheated instant pot at 350°F (180°C) for about 20 minutes or until the custard is set but still a little wobbly.
5. Serve at room temperature. Bon appétit!

Grit and Ham Fritters
Prep time: 15 minutes | Cook time: 20 minutes | Serves 6 to 8

- 4 cups water
- 1 cup quick-cooking grits
- ¼ teaspoon salt
- 2 tablespoons butter
- 2 cups grated Cheddar cheese, divided
- 1 cup finely diced ham
- 1 tablespoon chopped chives
- Salt and freshly ground black pepper, to taste
- 1 egg, beaten
- 2 cups panko bread crumbs
- Cooking spray

1. Bring the water to a boil in a saucepan. Whisk in the grits and ¼ teaspoon of salt, and cook for 7 minutes until the grits are soft. Remove the pan from the heat and stir in the butter and 1 cup of the grated Cheddar cheese. Transfer the grits to a bowl and let them cool for 10 to 15 minutes.
2. Stir the ham, chives and the rest of the cheese into the grits and season with salt and pepper to taste. Add the beaten egg and refrigerate the mixture for 30 minutes.
3. Put the panko bread crumbs in a shallow dish. Measure out ¼-cup portions of the grits mixture and shape them into patties. Coat all sides of the patties with the panko bread crumbs, patting them with the hands so the crumbs adhere to the patties. You should have about 16 patties. Spritz both sides of the patties with cooking spray.
4. Preheat the air fryer to 400°F (204°C).
5. In batches of 5 or 6, air fry the fritters for 8 minutes. Using a flat spatula, flip the fritters over and air fry for another 4 minutes.
6. Serve hot.

Ham and Corn Muffins

Prep time: 10 minutes | Cook time: 6 minutes | Makes 8 muffins

- ¾ cup yellow cornmeal
- ¼ cup flour
- 1½ teaspoons baking powder
- ¼ teaspoon salt
- 1 egg, beaten
- 2 tablespoons canola oil
- ½ cup milk
- ½ cup shredded sharp Cheddar cheese
- ½ cup diced ham

1. Preheat the air fryer to 390°F (199°C).
2. In a medium bowl, stir together the cornmeal, flour, baking powder, and salt.
3. Add the egg, oil, and milk to dry ingredients and mix well.
4. Stir in shredded cheese and diced ham.
5. Divide batter among 8 parchment-paper-lined muffin cups.
6. Put 4 filled muffin cups in air fryer basket and bake for 5 minutes.
7. Reduce temperature to 330°F (166°C) and bake for 1 minute or until a toothpick inserted in center of the muffin comes out clean.
8. Repeat steps 6 and 7 to bake remaining muffins.
9. Serve warm.

Nut and Seed Muffins

Prep time: 15 minutes | Cook time: 10 minutes | Makes 8 muffins

- ½ cup whole-wheat flour, plus 2 tablespoons
- ¼ cup oat bran
- 2 tablespoons flaxseed meal
- ¼ cup brown sugar
- ½ teaspoon baking soda
- ½ teaspoon baking powder
- ¼ teaspoon salt
- ½ teaspoon cinnamon
- ½ cup buttermilk
- 2 tablespoons melted butter
- 1 egg
- ½ teaspoon pure vanilla extract
- ½ cup grated carrots
- ¼ cup chopped pecans
- ¼ cup chopped walnuts
- 1 tablespoon pumpkin seeds
- 1 tablespoon sunflower seeds
- Cooking spray

SPECIAL EQUIPMENT:

16 foil muffin cups, paper liners removed

1. Preheat the air fryer to 330°F (166°C).
2. In a large bowl, stir together the flour, bran, flaxseed meal, sugar, baking soda, baking powder, salt, and cinnamon.
3. In a medium bowl, beat together the buttermilk, butter, egg, and vanilla. Pour into flour mixture and stir just until dry ingredients moisten. Do not beat.
4. Gently stir in carrots, nuts, and seeds.
5. Double up the foil cups so you have 8 total and spritz with cooking spray.
6. Put 4 foil cups in air fryer basket and divide half the batter among them.
7. Bake for 10 minutes or until a toothpick inserted in center comes out clean.
8. Repeat step 7 to bake remaining 4 muffins.
9. Serve warm.

Buttery Banana Muffins

Prep time: 10 minutes | Cook time: 15 minutes | Serves 4

- 1 large egg, whisked
- 1 ripe banana, peeled and mashed
- ¼ cup butter, melted
- ¼ cup agave nectar
- ½ cup all-purpose flour
- ¼ almond flour
- 1 teaspoon baking powder
- ¼ cup brown sugar
- ½ teaspoon vanilla essence
- 1 teaspoon cinnamon powder
- ¼ teaspoon ground cloves

1. Mix all ingredients in a bowl.
2. Scrape the batter into silicone baking molds; place them in the baking dish.
3. Place the baking dish in the air fryer basket. Put the air fryer lid on and bake in the preheated instant pot at 320°F (160°C) for 15 minutes or until a tester comes out dry and clean.
4. Allow the muffins to cool before unmolding and serving.

Chocolate Chips Honey Muffins

Prep time: 5 minutes | Cook time: 15 minutes | Serves 6

- ½ cup all-purpose flour
- ⅓ cup almond flour
- 1 teaspoon baking powder
- A pinch of sea salt
- A pinch of grated nutmeg
- 1 egg
- ¼ cup honey
- ¼ cup milk
- 1 teaspoon vanilla extract
- 4 tablespoons coconut oil
- ½ cup dark chocolate chips

1. Mix all ingredients in a bowl. Scrape the batter into silicone baking molds; place them in the baking dish.
2. Place the baking dish in the air fryer basket. Put the air fryer lid on and bake in the preheated instant pot at 320°F (160°C) for 15 minutes or until a tester comes out dry and clean.
3. Allow the muffins to cool before unmolding and serving. Bon appétit!

Apple and Walnut Muffins

Prep time: 15 minutes | Cook time: 10 minutes | Makes 8 muffins

- 1 cup flour
- ⅓ cup sugar
- 1 teaspoon baking powder
- ¼ teaspoon baking soda
- ¼ teaspoon salt
- 1 teaspoon cinnamon
- ¼ teaspoon ginger
- ¼ teaspoon nutmeg
- 1 egg
- 2 tablespoons pancake syrup, plus 2 teaspoons
- 2 tablespoons melted butter, plus 2 teaspoons
- ¾ cup unsweetened apple sauce
- ½ teaspoon vanilla extract
- ¼ cup chopped walnuts
- ¼ cup diced apple

1. Preheat the air fryer to 330°F (166°C).
2. In a large bowl, stir together the flour, sugar, baking powder, baking soda, salt, cinnamon, ginger, and nutmeg.
3. In a small bowl, beat egg until frothy. Add syrup, butter, applesauce, and vanilla and mix well.
4. Pour egg mixture into dry ingredients and stir just until moistened.
5. Gently stir in nuts and diced apple.
6. Divide batter among 8 parchment-paper-lined muffin cups.
7. Put 4 muffin cups in air fryer basket and bake for 10 minutes.
8. Repeat with remaining 4 muffins or until toothpick inserted in center comes out clean.
9. Serve warm.

Potato Bread Rolls

Prep time: 15 minutes | Cook time: 20 minutes | Serves 5

- 5 large potatoes, boiled and mashed
- Salt and ground black pepper, to taste
- ½ teaspoon mustard seeds
- 1 tablespoon olive oil
- 2 small onions, chopped
- 2 sprigs curry leaves
- ½ teaspoon turmeric powder
- 2 green chilis, seeded and chopped
- 1 bunch coriander, chopped
- 8 slices bread, brown sides discarded

1. Preheat the air fryer to 400°F (204°C).
2. Put the mashed potatoes in a bowl and sprinkle on salt and pepper. Set to one side.
3. Fry the mustard seeds in olive oil over a medium-low heat in a skillet, stirring continuously, until they sputter.
4. Add the onions and cook until they turn translucent. Add the curry leaves and turmeric powder and stir. Cook for a further 2 minutes until fragrant.
5. Remove the pan from the heat and combine with the potatoes. Mix in the green chilies and coriander.

6. Wet the bread slightly and drain of any excess liquid.
7. Spoon a small amount of the potato mixture into the center of the bread and enclose the bread around the filling, sealing it entirely. Continue until the rest of the bread and filling is used up. Brush each bread roll with some oil and transfer to the basket of the air fryer.
8. Air fry for 15 minutes, gently shaking the air fryer basket at the halfway point to ensure each roll is cooked evenly.
9. Serve immediately.

Creamy Cinnamon Rolls

Prep time: 10 minutes | Cook time: 9 minutes | Serves 8

- 1 pound (454 g) frozen bread dough, thawed
- ¼ cup butter, melted
- ¾ cup brown sugar
- 1½ tablespoons ground cinnamon
- Cream Cheese Glaze:
- 4 ounces (113 g) cream cheese, softened
- 2 tablespoons butter, softened
- 1¼ cups powdered sugar
- ½ teaspoon vanilla extract

1. Let the bread dough come to room temperature on the counter. On a lightly floured surface, roll the dough into a 13-inch by 11-inch rectangle. Position the rectangle so the 13-inch side is facing you. Brush the melted butter all over the dough, leaving a 1-inch border uncovered along the edge farthest away from you.
2. Combine the brown sugar and cinnamon in a small bowl. Sprinkle the mixture evenly over the buttered dough, keeping the 1-inch border uncovered. Roll the dough into a log, starting with the edge closest to you. Roll the dough tightly, rolling evenly, and push out any air pockets. When you get to the uncovered edge of the dough, press the dough onto the roll to seal it together.
3. Cut the log into 8 pieces, slicing slowly with a sawing motion so you don't flatten the dough. Turn the slices on their sides and cover with a clean kitchen towel. Let the rolls sit in the warmest part of the kitchen for 1½ to 2 hours to rise.
4. To make the glaze, place the cream cheese and butter in a microwave-safe bowl. Soften the mixture in the microwave for 30 seconds at a time until it is easy to stir. Gradually add the powdered sugar and stir to combine. Add the vanilla extract and whisk until smooth. Set aside.
5. When the rolls have risen, preheat the air fryer to 350°F (177°C).
6. Transfer 4 of the rolls to the air fryer basket. Air fry for 5 minutes. Turn the rolls over and air fry for another 4 minutes. Repeat with the remaining 4 rolls.
7. Let the rolls cool for two minutes before glazing. Spread large dollops of cream cheese glaze on top of the warm cinnamon rolls, allowing some glaze to drip down the side of the rolls. Serve warm.

Posh Orange Rolls

Prep time: 15 minutes | Cook time: 8 minutes | Makes 8 rolls

- 3 ounces (85 g) low-fat cream cheese
- 1 tablespoon low-fat sour cream or plain yogurt
- 2 teaspoons sugar
- ¼ teaspoon pure vanilla extract
- ¼ teaspoon orange extract
- 1 can (8 count) organic crescent roll dough
- ¼ cup chopped walnuts
- ¼ cup dried cranberries
- ¼ cup shredded, sweetened coconut
- Butter-flavored cooking spray
- Orange Glaze:
- ½ cup powdered sugar
- 1 tablespoon orange juice
- ¼ teaspoon orange extract
- Dash of salt

1. Cut a circular piece of parchment paper slightly smaller than the bottom of the air fryer basket. Set aside.
2. In a small bowl, combine the cream cheese, sour cream or yogurt, sugar, and vanilla and orange extracts. Stir until smooth.
3. Preheat the air fryer to 300°F (149°C).
4. Separate crescent roll dough into 8 triangles and divide cream cheese mixture among them. Starting at wide end, spread cheese mixture to within 1 inch of point.
5. Sprinkle nuts and cranberries evenly over cheese mixture.
6. Starting at wide end, roll up triangles, then sprinkle with coconut, pressing in lightly to make it stick. Spray tops of rolls with butter-flavored cooking spray.
7. Put parchment paper in air fryer basket, and place 4 rolls on top, spaced evenly.
8. Air fry for 8 minutes, until rolls are golden brown and cooked through.
9. Repeat steps 7 and 8 to air fry remaining 4 rolls. You should be able to use the same piece of parchment paper twice.
10. In a small bowl, stir together ingredients for glaze and drizzle over warm rolls. Serve warm.

Avocado Quesadillas

Prep time: 10 minutes | Cook time: 11 minutes | Serves 4

- 4 eggs
- 2 tablespoons skim milk
- Salt and ground black pepper, to taste
- Cooking spray
- 4 flour tortillas
- 4 tablespoons salsa
- 2 ounces (57 g) Cheddar cheese, grated
- ½ small avocado, peeled and thinly sliced

1. Preheat the air fryer to 270°F (132°C).
2. Beat together the eggs, milk, salt, and pepper.
3. Spray a baking pan lightly with cooking spray and add egg mixture.
4. Bake for 8 minutes, stirring every 1 to 2 minutes, until eggs are scrambled to the liking. Remove and set aside.
5. Spray one side of each tortilla with cooking spray. Flip over.
6. Divide eggs, salsa, cheese, and avocado among the tortillas, covering only half of each tortilla.
7. Fold each tortilla in half and press down lightly. Increase the temperature of the air fryer to 390°F (199°C).
8. Put 2 tortillas in air fryer basket and air fry for 3 minutes or until cheese melts and outside feels slightly crispy. Repeat with remaining two tortillas.
9. Cut each cooked tortilla into halves. Serve warm.

Banana Bread

Prep time: 10 minutes | Cook time: 22 minutes | Makes 3 loaves

- 3 ripe bananas, mashed
- 1 cup sugar
- 1 large egg
- 4 tablespoons (½ stick) unsalted butter, melted
- 1½ cups all-purpose flour
- 1 teaspoon baking soda
- 1 teaspoon salt

1. Coat the insides of 3 mini loaf pans with cooking spray.
2. In a large mixing bowl, mix the bananas and sugar.
3. In a separate large mixing bowl, combine the egg, butter, flour, baking soda, and salt and mix well.
4. Add the banana mixture to the egg and flour mixture. Mix well.
5. Divide the batter evenly among the prepared pans.
6. Preheat the air fryer to 310°F (154°C). Set the mini loaf pans into the air fryer basket.
7. Bake in the preheated air fryer for 22 minutes. Insert a toothpick into the center of each loaf; if it comes out clean, they are done.
8. When the loaves are cooked through, remove the pans from the air fryer basket. Turn out the loaves onto a wire rack to cool
9. Serve warm.

Rye and Quinoa Porridge

Prep time: 5 minutes | Cook time: 12 minutes | Serves 5

- ½ cup rolled oats
- ½ cup quinoa flakes
- ½ cup rye flakes
- 1 cup coconut milk
- 1 cup orange juice
- 2 eggs, whisked
- 4 tablespoons honey
- ½ teaspoon ground cinnamon

1. Thoroughly combine all ingredients in a mixing bowl. Spoon the mixture into a lightly greased baking dish.
2. Place the baking dish in the air fryer basket. Put the air fryer lid on and bake in the preheated instant pot at 380°F (193°C) for 12 minutes.
3. Serve immediately. Bon appétit!

Chapter 5
Poultry

Teriyaki Chicken and Bell Pepper Kebabs

Prep time: 15 minutes | Cook time: 14 minutes | Serves 4

- 1 pound (454 g) boneless, skinless chicken breasts, cut into 2-inch cubes
- 1 cup teriyaki sauce, divided
- 2 green bell peppers, seeded and cut into 1-inch cubes
- 2 cups fresh pineapple, cut into 1-inch cubes

1. Place the chicken and ½ cup of teriyaki sauce in a large resealable plastic bag or container. Toss to coat evenly. Refrigerate for at least 30 minutes.
2. Place the grill plate on the grill position. Select Grill, set the temperature to 350°F (177°C), and set the time to 14 minutes.
3. Assemble the kebabs by threading the chicken onto the wood skewers, alternating with the peppers and pineapple. Ensure the ingredients are pushed almost completely down to the end of the skewers.
4. Place the skewers on the grill plate. Grill for 10 to 14 minutes, occasionally basting the kebabs with the remaining ½ cup of teriyaki sauce while cooking.
5. Cooking is complete when the internal temperature of the chicken reaches 165°F (74°C) on a food thermometer.

Lemony Chicken and Veggie Kebabs

Prep time: 15 minutes | Cook time: 14 minutes | Serves 4

- 2 tablespoons plain Greek yogurt
- ¼ cup extra-virgin olive oil
- Juice of 4 lemons
- Grated zest of 1 lemon
- 4 garlic cloves, minced
- 2 tablespoons dried oregano
- 1 teaspoon sea salt
- ½ teaspoon freshly ground black pepper
- 1 pound (454 g) boneless, skinless chicken breasts, cut into 2-inch cubes
- 1 red onion, quartered
- 1 zucchini, sliced

1. In a large bowl, whisk together the Greek yogurt, oil, lemon juice, zest, garlic, oregano, salt, and pepper until well combined.
2. Place the chicken and half of the marinade into a large resealable plastic bag or container. Move the chicken around to coat evenly. Refrigerate for at least 30 minutes.
3. Place the grill plate on the grill position. Select Grill, set the temperature to 350°F (177°C), and set the time to 14 minutes.
4. Assemble the kebabs by threading the chicken on the wood skewers, alternating with the red onion and zucchini. Ensure the ingredients are pushed almost completely down to the end of the skewers.
5. Place the skewers on the grill plate. Grill for 10 to 14 minutes, occasionally basting the kebabs with the remaining marinade while cooking.
6. Cooking is complete when the internal temperature of the chicken reaches 165°F (74°C) on a food thermometer.

Spicy Chicken Kebabs

Prep time: 15 minutes | Cook time: 14 minutes | Serves 4

- 1 tablespoon ground cumin
- 1 tablespoon garlic powder
- 1 tablespoon chili powder
- 2 teaspoons paprika
- ¼ teaspoon sea salt
- 1 pound (454 g) boneless, skinless chicken breasts, cut in 2-inch cubes
- 2 tablespoons extra-virgin olive oil, divided
- 2 red bell peppers, seeded and cut into 1-inch cubes
- 1 red onion, quartered
- Juice of 1 lime

1. In a small mixing bowl, combine the cumin, garlic powder, chili powder, paprika, salt, and pepper, and mix well.
2. Place the chicken, 1 tablespoon oil, and half of the spice mixture into a large resealable plastic bag or container. Toss to coat evenly.
3. Place the bell pepper, onion, remaining 1 tablespoon of oil, and remaining spice mixture into a large resealable plastic bag or container. Toss to coat evenly. Refrigerate the chicken and vegetables for at least 30 minutes.
4. Place the grill plate on the grill position. Select Grill, set the temperature to 400°F (204°C), and set the time to 14 minutes.
5. Assemble the kebabs by threading the chicken onto the wood skewers, alternating with the peppers and onion. Ensure the ingredients are pushed almost completely down to the end of the skewers.
6. Place the skewers on the grill plate. Grill for 10 to 14 minutes.
7. Cooking is complete when the internal temperature of the chicken reaches 165°F (74°C). When cooking is complete, remove from the heat, and drizzle with lime juice.

Tempero Baiano Brazilian Chicken

Prep time: 5 minutes | Cook time: 20 minutes | Serves 4

- 1 teaspoon cumin seeds
- 1 teaspoon dried oregano
- 1 teaspoon dried parsley
- 1 teaspoon ground turmeric
- 2 tablespoons olive oil
- 1½ pounds (680 g) chicken drumsticks

1. In a clean coffee grinder or spice mill, combine the cumin, oregano, parsley, turmeric, coriander seeds, salt, peppercorns, and cayenne. Process until finely ground.
2. In a small bowl, combine the ground spices with the lime juice and oil. Place the chicken in a resealable plastic bag. Add the marinade, seal, and massage until the chicken is well coated. Marinate at room temperature for 30 minutes or in the refrigerator for up to 24 hours.
3. Preheat the air fryer to 400°F (204°C).

Sriracha-Honey Glazed Chicken Thighs
Prep time: 5 minutes | Cook time: 17 minutes | Serves 4

- 1 cup sriracha
- Juice of 2 lemons
- ¼ cup honey
- 4 bone-in chicken thighs

1. Place the sriracha, lemon juice, and honey in a large resealable plastic bag or container. Add the chicken thighs and toss to coat evenly. Refrigerate for 30 minutes.
2. Place the grill plate on the grill position. Select Grill, set the temperature to 350°F (177°C), and set the time to 14 minutes.
3. Place the chicken thighs onto the grill plate, gently pressing them down to maximize grill marks. Grill for 7 minutes.
4. After 7 minutes, flip the chicken thighs using tongs. Grill for 7 minutes more.
5. Cooking is complete when the internal temperature of the meat reaches at least 165°F (74°C) on a food thermometer. If necessary, continue grilling for 2 to 3 minutes more.
6. When cooking is complete, remove the chicken from the grill, and let it rest for 5 minutes before serving.

Lime-Garlic Grilled Chicken
Prep time: 5 minutes | Cook time: 18 minutes | Serves 4

- 1½ tablespoons extra-virgin olive oil
- 3 garlic cloves, minced
- ¼ teaspoon ground cumin
- Sea salt, to taste
- Freshly ground black pepper, to taste
- Grated zest of 1 lime
- Juice of 1 lime
- 4 boneless, skinless chicken breasts

1. In a large shallow bowl, stir together the oil, garlic, cumin, salt, pepper, zest, and lime juice. Add the chicken breasts and coat well. Cover and marinate in the refrigerator for 30 minutes.
2. Place the grill plate on the grill position. Select Grill, set the temperature to 350°F (177°C), and set the time to 18 minutes.
3. Place the chicken breasts on the grill plate. Grill for 7 minutes. After 7 minutes, flip the chicken and grill for an additional 7 minutes.
4. Check the chicken for doneness. If needed, grill up to 4 minutes more. Cooking is complete when the internal temperature of the chicken reaches at least 165°F (74°C) on a food thermometer.
5. Remove from the grill, and place on a cutting board or platter to rest for 5inutes. Serve.

Herbed Grilled Chicken Thighs
Prep time: 10 minutes | Cook time: 13 minutes | Serves 4

- Grated zest of 2 lemons
- Juice of 2 lemons
- 3 sprigs fresh rosemary, leaves finely chopped
- 3 sprigs fresh sage, leaves finely chopped
- 2 garlic cloves, minced
- ¼ teaspoon red pepper flakes
- ¼ cup canola oil
- Sea salt
- 4 (4- to 7-ounce / 113- to 198-g) boneless chicken thighs

1. In a small bowl, whisk together the lemon zest and juice, rosemary, sage, garlic, red pepper flakes, and oil. Season with salt.
2. Place the chicken and lemon-herb mixture in a large resealable plastic bag or container. Toss to coat evenly. Refrigerate the chicken for at least 30 minutes.
3. Place the grill plate on the grill position. Select Grill, set the temperature to 400°F (204°C), and set the time to 13 minutes.
4. Place the chicken on the grill plate. Grill for 10 to 13 minutes.
5. Cooking is complete when the internal temperature of the chicken reaches at least 165°F (74°C) on a food thermometer.

Piri-Piri Chicken Thighs
Prep time: 5 minutes | Cook time: 25 minutes | Serves 4

- ¼ cup piri-piri sauce
- 1 tablespoon freshly squeezed lemon juice
- 2 tablespoons brown sugar, divided
- 2 cloves garlic, minced
- 1 tablespoon extra-virgin olive oil
- 4 bone-in, skin-on chicken thighs, each weighing approximately 7 to 8 ounces (198 to 227 g)
- ½ teaspoon cornstarch

1. To make the marinade, whisk together the piri-piri sauce, lemon juice, 1 tablespoon of brown sugar, and the garlic in a small bowl. While whisking, slowly pour in the oil in a steady stream and continue to whisk until emulsified. Using a skewer, poke holes in the chicken thighs and place them in a small glass dish. Pour the marinade over the chicken and turn the thighs to coat them with the sauce. Cover the dish and refrigerate for at least 15 minutes and up to 1 hour.
2. Meanwhile, whisk the remaining brown sugar and the cornstarch into the marinade and microwave it on high power for 1 minute until it is bubbling and thickened to a glaze.
3. Once the chicken is cooked, turn the thighs over and brush them with the glaze. Air fry for a few additional minutes until the glaze browns and begins to char in spots.
4. Remove the chicken to a platter and serve with additional piri-piri sauce, if desired.

Ginger Chicken Thighs

Prep time: 10 minutes | Cook time: 10 minutes | Serves 4

- ¼ cup julienned peeled fresh ginger
- 2 tablespoons vegetable oil
- 1 tablespoon honey
- 1 tablespoon soy sauce
- 1 tablespoon ketchup
- 1 teaspoon garam masala
- 1 teaspoon ground turmeric
- ¼ teaspoon kosher salt
- ½ teaspoon cayenne pepper
- Vegetable oil spray
- 1 pound (454 g) boneless, skinless chicken thighs, cut crosswise into thirds
- ¼ cup chopped fresh cilantro, for garnish

1. In a small bowl, combine the ginger, oil, honey, soy sauce, ketchup, garam masala, turmeric, salt, and cayenne. Whisk until well combined. Place the chicken in a resealable plastic bag and pour the marinade over. Seal the bag and massage to cover all of the chicken with the marinade. Marinate at room temperature for 30 minutes or in the refrigerator for up to 24 hours.
2. Preheat the air fryer to 350°F (177°C).
3. Spray the air fryer basket with vegetable oil spray and add the chicken and as much of the marinade and julienned ginger as possible. Bake for 10 minutes. Use a meat thermometer to ensure the chicken has reached an internal temperature of 165°F (74°C).
4. To serve, garnish with cilantro.

Spicy BBQ Chicken Drumsticks

Prep time: 10 minutes | Cook time: 20 minutes | Serves 4

- 2 cups barbecue sauce
- Juice of 1 lime
- 2 tablespoons honey
- 1 tablespoon hot sauce
- Sea salt, to taste
- Freshly ground black pepper, to taste
- 1 pound (454 g) chicken drumsticks

1. In a large bowl, combine the barbecue sauce, lime juice, honey, and hot sauce. Season with salt and pepper. Set aside ½ cup of the sauce. Add the drumsticks to the bowl, and toss until evenly coated.
2. Place the grill plate on the grill position. Select Grill, set the temperature to 350°F (177°C), and set the time to 20 minutes.
3. Place the drumsticks on the grill plate. Grill for 18 minutes, basting often during cooking.
4. Cooking is complete when the internal temperature of the meat reaches at least 165°F (74°C) on a food thermometer. If necessary, continue grilling for 2 minutes more.

Air Fryer Naked Chicken Tenders

Prep time: 5 minutes | Cook time: 7 minutes | Serves 4

SEASONING:
- 1 teaspoon kosher salt
- ½ teaspoon garlic powder
- ½ teaspoon onion powder
- ½ teaspoon chili powder
- ¼ teaspoon sweet paprika
- ¼ teaspoon freshly ground black pepper

CHICKEN:
- 8 chicken breast tenders (1 pound / 454 g total)
- 2 tablespoons mayonnaise

1. Preheat the air fryer to 375°F (191°C).
2. For the seasoning: In a small bowl, combine the salt, garlic powder, onion powder, chili powder, paprika, and pepper.
3. For the chicken: Place the chicken in a medium bowl and add the mayonnaise. Mix well to coat all over, then sprinkle with the seasoning mix.
4. Working in batches, arrange a single layer of the chicken in the air fryer basket. Air fry for 6 to 7 minutes, flipping halfway, until cooked through in the center. Serve immediately.

Maple-Teriyaki Chicken Wings

Prep time: 5 minutes | Cook time: 14 minutes | Serves 4

- 1 cup maple syrup
- ⅓ cup soy sauce
- ¼ cup teriyaki sauce
- 3 garlic cloves, minced
- 2 teaspoons garlic powder
- 2 teaspoons onion powder
- 1 teaspoon freshly ground black pepper
- 2 pounds (907 g) bone-in chicken wings (drumettes and flats)

1. Place the grill plate on the grill position. Select Grill, set the temperature to 350°F (177°C), and set the time to 14 minutes.
2. Meanwhile, in a large bowl, whisk together the maple syrup, soy sauce, teriyaki sauce, garlic, garlic powder, onion powder, and black pepper. Add the wings, and use tongs to toss and coat.
3. Place the chicken wings on the grill plate. Grill for 5 minutes. After 5 minutes, flip the wings and grill for an additional 5 minutes.
4. Check the wings for doneness. Cooking is complete when the internal temperature of the meat reaches at least 165°F (74°C) on a food thermometer. If needed, grill for up to 4 minutes more.
5. Remove from the grill and serve.

Crispy Dill Pickle Chicken Wings

Prep time: 5 minutes | Cook time: 26 minutes | Serves 4

- 2 pounds (907 g) bone-in chicken wings (drumettes and flats)
- 1½ cups dill pickle juice
- 1½ tablespoons vegetable oil
- ½ tablespoon dried dill
- ¾ teaspoon garlic powder
- Sea salt, to taste
- Freshly ground black pepper, to taste

1. Place the chicken wings in a large shallow bowl. Pour the pickle juice over the top, ensuring all of the wings are coated and as submerged as possible. Cover and refrigerate for 2 hours.
2. Place the crisper tray on the air fry position. Select Air Fry, set the temperature to 390°F (199°C), and set the time to 26 minutes.
3. Rinse the brined chicken wings under cool water, then pat them dry with a paper towel. Place in a large bowl.
4. In a small bowl, whisk together the oil, dill, garlic powder, salt, and pepper. Drizzle over the wings and toss to fully coat them.
5. Place the wings in the crisper tray, spreading them out evenly. Air fry for 11 minutes.
6. After 11 minutes, flip the wings with tongs. Air fry for 11 minutes more.
7. Check the wings for doneness. Cooking is complete when the internal temperature of the chicken reaches at least 165°F (74°C) on a food thermometer. If needed Air fry for up to 4 more minutes.
8. Remove the wings from the crisper tray and serve immediately.

Chicken Fried Steak

Prep time: 15 minutes | Cook time: 10 minutes | Serves 4

- ½ cup flour
- 2 teaspoons salt, divided
- Freshly ground black pepper, to taste
- ¼ teaspoon garlic powder
- 1 cup buttermilk
- 1 cup fine bread crumbs
- 4 (6-ounce / 170-g) tenderized top round steaks, ½-inch thick
- Vegetable or canola oil
- For the Gravy:
- 2 tablespoons butter or bacon drippings
- ¼ onion, minced
- 1 clove garlic, smashed
- ¼ teaspoon dried thyme
- 3 tablespoons flour
- 1 cup milk
- Salt and freshly ground black pepper, to taste
- Dashes of Worcestershire sauce

1. Set up a dredging station. Combine the flour, 1 teaspoon of salt, black pepper and garlic powder in a shallow bowl. Pour the buttermilk into a second shallow bowl. Finally, put the bread crumbs and 1 teaspoon of salt in a third shallow bowl.
2. Dip the tenderized steaks into the flour, then the buttermilk, and then the bread crumb mixture, pressing the crumbs onto the steak. Put them on a baking sheet and spray both sides generously with vegetable or canola oil.
3. Preheat the air fryer to 400°F (204°C).
4. Transfer the steaks to the air fryer basket, two at a time, and air fry for 10 minutes, flipping the steaks over halfway through the cooking time. Hold the first batch of steaks warm in a 170°F (77°C) oven while you air fry the second batch.
5. While the steaks are cooking, make the gravy. Melt the butter in a small saucepan over medium heat on the stovetop. Add the onion, garlic and thyme and cook for five minutes, until the onion is soft and just starting to brown. Stir in the flour and cook for another five minutes, stirring regularly, until the mixture starts to brown. Whisk in the milk and bring the mixture to a boil to thicken. Season to taste with salt, lots of freshly ground black pepper, and a few dashes of Worcestershire sauce.
6. Pour the gravy over the chicken fried steaks and serve.

Roasted Chicken and Vegetable Salad

Prep time: 10 minutes | Cook time: 10 to 13 minutes | Serves 4

- 3 (4-ounce / 113-g) low-sodium boneless, skinless chicken breasts, cut into 1-inch cubes
- 1 small red onion, sliced
- 1 red bell pepper, sliced
- 1 cup green beans, cut into 1-inch pieces
- 2 tablespoons low-fat ranch salad dressing
- 2 tablespoons freshly squeezed lemon juice
- ½ teaspoon dried basil
- 4 cups mixed lettuce

1. Preheat the air fryer to 400°F (204°C).
2. In the air fryer basket, roast the chicken, red onion, red bell pepper, and green beans for 10 to 13 minutes, or until the chicken reaches an internal temperature of 165°F (74°C) on a meat thermometer, tossing the food in the basket once during cooking.
3. While the chicken cooks, in a serving bowl, mix the ranch dressing, lemon juice, and basil.
4. Transfer the chicken and vegetables to a serving bowl and toss with the dressing to coat. Serve immediately on lettuce leaves.

Lemon Chicken and Spinach Salad

Prep time: 10 minutes | Cook time: 16 to 20 minutes | Serves 4

- 3 (5-ounce / 142-g) low-sodium boneless, skinless chicken breasts, cut into 1-inch cubes
- 5 teaspoons olive oil
- ½ teaspoon dried thyme
- 1 medium red onion, sliced
- 1 red bell pepper, sliced
- 1 small zucchini, cut into strips
- 3 tablespoons freshly squeezed lemon juice
- 6 cups fresh baby spinach

1. Preheat the air fryer to 400°F (204°C).
2. In a large bowl, mix the chicken with the olive oil and thyme. Toss to coat. Transfer to a medium metal bowl and roast for 8 minutes in the air fryer.
3. Add the red onion, red bell pepper, and zucchini. Roast for 8 to 12 minutes more, stirring once during cooking, or until the chicken reaches an internal temperature of 165°F (74°C) on a meat thermometer.
4. Remove the bowl from the air fryer and stir in the lemon juice.
5. Put the spinach in a serving bowl and top with the chicken mixture. Toss to combine and serve immediately.

Almond-Crusted Chicken Nuggets

Prep time: 10 minutes | Cook time: 10 to 13 minutes | Serves 4

- 1 egg white
- 1 tablespoon freshly squeezed lemon juice
- ½ teaspoon dried basil
- ½ teaspoon ground paprika
- 1 pound (454 g) low-sodium boneless, skinless chicken breasts, cut into 1½-inch cubes
- ½ cup ground almonds
- 2 slices low-sodium whole-wheat bread, crumbled

1. Preheat the air fryer to 400°F (204°C).
2. In a shallow bowl, beat the egg white, lemon juice, basil, and paprika with a fork until foamy.
3. Add the chicken and stir to coat.
4. On a plate, mix the almonds and bread crumbs.
5. Toss the chicken cubes in the almond and bread crumb mixture until coated.
6. Bake the nuggets in the air fryer, in two batches, for 10 to 13 minutes, or until the chicken reaches an internal temperature of 165°F (74°C) on a meat thermometer. Serve immediately.

Easy Tandoori Chicken

Prep time: 5 minutes | Cook time: 18 to 23 minutes | Serves 4

- ⅔ cup plain low-fat yogurt
- 2 tablespoons freshly squeezed lemon juice
- 2 teaspoons curry powder
- ½ teaspoon ground cinnamon
- 2 garlic cloves, minced
- 2 teaspoons olive oil
- 4 (5-ounce / 142-g) low-sodium boneless, skinless chicken breasts

1. In a medium bowl, whisk the yogurt, lemon juice, curry powder, cinnamon, garlic, and olive oil.
2. With a sharp knife, cut thin slashes into the chicken. Add it to the yogurt mixture and turn to coat. Let stand for 10 minutes at room temperature. You can also prepare this ahead of time and marinate the chicken in the refrigerator for up to 24 hours.
3. Preheat the air fryer to 360°F (182°C).
4. Remove the chicken from the marinade and shake off any excess liquid. Discard any remaining marinade.
5. Roast the chicken for 10 minutes. With tongs, carefully turn each piece. Roast for 8 to 13 minutes more, or until the chicken reaches an internal temperature of 165°F (74°C) on a meat thermometer. Serve immediately.

Roasted Chicken Tenders with Veggies

Prep time: 10 minutes | Cook time: 18 to 20 minutes | Serves 4

- 1 pound (454 g) chicken tenders
- 1 tablespoon honey
- Pinch salt
- Freshly ground black pepper, to taste
- ½ cup soft fresh bread crumbs
- ½ teaspoon dried thyme
- 1 tablespoon olive oil
- 2 carrots, sliced
- 12 small red potatoes

1. Preheat the air fryer to 380°F (193°C).
2. In a medium bowl, toss the chicken tenders with the honey, salt, and pepper.
3. In a shallow bowl, combine the bread crumbs, thyme, and olive oil, and mix.
4. Coat the tenders in the bread crumbs, pressing firmly onto the meat.
5. Place the carrots and potatoes in the air fryer basket and top with the chicken tenders.
6. Roast for 18 to 20 minutes or until the chicken is cooked to 165°F (74°C) and the vegetables are tender, shaking the basket halfway during the cooking time.
7. Serve warm.

Dill Chicken Strips

Prep time: 15 minutes | Cook time: 10 minutes | Serves 4

- 2 whole boneless, skinless chicken breasts, halved lengthwise
- 1 cup Italian dressing
- 3 cups finely crushed potato chips
- 1 tablespoon dried dill weed
- 1 tablespoon garlic powder
- 1 large egg, beaten
- Cooking spray

1. In a large resealable bag, combine the chicken and Italian dressing. Seal the bag and refrigerate to marinate at least 1 hour.
2. In a shallow dish, stir together the potato chips, dill, and garlic powder. Place the beaten egg in a second shallow dish.
3. Remove the chicken from the marinade. Roll the chicken pieces in the egg and the potato chip mixture, coating thoroughly.
4. Preheat the air fryer to 325°F (163°C). Line the air fryer basket with parchment paper.
5. Place the coated chicken on the parchment and spritz with cooking spray.
6. Bake for 5 minutes. Flip the chicken, spritz it with cooking spray, and bake for 5 minutes more until the outsides are crispy and the insides are no longer pink. Serve immediately.

Blackened Chicken Breasts

Prep time: 10 minutes | Cook time: 20 minutes | Serves 4

- 1 large egg, beaten
- ¾ cup Blackened seasoning
- 2 whole boneless, skinless chicken breasts (about 1 pound / 454 g each), halved
- Cooking spray

1. Preheat the air fryer to 360°F (182°C). Line the air fryer basket with parchment paper.
2. Place the beaten egg in one shallow bowl and the Blackened seasoning in another shallow bowl.
3. One at a time, dip the chicken pieces in the beaten egg and the Blackened seasoning, coating thoroughly.
4. Place the chicken pieces on the parchment and spritz with cooking spray.
5. Air fry for 10 minutes. Flip the chicken, spritz it with cooking spray, and air fry for 10 minutes more until the internal temperature reaches 165°F (74°C) and the chicken is no longer pink inside. Let sit for 5 minutes before serving.

Israeli Chicken Schnitzel

Prep time: 5 minutes | Cook time: 10 minutes | Serves 4

- 2 large boneless, skinless chicken breasts, each weighing about 1 pound (454 g)
- 1 cup all-purpose flour
- 2 teaspoons garlic powder
- 2 teaspoons kosher salt
- 1 teaspoon black pepper
- 1 teaspoon paprika
- 2 eggs beaten with 2 tablespoons water
- 2 cups panko bread crumbs
- Vegetable oil spray
- Lemon juice, for serving

1. Preheat the air fryer to 375°F (191°C).
2. Place 1 chicken breast between 2 pieces of plastic wrap. Use a mallet or a rolling pin to pound the chicken until it is ¼ inch thick. Set aside. Repeat with the second breast. Whisk together the flour, garlic powder, salt, pepper, and paprika on a large plate. Place the panko in a separate shallow bowl or pie plate.
3. Dredge 1 chicken breast in the flour, shaking off any excess, then dip it in the egg mixture. Dredge the chicken breast in the panko, making sure to coat it completely. Shake off any excess panko. Place the battered chicken breast on a plate. Repeat with the second chicken breast.
4. Spray the air fryer basket with oil spray. Place 1 of the battered chicken breasts in the basket and spray the top with oil spray. Air fry until the top is browned, about 5 minutes. Flip the chicken and spray the second side with oil spray. Air fry until the second side is browned and crispy and the internal temperature reaches 165°F (74°C). Remove the first chicken breast from the air fryer and repeat with the second chicken breast.
5. Serve hot with lemon juice.

Mayonnaise-Mustard Chicken

Prep time: 10 minutes | Cook time: 15 minutes | Serves 4

- 6 tablespoons mayonnaise
- 2 tablespoons coarse-ground mustard
- 2 teaspoons honey (optional)
- 2 teaspoons curry powder
- 1 teaspoon kosher salt
- 1 teaspoon cayenne pepper
- 1 pound (454 g) chicken tenders

1. Preheat the air fryer to 350°F (177°C).
2. In a large bowl, whisk together the mayonnaise, mustard, honey (if using), curry powder, salt, and cayenne. Transfer half of the mixture to a serving bowl to serve as a dipping sauce. Add the chicken tenders to the large bowl and toss until well coated.
3. Place the tenders in the air fryer basket and bake for 15 minutes. Use a meat thermometer to ensure the chicken has reached an internal temperature of 165°F (74°C).
4. Serve the chicken with the dipping sauce.

Chapter 6
Fish and Seafood

Honey-Lemon Snapper with Grapes

Prep time: 15 minutes | Cook time: 12 minutes | Serves 4

- 4 (4-ounce / 113-g) red snapper fillets
- 2 teaspoons olive oil
- 3 plums, halved and pitted
- 3 nectarines, halved and pitted
- 1 cup red grapes
- 1 tablespoon freshly squeezed lemon juice
- 1 tablespoon honey
- ½ teaspoon dried thyme

1. Arrange the red snapper fillets in the perforated pan and drizzle the olive oil over the top.
2. Select Air Fry. Set temperature to 390°F (199°C) and set time to 12 minutes. Press Start to begin preheating.
3. Once preheated, place the pan into the oven.
4. After 4 minutes, remove the pan from the oven. Top the fillets with the plums and nectarines. Scatter the red grapes all over the fillets. Drizzle with the lemon juice and honey and sprinkle the thyme on top. Return the pan to the oven and continue cooking for 8 minutes, or until the fish is flaky.
5. When cooking is complete, remove from the oven and serve warm.

Miso-Glazed Cod with Bok Choy

Prep time: 5 minutes | Cook time: 17 minutes | Serves 4

- 4 (6-ounce / 170-g) cod fillets
- ¼ cup miso
- 3 tablespoons brown sugar
- 1 teaspoon sesame oil, divided
- 1 tablespoon white wine or mirin
- 2 tablespoons soy sauce
- ¼ teaspoon red pepper flakes
- 1 pound (454 g) baby bok choy, halved lengthwise

1. Place the cod, miso, brown sugar, ¾ teaspoon of sesame oil, and white wine in a large resealable plastic bag or container. Move the fillets around to coat evenly with the marinade. Refrigerate for 30 minutes.
2. Place the grill plate on the grill position. Select Grill, set the temperature to 450°F (232°C), and set the time to 8 minutes.
3. Place the fillets on the grill plate. Gently press them down to maximize grill marks. Grill for 8 minutes. (There is no need to flip the fish during grilling.)
4. While the cod grills, in a small bowl, whisk together the remaining ¼ teaspoon of sesame oil, soy sauce, and red pepper flakes. Brush the bok choy halves with the soy sauce mixture on all sides.
5. Remove the cod from the grill and set aside on a cutting board to rest. Tent with aluminum foil to keep warm.
6. Place the bok choy on the grill plate, cut-side down. Grill for 9 minutes. (There is no need to flip the bok choy during grilling.)
7. Remove the bok choy from the grill, plate with the cod, and serve.

Ginger Swordfish Steaks with Jalapeño

Prep time: 10 minutes | Cook time: 8 minutes | Serves 4

- 4 (4-ounce / 113-g) swordfish steaks
- ½ teaspoon toasted sesame oil
- 1 jalapeño pepper, finely minced
- 2 garlic cloves, grated
- 2 tablespoons freshly squeezed lemon juice
- 1 tablespoon grated fresh ginger
- ½ teaspoon Chinese five-spice powder
- ⅛ teaspoon freshly ground black pepper

1. On a clean work surface, place the swordfish steaks and brush both sides of the fish with the sesame oil.
2. Combine the jalapeño, garlic, lemon juice, ginger, five-spice powder, and black pepper in a small bowl and stir to mix well. Rub the mixture all over the fish until completely coated. Allow to sit for 10 minutes.
3. When ready, arrange the swordfish steaks in the perforated pan.
4. Select Air Fry. Set temperature to 380°F (193°C) and set time to 8 minutes. Press Start to begin preheating.
5. Once preheated, place the pan into the oven. Flip the steaks halfway through.
6. When cooking is complete, remove from the oven and cool for 5 minutes before serving.

Fried Cod Fillets in Beer

Prep time: 5 minutes | Cook time: 15 minutes | Serves 4

- 2 eggs
- 1 cup malty beer
- 1 cup all-purpose flour
- ½ cup cornstarch
- 1 teaspoon garlic powder
- Salt and pepper, to taste
- 4 (4-ounce / 113-g) cod fillets
- Cooking spray

1. In a shallow bowl, beat together the eggs with the beer. In another shallow bowl, thoroughly combine the flour and cornstarch. Sprinkle with the garlic powder, salt, and pepper.
2. Dredge each cod fillet in the flour mixture, then in the egg mixture. Dip each piece of fish in the flour mixture a second time.
3. Spritz the perforated pan with cooking spray. Arrange the cod fillets in the pan in a single layer.
4. Select Air Fry. Set temperature to 400°F (205°C) and set time to 15 minutes. Press Start to begin preheating.
5. Once preheated, place the pan into the oven. Flip the fillets halfway through the cooking time.
6. When cooking is complete, the cod should reach an internal temperature of 145°F (63°C) on a meat thermometer and the outside should be crispy. Let the fish cool for 5 minutes and serve.

Parmesan Fish Fillets with Tarragon

Prep time: 8 minutes | Cook time: 17 minutes | Serves 4

- ⅓ cup grated Parmesan cheese
- ½ teaspoon fennel seed
- ½ teaspoon tarragon
- ⅓ teaspoon mixed peppercorns
- 2 eggs, beaten
- 4 (4-ounce / 113-g) fish fillets, halved
- 2 tablespoons dry white wine
- 1 teaspoon seasoned salt

1. Place the grated Parmesan cheese, fennel seed, tarragon, and mixed peppercorns in a food processor and pulse for about 20 seconds until well combined. Transfer the cheese mixture to a shallow dish.
2. Place the beaten eggs in another shallow dish.
3. Drizzle the dry white wine over the top of fish fillets. Dredge each fillet in the beaten eggs on both sides, shaking off any excess, then roll them in the cheese mixture until fully coated. Season with the salt.
4. Arrange the fillets in the perforated pan.
5. Select Air Fry. Set temperature to 345°F (174°C) and set time to 17 minutes. Press Start to begin preheating.
6. Once preheated, place the pan into the oven. Flip the fillets once halfway through the cooking time.
7. When cooking is complete, the fish should be cooked through no longer translucent. Remove from the oven and cool for 5 minutes before serving.

Cornmeal-Crusted Trout Fingers

Prep time: 15 minutes | Cook time: 6 minutes | Serves: 2

- ½ cup yellow cornmeal, medium or finely ground (not coarse)
- ⅓ cup all-purpose flour
- 1½ teaspoons baking powder
- 1 teaspoon kosher salt, plus more as needed
- ½ teaspoon freshly ground black pepper, plus more as needed
- ⅛ teaspoon cayenne pepper
- ¾ pound (340 g) skinless trout fillets, cut into strips 1 inch wide and 3 inches long
- 3 large eggs, lightly beaten
- Cooking spray
- ½ cup mayonnaise
- 2 tablespoons capers, rinsed and finely chopped
- 1 tablespoon fresh tarragon
- 1 teaspoon fresh lemon juice, plus lemon wedges, for serving

1. Preheat the air fryer to 400°F (204°C).
2. In a large bowl, whisk together the cornmeal, flour, baking powder, salt, black pepper, and cayenne. Dip the trout strips in the egg, then toss them in the cornmeal mixture until fully coated. Transfer the trout to a rack set over a baking sheet and liberally spray all over with cooking spray.

3. Transfer half the fish to the air fryer and air fry until the fish is cooked through and golden brown, about 6 minutes. Transfer the fish sticks to a plate and repeat with the remaining fish.
4. Meanwhile, in a bowl, whisk together the mayonnaise, capers, tarragon, and lemon juice. Season the tartar sauce with salt and black pepper.
5. Serve the trout fingers hot along with the tartar sauce and lemon wedges.

Southwest Shrimp and Cabbage Tacos

Prep time: 15 minutes | Cook time: 10 minutes | Serves 4

- 4 corn tortillas
- Nonstick cooking spray
- 1 pound (454 g) fresh jumbo shrimp
- Juice of ½ lemon
- 1 teaspoon chili powder
- 1 teaspoon ground cumin
- 1 teaspoon Southwestern seasoning
- ¼ teaspoon cayenne pepper
- 2 cups shredded green cabbage
- 1 avocado, peeled and sliced

1. Place the grill plate on the grill position. Select Grill, set the temperature to 450°F (232°C), and set the time to 10 minutes.
2. Spray both sides of the tortillas with cooking spray, and in a large bowl, toss the shrimp with the lemon juice, chili powder, cumin, Southwestern seasoning, and cayenne pepper, until evenly coated. Let marinate while grilling the tortillas in the next step.
3. Place 1 tortilla on the grill plate. Grill for 1 minute. After 1 minute, remove the tortilla; set aside. Repeat with the remaining 3 tortillas.
4. After removing the final tortilla, carefully place the shrimp on the grill plate. Grill for 5 minutes. (There is no need to flip the shrimp during grilling.)
5. Remove the shrimp from the grill, arrange on the grilled tortillas, and top with cabbage and avocado. Feel free to include other toppings, such as cotija cheese, cilantro, and lime wedges.

Tandoori-Spiced Salmon and Potatoes

Prep time: 10 minutes | Cook time: 28 minutes | Serves: 2

- 1 pound (454 g) fingerling potatoes
- 2 tablespoons vegetable oil
- Kosher salt and freshly ground black pepper, to taste
- 1 teaspoon ground turmeric
- 1 teaspoon ground cumin
- 1 teaspoon ground ginger
- ½ teaspoon smoked paprika
- ¼ teaspoon cayenne pepper
- 2 (6-ounce / 170-g) skin-on salmon fillets

1. Preheat the air fryer to 375°F (191°C).
2. In a bowl, toss the potatoes with 1 tablespoon of the oil until evenly coated. Season with salt and pepper. Transfer the potatoes to the air fryer and air fry for 20 minutes.
3. Meanwhile, in a bowl, combine the remaining 1 tablespoon oil, the turmeric, cumin, ginger, paprika, and cayenne. Add the salmon fillets and turn in the spice mixture until fully coated all over.
4. After the potatoes have cooked 20 minutes, place the salmon fillets, skin-side up, on top of the potatoes, and continue cooking until the potatoes are tender, the salmon is cooked, and the salmon skin is slightly crisp, 5 to 8 minutes for medium to well-done.
5. Transfer the salmon fillets to two plates and serve with the potatoes while both are warm.

Baked Salmon in Wine

Prep time: 5 minutes | Cook time: 10 minutes | Serves 4

- 4 tablespoons butter, melted
- 2 cloves garlic, minced
- Sea salt and ground black pepper, to taste
- ¼ cup dry white wine
- 1 tablespoon lime juice
- 1 teaspoon smoked paprika
- ½ teaspoon onion powder
- 4 salmon steaks
- Cooking spray

1. Place all the ingredients except the salmon and oil in a shallow dish and stir to mix well.
2. Add the salmon steaks, turning to coat well on both sides. Transfer the salmon to the refrigerator to marinate for 30 minutes.
3. When ready, put the salmon steaks in the perforated pan, discarding any excess marinade. Spray the salmon steaks with cooking spray.
4. Select Air Fry. Set temperature to 360°F (182°C) and set time to 10 minutes. Press Start to begin preheating.
5. Once preheated, place the pan into the oven. Flip the salmon steaks halfway through.
6. When cooking is complete, remove from the oven and divide the salmon steaks among four plates. Serve warm.

Garlicky Shrimp Caesar Salad

Prep time: 10 minutes | Cook time: 5 minutes | Serves 4

- 1 pound (454 g) fresh jumbo shrimp
- Juice of ½ lemon
- 3 garlic cloves, minced
- Sea salt, to taste
- Freshly ground black pepper, to taste
- 2 heads romaine lettuce, chopped
- ¾ cup Caesar dressing
- ½ cup grated Parmesan cheese

1. Place the grill plate on the grill position. Select Grill, set the temperature to 450°F (232°C), and set the time to 5 minutes.
2. In a large bowl, toss the shrimp with the lemon juice, garlic, salt, and pepper. Let marinate for 10 minutes.
3. Place the shrimp on the grill plate. Grill for 5 minutes. (There is no need to flip the shrimp during grilling.)
4. While the shrimp grills, toss the romaine lettuce with the Caesar dressing, then divide evenly among four plates or bowls.
5. When cooking is complete, use tongs to remove the shrimp from the grill and place on top of each salad. Sprinkle with the Parmesan cheese and serve.

Lime-Chili Shrimp Bowl

Prep time: 10 minutes | Cook time: 10 to 15 minutes | Serves 4

- 1 teaspoon olive oil, plus more for spraying
- 2 teaspoons lime juice
- 1 teaspoon honey
- 1 teaspoon minced garlic
- 1 teaspoon chili powder
- Salt, to taste
- 12 ounces (340 g) medium cooked shrimp, thawed, deveined, peeled
- 2 cups cooked brown rice
- 1 (15-ounce / 425-g) can seasoned black beans, warmed
- 1 large avocado, chopped
- 1 cup sliced cherry tomatoes

1. Preheat the air fryer to 400°F (204°C). Spray the air fryer basket lightly with olive oil.
2. In a medium bowl, mix together the lime juice, 1 teaspoon of olive oil, honey, garlic, chili powder, and salt to make a marinade.
3. Add the shrimp and toss to coat evenly in the marinade.
4. Place the shrimp in the fryer basket. Air fry for 5 minutes. Shake the basket and air fry until the shrimp are cooked through and starting to brown, an additional 5 to 10 minutes.
5. To assemble the bowls, spoon ¼ of the rice, black beans, avocado, and cherry tomatoes into each of four bowls. Top with the shrimp and serve.

Seasoned Breaded Shrimp

Prep time: 15 minutes | Cook time: 10 to 15 minutes | Serves 4

- 2 teaspoons Old Bay seasoning, divided
- ½ teaspoon garlic powder
- ½ teaspoon onion powder
- 1 pound (454 g) large shrimp, deveined, with tails on
- 2 large eggs
- ½ cup whole-wheat panko bread crumbs
- Cooking spray

1. Preheat the air fryer to 380°F (193°C).
2. Spray the air fryer basket lightly with cooking spray.
3. In a medium bowl, mix together 1 teaspoon of Old Bay seasoning, garlic powder, and onion powder. Add the shrimp and toss with the seasoning mix to lightly coat.
4. In a separate small bowl, whisk the eggs with 1 teaspoon water.
5. In a shallow bowl, mix together the remaining 1 teaspoon Old Bay seasoning and the panko bread crumbs.
6. Dip each shrimp in the egg mixture and dredge in the bread crumb mixture to evenly coat.
7. Place the shrimp in the fryer basket, in a single layer. Lightly spray the shrimp with oil. You many need to cook the shrimp in batches.
8. Air fry for 10 to 15 minutes, or until the shrimp is cooked through and crispy, shaking the basket at 5-minute intervals to redistribute and evenly cook.
9. Serve immediately.

Country Shrimp

Prep time: 10 minutes | Cook time: 15 to 20 minutes | Serves 4

- 2 tablespoons olive oil, plus more for spraying
- 1 pound (454 g) large shrimp, deveined, tail on
- 1 pound (454 g) smoked turkey sausage, cut into thick slices
- 2 corn cobs, quartered
- 1 zucchini, cut into bite-sized pieces
- 1 red bell pepper, cut into chunks
- 1 tablespoon Old Bay seasoning

1. Preheat the air fryer to 400°F (204°C). Spray the fryer basket lightly with olive oil.
2. In a large bowl, mix the shrimp, turkey sausage, corn, zucchini, bell pepper, and Old Bay seasoning, and toss to coat with the spices. Add the 2 tablespoons of olive oil and toss again until evenly coated.
3. Spread the mixture in the fryer basket in a single layer. You will need to cook in batches.
4. Air fry for 15 to 20 minutes, or until cooked through, shaking the basket every 5 minutes for even cooking.
5. Serve immediately.

Spicy Orange Shrimp

Prep time: 20 minutes | Cook time: 10 to 15 minutes | Serves 4

- ⅓ cup orange juice
- 3 teaspoons minced garlic
- 1 teaspoon Old Bay seasoning
- ¼ to ½ teaspoon cayenne pepper
- 1 pound (454 g) medium shrimp, thawed, deveined, peeled, with tails off
- Cooking spray

1. In a medium bowl, combine the orange juice, garlic, Old Bay seasoning, and cayenne pepper.
2. Dry the shrimp with paper towels to remove excess water.
3. Add the shrimp to the marinade and stir to evenly coat. Cover with plastic wrap and place in the refrigerator for 30 minutes so the shrimp can soak up the marinade.
4. Preheat the air fryer to 400°F (204°C). Spray the air fryer basket lightly with olive oil.
5. Place the shrimp into the fryer basket. Air fry for 5 minutes. Shake the basket and lightly spray with olive oil. Air fry until the shrimp are opaque and crisp, 5 to 10 more minutes.
6. Serve immediately.

Air Fried Spring Rolls

Prep time: 10 minutes | Cook time: 17 to 22 minutes | Serves 4

- 2 teaspoons minced garlic
- 2 cups finely sliced cabbage
- 2 (4-ounce / 113-g) cans tiny shrimp, drained
- 4 teaspoons soy sauce
- Salt and freshly ground black pepper, to taste
- 16 square spring roll wrappers
- Cooking spray

1. Preheat the air fryer to 370°F (188°C).
2. Spray the air fryer basket lightly with olive oil. Spray a medium sauté pan with olive oil.
3. Add the garlic to the sauté pan and cook over medium heat until fragrant, 30 to 45 seconds. Add the cabbage and carrots and sauté until the vegetables are slightly tender, about 5 minutes.
4. Add the shrimp and soy sauce and season with salt and pepper, then stir to combine. Sauté until the moisture has evaporated, 2 more minutes. Set aside to cool.
5. Place a spring roll wrapper on a work surface so it looks like a diamond. Place 1 tablespoon of the shrimp mixture on the lower end of the wrapper.
6. Roll the wrapper away from you halfway, then fold in the right and left sides, like an envelope. Continue to roll to the very end, using a little water to seal the edge. Repeat with the remaining wrappers and filling.
7. Place the spring rolls in the fryer basket in a single layer, leaving room between each roll. Lightly spray with olive oil. You may need to cook them in batches.
8. Air fry for 5 minutes. Turn the rolls over, lightly spray with olive oil, and air fry until heated through and the rolls start to brown, 5 to 10 more minutes.

Cajun-Style Fish Tacos

Prep time: 5 minutes | Cook time: 10 to 15 minutes | Serves 6

- 2 teaspoons avocado oil
- 1 tablespoon Cajun seasoning
- 4 tilapia fillets
- 1 (14-ounce / 397-g) package coleslaw mix
- 12 corn tortillas
- 2 limes, cut into wedges

1. Preheat the air fryer to 380°F (193°C). Line the air fryer basket with a perforated air fryer liner.
2. In a medium, shallow bowl mix the avocado oil and the Cajun seasoning to make a marinade. Add the tilapia fillets and coat evenly.
3. Place the fillets in the basket in a single layer, leaving room between each fillet. You may need to cook in batches.
4. Air fry until the fish is cooked and easily flakes with a fork, 10 to 15 minutes.
5. Assemble the tacos by placing some of the coleslaw mix in each tortilla. Add ⅓ of a tilapia fillet to each tortilla. Squeeze some lime juice over the top of each taco and serve.

Homemade Fish Sticks

Prep time: 15 minutes | Cook time: 10 to 15 minutes | Serves 4

- 4 fish fillets
- ½ cup whole-wheat flour
- 1 teaspoon seasoned salt
- 2 eggs
- 1½ cups whole-wheat panko bread crumbs
- ½ tablespoon dried parsley flakes
- Cooking spray

1. Preheat the air fryer to 400°F (204°C). Spray the air fryer basket lightly with olive oil.
2. Cut the fish fillets lengthwise into "sticks."
3. In a shallow bowl, mix the whole-wheat flour and seasoned salt.
4. In a small bowl, whisk the eggs with 1 teaspoon of water.
5. In another shallow bowl, mix the panko bread crumbs and parsley flakes.
6. Coat each fish stick in the seasoned flour, then in the egg mixture, and dredge them in the panko bread crumbs.
7. Place the fish sticks in the fryer basket in a single layer and lightly spray the fish sticks with olive oil. You may need to cook them in batches.
8. Air fry for 5 to 8 minutes. Flip the fish sticks over and lightly spray with the olive oil. Air fry until golden brown and crispy, 5 to 7 more minutes.
9. Serve warm.

Crispy Catfish Strips

Prep time: 5 minutes | Cook time: 16 to 18 minutes | Serves 4

- 1 cup buttermilk
- 5 catfish fillets, cut into 1½-inch strips
- Cooking spray
- 1 cup cornmeal
- 1 tablespoon Creole, Cajun, or Old Bay seasoning

1. Pour the buttermilk into a shallow baking dish. Place the catfish in the dish and refrigerate for at least 1 hour to help remove any fishy taste.
2. Preheat the air fryer to 400°F (204°C). Spray the air fryer basket lightly with cooking spray.
3. In a shallow bowl, combine cornmeal and Creole seasoning.
4. Shake any excess buttermilk off the catfish. Place each strip in the cornmeal mixture and coat completely. Press the cornmeal into the catfish gently to help it stick.
5. Place the strips in the fryer basket in a single layer. Lightly spray the catfish with olive oil. You may need to cook the catfish in more than one batch.
6. Air fry for 8 minutes. Turn the catfish strips over and lightly spray with olive oil. Air fry until golden brown and crispy, 8 to 10 more minutes.
7. Serve warm.

Garlic-Lemon Tilapia

Prep time: 5 minutes | Cook time: 10 to 15 minutes | Serves 4

1 tablespoon lemon juice
1 tablespoon olive oil
1 teaspoon minced garlic
½ teaspoon chili powder
4 (6-ounce / 170-g) tilapia fillets

1. Preheat the air fryer to 380°F (193°C). Line the air fryer basket with perforated air fryer liners.
2. In a large, shallow bowl, mix together the lemon juice, olive oil, garlic, and chili powder to make a marinade. Place the tilapia fillets in the bowl and coat evenly.
3. Place the fillets in the basket in a single layer, leaving space between each fillet. You may need to cook in more than one batch.
4. Air fry until the fish is cooked and flakes easily with a fork, 10 to 15 minutes.
5. Serve hot.

Tuna and Cucumber Salad

Prep time: 10 minutes | Cook time: 6 minutes | Serves 4

- 2 tablespoons rice wine vinegar
- ¼ teaspoon sea salt, plus additional for seasoning
- ½ teaspoon freshly ground black pepper, plus additional for seasoning
- 6 tablespoons extra-virgin olive oil
- 1½ pounds (680 g) ahi tuna, cut into four strips
- 2 tablespoons sesame oil
- 1 (10-ounce / 284-g) bag baby greens
- ½ English cucumber, sliced

1. Place the grill plate on the grill position. Select Grill, set the temperature to 450°F (232°C), and set the time to 6 minutes.
2. Meanwhile, in a small bowl, whisk together the rice vinegar, ¼ teaspoon of salt, and ½ teaspoon of pepper. Slowly pour in the oil while whisking, until the vinaigrette is fully combined.
3. Season the tuna with salt and pepper, and drizzle with the sesame oil.
4. Place the tuna strips on the grill plate. Grill for 4 to 6 minutes. (There is no need to flip during cooking.)
5. While the tuna cooks, divide the baby greens and cucumber slices evenly among four plates or bowls.
6. When cooking is complete, top each salad with one tuna strip. Drizzle the vinaigrette over the top, and serve immediately.

Tuna Patty Sliders

Prep time: 15 minutes | Cook time: 10 to 15 minutes | Serves 4

- 3 (5-ounce / 142-g) cans tuna, packed in water
- ⅔ cup whole-wheat panko bread crumbs
- ⅓ cup shredded Parmesan cheese
- 1 tablespoon sriracha
- ¾ teaspoon black pepper
- 10 whole-wheat slider buns
- Cooking spray

1. Preheat the air fryer to 350°F (177°C).
2. Spray the air fryer basket lightly with cooking spray.
3. In a medium bowl combine the tuna, bread crumbs, Parmesan cheese, sriracha, and black pepper and stir to combine.
4. Form the mixture into 10 patties.
5. Place the patties in the fryer basket in a single layer. Spray the patties lightly with cooking spray. You may need to cook them in batches.
6. Air fry for 6 to 8 minutes. Turn the patties over and lightly spray with olive oil. Air fry until golden brown and crisp, another 4 to 7 more minutes.

Marinated Salmon Fillets

Prep time: 10 minutes | Cook time: 15 to 20 minutes | Serves 4

- 1 tablespoon olive oil, plus more for spraying
- ¼ cup soy sauce
- ¼ cup rice wine vinegar
- 1 tablespoon brown sugar
- 1 teaspoon mustard powder
- 1 teaspoon ground ginger
- ½ teaspoon freshly ground black pepper
- ½ teaspoon minced garlic
- 4 (6-ounce / 170-g) salmon fillets, skin-on

1. Preheat the air fryer to 370°F (188°C). Spray the air fryer basket lightly with olive oil.
2. In a small bowl combine the soy sauce, rice wine vinegar, brown sugar, 1 tablespoon of olive oil, mustard powder, ginger, black pepper, and garlic to make a marinade.
3. Place the fillets in a shallow baking dish and pour the marinade over them. Cover the baking dish and marinate for at least 1 hour in the refrigerator, turning the fillets occasionally to keep them coated in the marinade.
4. Shake off as much marinade as possible from the fillets and place them, skin side down, in the fryer basket in a single layer. You may need to cook the fillets in batches.
5. Air fry for 15 to 20 minutes for well done. The minimum internal temperature should be 145°F (63°C) at the thickest part of the fillet.
6. Serve hot.

Cajun-Style Salmon Burgers

Prep time: 10 minutes | Cook time: 10 to 15 minutes | Serves 4

4 (5-ounce / 142-g) cans pink salmon in water, any skin and bones removed, drained
2 eggs, beaten
1 cup whole-wheat bread crumbs
4 tablespoons light mayonnaise
2 teaspoons Cajun seasoning
2 teaspoons dry mustard
4 whole-wheat buns
Cooking spray

1. In a medium bowl, mix the salmon, egg, bread crumbs, mayonnaise, Cajun seasoning, and dry mustard. Cover with plastic wrap and refrigerate for 30 minutes.
2. Preheat the air fryer to 360°F (182°C). Spray the air fryer basket lightly with cooking spray.
3. Shape the mixture into four ½-inch-thick patties about the same size as the buns.
4. Place the salmon patties in the fryer basket in a single layer and lightly spray the tops with olive oil. You may need to cook them in batches.
5. Air fry for 6 to 8 minutes. Turn the patties over and lightly spray with olive oil. Air fry until crispy on the outside, 4 to 7 more minutes.
6. Serve on whole-wheat buns.

Chapter 7
Pork, Beef, and Lamb

Air Fried Vegetables and Chorizo

Prep time: 5 minutes | Cook time: 15 minutes | Serves 4

- ½ pound (227 g) Brussels sprouts, trimmed and halved
- 1 red onion, sliced
- 2 mixed bell peppers, sliced
- ½ teaspoon thyme
- 4 chorizo sausages
- Salt and ground black pepper, to taste

1. Preheat the air fryer to 350°F (180°C). Spritz the air fryer basket with cooking spray.
2. Combine the vegetables in a large bowl, then season with thyme, salt, and black pepper. Set aside.
3. Cook the sausages in the preheated air fryer for 6 minutes. Flip the sausages with tongs and add the seasoned vegetables in the basket and cook for 8 minutes more or until the sausages are well browned and the vegetables are tender.
4. Transfer them onto a large plate and serve warm.

Air Fried Pork Tenderloins with Apple

Prep time: 5 minutes | Cook time: 15 minutes | Serves 4

- 1 teaspoon cinnamon
- 4 pork tenderloins
- 1 apple, sliced
- 1 tablespoon soy sauce
- 2 tablespoons olive oil
- Salt and ground black pepper, to taste

1. Combine the cinnamon, soy sauce, olive oil, salt, and black pepper in a large bowl. Stir to mix well.
2. Dunk the pork tenderloins in the mixture, then wrap the bowl in plastic and sit under room temperature for at least 20 minutes.
3. Preheat the air fryer to 380°F (193°C).
4. Remove the pork tenderloins from the marinade and place in the air fryer basket. Spread the apple slices on top of the tenderloins. Baste them with some marinade.
5. Cook for 14 minutes or until well browned on both sides. Flip the pork tenderloins halfway through the cooking time.
6. Transfer them onto a plate and serve warm.

Air Fried Pork Escalops

Prep time: 5 minutes | Cook time: 15 minutes | Serves 4

- 4 boneless pork chops
- ¼ cup Parmesan cheese, grated
- 2 tablespoons Italian bread crumbs
- Salt and ground black pepper, to taste

1. Preheat the air fryer to 390°F (199°C). Spritz the air fryer basket with cooking spray.
2. Combine the cheese, bread crumbs, salt, and black pepper in a large bowl. Stir to mix well.
3. Dredge the pork chops in the mixture and press to coat well.
4. Arrange the pork in the preheated air fryer and cook for 15 minutes or until golden brown. Flip the pork halfway through the cooking time.
5. Transfer the pork chops to a plate and serve immediately.

Five Spice Pork Belly

Prep time: 10 minutes | Cook time: 30 minutes | Serves 6

- 1½ pounds (680 g) pork belly, blanched
- 1 teaspoon five spice powder
- ¾ teaspoon garlic powder
- 1 teaspoon salt
- ½ teaspoon white pepper

1. Preheat the air fryer to 330°F (166°C). Spritz the air fryer basket with cooking spray.
2. On a clean work surface, pierce the skin of the pork belly with a skewer as many times as possible to increase the crispiness.
3. Rub the pork belly with five spice powder, garlic powder, salt, and white pepper.
4. Arrange the seasoned pork belly in the air fryer basket and cook for 20 minutes. Flip the belly with tongs and increase the temperature to 350°F (180°C) and cook for an additional 10 minutes until the belly is well browned.
5. Transfer the cooked belly onto a plate and serve immediately.

Bbq Pork Empanadas

Prep time: 20 minutes | Cook time: 35 to 40 minutes | Serves 4

- 6 ounces (170 g) pork tenderloin
- 2 tablespoons spicy BBQ sauce
- 8 ounces (227 g) store-bought pie crust
- Kosher salt and ground black pepper, to taste

1. Preheat the air fryer to 360°F (182°C). Spritz the air fryer basket with cooking spray.
2. Arrange the pork tenderloin in the preheated air fryer and sprinkle with salt and black pepper.
3. Cook for 20 minutes or until an instant-read thermometer inserted in the thickest part of the tenderloin registers at least 145°F (63°C). Flip the pork tenderloin halfway through the cooking time.
4. Transfer the pork tenderloin to a plate lined with parchment paper. Allow to cool for 10 minutes.
5. Clean the air fryer and preheat to 390°F (199°C). Spritz the basket with cooking spray.
6. Put the BBQ sauce in a bowl, slice the pork tenderloin into strips, and dunk the strips in the BBQ sauce.
7. Make the empanadas: Roll the pie crust out, then cut it into 8 4-inch circles. Divide and spoon the pork with BBQ sauce in the middle of circles.
8. Fold the circles over to make pockets, then poke three holes into each pocket and crimp the edge to close with a fork.
9. Arrange the empanadas in the air fryer basket and cook for 5 minutes or until lightly browned and crisp. Flip the empanadas halfway through the cooking time. You may need to work in batches to avoid overcrowding.
10. Transfer the empanadas to a plate lined with parchment paper. Allow to cool for a few minutes before serving.

Pork Liver and Buns Soufflé

Prep time: 30 minutes | Cook time: 20 minutes | Serves 4

- ½ pound (227 g) pork liver, cut into cubes
- 3 ounces (85 g) buns
- 1 cup warm milk
- 3 eggs yolks
- Salt and ground black pepper, to taste

SPECIAL EQUIPMENT:
- 4 ramekins

1. Put the liver in a bowl and refrigerate for 15 minutes.
2. Soak the buns in a separate bowl of the warm milk for 10 minutes.
3. Preheat the air fryer to 350°F (180°C).
4. Put the buns, liver, and remaining ingredients in a food processor. Pulse to combine well.
5. Divide the mixture into the ramekins, then arrange the ramekins into the air fryer basket.
6. Cook in the preheated air fryer for 20minutes or until a toothpick inserted in the soufflé comes out clean.
7. Serve the soufflé warm.

Bacon and Potato Roast

Prep time: 5 minutes | Cook time: 25 to 30 minutes | Serves 4

- 4 streaky cut rashers bacon
- 4 potatoes, halved
- 2 sprigs rosemary
- 6 garlic cloves, squashed
- 1 tablespoon olive oil
- Salt and ground black pepper, to taste

1. Preheat the air fryer to 390°F (199°C). Spritz the air fryer basket with cooking spray.
2. Combine all the ingredients in a large bowl, then toss to coat them well with olive oil, salt, and black pepper.
3. Place them in the air fryer basket and roast for 25 to 30 minutes or until the potato halves are brown and crisp and the bacon curls and buckles.
4. Serve them immediately on a large platter.

Balsamic Steaks

Prep time: 5 minutes | Cook time: 10 minutes | Serves 4

- ½ tablespoon Italian seasoning
- 1 tablespoon balsamic vinegar
- 4 ribeye steaks
- 2 tablespoons olive oil
- Salt and ground black pepper, to taste

1. Combine the Italian seasoning, balsamic vinegar, olive oil, salt, and black pepper in a large bowl. Stir to mix well.
2. Dunk the ribeye steaks in the bowl of mixture, then wrap the bowl in plastic and refrigerate to marinate for at least 30 minutes.
3. Preheat the air fryer to 360°F (182°C).
4. Remove the steaks from the marinade and place in the air fryer basket. Cook for 10 minutes or until the steaks are well browned on both sides. Flip the steaks with tongs halfway through the cooking time.
5. Remove the steaks from the basket and serve immediately.

Ham and Pear Bake

Prep time: 5 minutes | Cook time: 20 minutes | Serves 4

- 1½ pounds (680 g) smoked ham sliced
- 1 pound (454 g) pears, peeled and halved
- ¾ tablespoon allspice
- 1½ cups brown sugar
- 1 tablespoon apple cider vinegar
- 1 teaspoon ground black pepper

1. Preheat the air fryer to 330°F (166°C). Put the ham on a lightly greased 6-inch baking dish.
2. Combine the remaining ingredients in a frying pan, then fry the pears for 2 to 3 minutes over medium heat. Flip the pears halfway through.
3. Arrange the pears on the baking dish, cut sides down, then arrange the dish in the air fryer and cook for 10 minutes. Flip the ham and pears, then cook for 5 minutes more or until the pears are caramelized.
4. Remove them from the air fryer and serve warm.

Crispy Sausage Balls

Prep time: 5 minutes | Cook time: 15 minutes | Serves 4

- 3 tablespoons bread crumbs
- 1 pound (454 g) pork sausages, crumbled
- ½ teaspoon garlic purée
- 1 teaspoon oregano
- 1 onion, chopped
- Salt and ground black pepper, to taste

1. Preheat the air fryer to 340°F (171°C). Spritz the air fryer basket with cooking spray.
2. Put the bread crumbs in a bowl. Combine the remaining ingredients in another bowl and stir to mix well.
3. Form the sausage mixture into balls with your hands, then roll them in the bowl of bread crumbs to coat well.
4. Place the balls in the preheated air fryer and cook for 15 minutes or until crispy. Shake the basket once halfway through the cooking time.
5. Remove the balls from the basket and serve immediately.

Air Fried Steaks with Pesto

Prep time: 25 minutes | Cook time: 15 minutes | Serves 4

- 4 boneless beef steaks
- 1 tablespoon smoked paprika
- 4 tablespoons pesto, for serving
- Salt and ground black pepper, to taste

1. Rub the beef steaks with paprika, salt, and black pepper. Wrap the steaks in plastic and let them sit under room temperature for at least 20 minutes.
2. Preheat the air fryer to 390°F (199°C). Spritz the air fryer basket with cooking spray.
3. Put the steaks in the air fryer basket and cook for 12 minutes or until well browned. Flip the steaks halfway through the cooking time.
4. Transfer the steaks onto a plate. Baste with pesto and slice to serve.

Bacon-wrapped Filets Mignons

Prep time: 5 minutes | Cook time: 18 minutes | Serves 4

- 4 slices bacon
- 1 tablespoon fresh thyme leaves
- 4 (8-ounce / 227-g) filets mignons
- Salt and ground black pepper, to taste

SPECIAL EQUIPMENT:
- 4 or 8 toothpicks, soaked for at least 30 minutes

1. Preheat the air fryer to 400°F (205°C).
2. Unroll the bacon slices on a clean work surface and sprinkle with thyme leaves.
3. Place each filet on one end of each bacon slice, then roll the bacon slices up to wrap around the side of the filets mignons. Secure with one or two toothpicks.
4. Place the bacon-wrapped filets mignons in the air fryer basket and sprinkle with salt and black pepper to season.
5. Cook for 18 minutes or until well browned. Flip them halfway through the cooking time.
6. Remove the bacon-wrapped filets mignons from the basket. Discard the toothpicks and serve immediately.

Air Fried Lamb and Asparagus

Prep time: 5 minutes | Cook time: 15 minutes | Serves 4

- 1 pound (454 g) lamb chops
- 1 garlic clove, minced
- 4 asparagus spears, trimmed
- 2 teaspoons fresh thyme, chopped
- Salt and ground black pepper, to taste

1. Preheat the air fryer to 400°F (205°C). Spritz the air fryer basket with cooking spray.
2. Put the lamb chops in the air fryer basket. Sprinkle with minced garlic and salt. Cook for 10 minutes.
3. Add the asparagus to the air fryer basket, and sprinkle with salt and black pepper. Spritz them with cooking spray.
4. Flip the lamb and cook for an additional 5 minutes or until the lamb chops are well browned and the asparagus is tender.
5. Remove them from the basket and serve with thyme on top.

Lamb Koftas

Prep time: 15 minutes | Cook time: 8 minutes | Serves 3 to 4

- 1 pound (454 g) ground lamb
- 1 egg, beaten
- 1 teaspoon ground coriander
- 1 teaspoon ground cumin
- 2 tablespoons chopped fresh mint
- ½ teaspoon salt
- Freshly ground black pepper, to taste

SPECIAL EQUIPMENT:

- 5 wooden skewers, soaked for at least 30 minutes

1. Preheat the air fryer to 400°F (205°C). Spritz the air fryer basket with cooking spray.
2. Put all the ingredients in a bowl. Stir to mix well. Then divide and shape the mixture into 10 ovals.
3. Snap the skewers in half and run the skewers through each lamb oval to make the koftas
4. Arrange the koftas in the preheated air fryer and cook for 8 minutes or until well browned on both sides. Flip the koftas halfway through the cooking time.
5. Remove the koftas from the air fryer and serve warm.

Air Fried Lamb Steaks and Red Potatoes

Prep time: 10 minutes | Cook time: 15 minutes | Serves 2

- 2 lamb steaks
- 2 red potatoes, sliced
- 2 garlic cloves, crushed
- 2 tablespoons fresh thyme, chopped
- Salt and ground black pepper, to taste

1. Preheat the air fryer to 360°F (182°C). Spritz the air fryer basket with cooking spray.
2. Arrange the lamb steaks and potatoes in the air fryer basket and sprinkle with crushed garlic, salt, and black pepper.
3. Cook in the preheated air fryer for 14 to 16 minutes or until the lamb steaks are well browned. Flip the lamb steaks and potatoes with tongs halfway through the cooking time.
4. Serve them immediately on a platter with thyme on top.

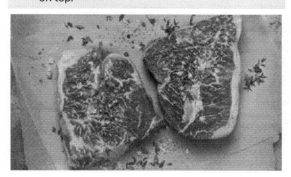

Herbed Lamb Chops with Roasted Garlic

Prep time: 5 minutes | Cook time: 25 minutes | Serves 4

- 1 garlic head, halved lengthwise
- ½ tablespoon thyme
- ½ tablespoon oregano
- 4 lamb chops
- 1 tablespoons olive oil
- Salt and ground black pepper, to taste

1. Preheat the air fryer to 390°F (199°C). Spritz the air fryer basket with cooking spray.
2. Roast the garlic in the greased air fryer basket for 10 minutes until the garlic head is soft.
3. Meanwhile, combine the thyme, oregano, olive oil, salt, and black pepper in a bowl.
4. Remove the garlic from the basket and allow to cool for a few minutes. Squeeze the roasted garlic in the herb mixture. Stir to mix well.
5. Dunk the lamb chops in the bowl of mixture to coat well. Then Place the lamb chops in the air fryer basket.
6. Cook for 12 minutes or until the lamb chops are well browned. Flip the lamb chops with tongs halfway through the cooking time.
7. Serve the lamb chops immediately.

Red Curry Stack

Prep time: 6 hours to 8 hours | Cook time: 12 to 18 minutes | Serves 4

- 3 tablespoons red curry paste
- 2 teaspoons fresh ginger, grated
- 3 scallions, minced
- 1½ pounds (680 g) flank steak
- Fresh cilantro leaves, for garnish
- ¼ cup olive oil
- 2 tablespoons soy sauce
- 2 tablespoons rice wine vinegar
- Salt and ground black pepper, to taste

1. Combine the red curry paste, ginger, soy sauce, rice vinegar, scallions, and olive oil in a bowl.
2. Put the flank steak on a large plate, then pierce with a skewer as many times as possible. Baste half of the paste mixture over the steak. Flip the steak and repeat the instructions above.
3. Wrap the plate in plastic and refrigerate to marinate for 6 to 8 hours.
4. Remove the marinated steak from the refrigerator and let stand for 30 minutes.
5. Meanwhile, preheat the air fryer to 400°F (205°C).
6. Arrange the steak in the air fryer basket and baste with marinade. Sprinkle with salt and black pepper.
7. Cook for 12 to 18 minutes or until the flank steak reaches your desired doneness. Flip the steak halfway through the cooking time.
8. Remove the steak from the air fryer and slice to serve.

Air Fried Pork Tenderloin with Godlen Apples

Prep time: 10 minutes | Cook time: 30 minutes | Serves 2 to 3

- 1 (1-pound / 454-g) pork tenderloin
- 2 tablespoons coarse brown mustard
- 1½ teaspoons finely chopped fresh rosemary, plus sprigs for garnish
- 2 apples, cored and cut into 8 wedges
- Salt and ground black pepper, to taste
- 1 teaspoon brown sugar
- 1 tablespoon butter, melted

1. Preheat the air fryer to 370°F (188°C). Spritz the air fryer basket with cooking spray.
2. On a clean work surface, brush the pork tenderloin with brown mustard, then sprinkle with rosemary, salt, and black pepper.
3. Place the pork tenderloin in the air fryer basket and cook for 15 to 18 minutes or until an instant-read thermometer inserted in the thickest part of the pork tenderloin registers at least 145°F (63°C). Flip the pork tenderloin halfway through the cooking time.
4. Meanwhile, combine the brown sugar and butter in a bowl, then put the apple wedges in the mixture and toss to coat well.
5. Remove the pork tenderloin from the air fryer basket and increase the temperature of the air fryer to 400°F (205°C).
6. Cook the apple in the air fryer basket for 8 minutes or until the apples are golden brown. Shake the basket twice during the cooking.
7. Transfer the pork tenderloin and apples onto a large plate and spread the rosemary sprigs before serving.

Beef Eggs

Prep time: 15 minutes | Cook time: 15 minutes | Serves 4

- 1 (8-ounce / 227-g) package cream cheese, softened
- 8 medium jalapeño peppers, stemmed, halved, and seeded
- 2 pounds (907 g) ground beef (85% lean)
- 8 slices thin-cut bacon
- Fresh cilantro leaves, for garnish
- 1 teaspoon fine sea salt
- ½ teaspoon ground black pepper

SPECIAL EQUIPMENT:
- 8 toothpicks, soaked for at least 30 minutes

1. Preheat the air fryer to 400°F (205°C). Spray the air fryer basket with cooking spray.
2. Divide the cream cheese in all the jalapeño halves, then assemble the jalapeño halves back to 8 jalapeños.
3. Combine the ground beef with salt and pepper on a clean work surface, then divide the ground beef into 8 portions.
4. Wrap each jalapeño with each portion of ground beef and form them into egg shape, then wrap each of them with a slice of bacon and secure with a toothpick.
5. Arrange them in the preheated air fryer and cook for 15 minutes or until the bacon is well browned and crispy. Flip them halfway through. You may need to work in batches to avoid overcrowding.
6. Transfer them onto a large plate. Discard the toothpicks and serve with cilantro on top.
7. Store leftovers in an airtight container in the fridge for 3 days or in the freezer for up to a month. Reheat in a preheated 350°F air fryer for 4 minutes, or until heated through and the bacon is crispy.

Classic Beef Sliders

Prep time: 10 minutes | Cook time: 30 minutes | Serves 6

- 1 pound (454 g) 90% lean ground sirloin beef
- 6 whole wheat dinner rolls, sliced
- ½ teaspoon kosher salt
- Freshly ground black pepper, to taste

1. Preheat the air fryer to 360°F (182°C). Spritz the air fryer basket with cooking spray.
2. Combine the ground beef with salt and black pepper, then divide and form the ground beef into 6 patties.
3. Arrange the patties in the air fryer basket and cook for 8 minutes or until well browned. Flip the patties halfway through. You may need to work in batches to avoid overcrowding.
4. Remove the patties from the air fryer basket and allow to cool for a few minutes on a platter lined with parchment paper.
5. Assemble the patties with dinner rolls and serve.

Godlen Scotch Eggs

Prep time: 10 minutes | Cook time: 15 minutes | Serves 8

- 2 pounds (907 g) ground beef
- 8 large hard-boiled eggs, peeled
- 2 cups pork dust
- Dijon mustard, for serving
- 2 teaspoons fine sea salt
- ½ teaspoon ground black pepper

1. Preheat the air fryer to 400°F (205°C). Spray the air fryer basket with cooking spray.
2. Combine the ground beef with salt and black pepper on a clean work surface, then divide them into 8 portions.
3. Wrap each hard-boiled egg with a portion of ground beef.
4. Pour the pork dust in a bowl, then dunk the beef-wrapped eggs in the pork dust to coat.
5. Put the eggs in the preheated air fryer and spritz with cooking spray.
6. Cook for 15 minutes or until golden brown. Flip the eggs halfway through.
7. Remove the eggs from the air fryer and serve with Dijon mustard.

Air Fried Baby Back Ribs

Prep time: 5 minutes | Cook time: 35 minutes | Serves 2

- ½ teaspoon chili powder
- 1 teaspoon onion powder
- 2 teaspoons smoked paprika
- 1 teaspoon garlic powder
- 1 rack baby back ribs, cut in half crosswise
- 2 teaspoons fine sea salt
- 1 teaspoon ground black pepper

1. Preheat the air fryer to 350°F (180°C). Spray the air fryer basket with cooking spray.
2. Combine the chili powder, onion powder, paprika, garlic powder, salt, and black pepper in a bowl, then rub the ribs with this seasoning mixture.
3. Arrange the ribs in the preheated air fryer and cook for 30 to 35 minutes or until an instant-read thermometer inserted in the thickest part of the ribs registers at least 145°F (63°C). Flip the ribs halfway through the cooking time.
4. Remove the ribs from the air fryer basket and serve warm.

Ham and Apple Panini

Prep time: 5 minutes | Cook time: 5 minutes | Serves 1

- 2 slices whole grain bread
- 2 teaspoons Dijon mustard
- 1 ounce (28 g) cooked low-sodium ham, thinly sliced
- 2 thin slices Cheddar cheese
- 3 thin slices apple

1. Preheat the air fryer to 300°F (150°C). Spritz the air fryer basket with cooking spray.
2. On a dish, brush the bread with Dijon mustard on both sides.
3. Assemble the ham, cheese, and apple slices between the bread slices to make the panini.
4. Arrange the panini in the air fryer basket and cook for 5 minutes or until the cheese melts and the bread slices are lightly browned.
5. Transfer the panini on a plate and serve warm.

Bratwurst Curry

Prep time: 15 minutes | Cook time: 12 minutes | Serves 4

- 1 cup tomato sauce
- 2 teaspoons sweet paprika
- 2 teaspoons curry powder
- 1 pound (454 g) bratwurst, sliced diagonally into 1-inch pieces
- 1 small onion, diced
- 2 tablespoons cider vinegar
- ¼ teaspoon cayenne pepper
- Salt, to taste
- 1 teaspoon sugar

1. Preheat the air fryer to 400°F (205°C). Spritz the air fryer basket with cooking spray.
2. Mix the tomato sauce, paprika, curry powder, vinegar, cayenne pepper, salt, and sugar in a large bowl. Stir to combine well, then mix in the bratwurst and onion.
3. Pour the mixture in a 6-inch baking pan, then place the pan in the air fryer.
4. Cook for 12 minutes or until the mixture has a thick consistency and bubbles.
5. Remove the pan from the air fryer and serve the bratwurst curry warm.

Chapter 8
Vegan and Vegetarian

Black Bean and Tomato Chili

Prep time: 15 minutes | Cook time: 23 minutes | Serves 6

- 1 tablespoon olive oil
- 1 medium onion, diced
- 3 garlic cloves, minced
- 1 cup vegetable broth
- 3 cans black beans, drained and rinsed
- 2 cans diced tomatoes
- 2 chipanle peppers, chopped
- 2 teaspoons cumin
- 2 teaspoons chili powder
- 1 teaspoon dried oregano
- ½ teaspoon salt

1. Over a medium heat, fry the garlic and onions in the olive oil for 3 minutes.
2. Add the remaining ingredients, stirring constantly and scraping the bottom to prevent sticking.
3. Place the baking pan on the bake position. Select Bake, set the temperature to 400°F (204°C), and set the time to 20 minutes.
4. Take the baking pan and place the mixture inside. Put a sheet of aluminum foil on top.
5. Bake for 20 minutes.
6. When ready, plate up and serve immediately.

Corn and Potato Chowder

Prep time: 15 minutes | Cook time: 50 minutes | Serves 4

- 4 ears corn, shucked
- 2 tablespoons canola oil
- 1½ teaspoons sea salt, plus additional to season the corn
- ½ teaspoon freshly ground black pepper, plus additional to season the corn
- 3 tablespoons unsalted butter
- 1 small onion, finely chopped
- 2½ cups vegetable broth
- 1½ cups milk
- 4 cups diced panatoes
- 2 cups half-and-half
- 1½ teaspoons chopped fresh thyme

1. Place the grill plate on the grill position. Select Grill, set the temperature to 450°F (232°C), and set the time to 12 minutes.
2. Brush each ear of corn with ½ tablespoon of oil. Season the corn with salt and pepper to taste.
3. Place the corn on the grill plate. Grill for 6 minutes.
4. After 6 minutes, flip the corn. Continue cooking for the remaining 6 minutes.
5. When cooking is complete, remove the corn and let cool. Cut the kernels from the cobs.
6. In a food processor, purée 1 cup of corn kernels until smooth.
7. In a large pan over medium-high heat, melt the butter. Add the onion and sauté until soft, 5 to 7 minutes. Add the broth, milk, and panatoes. Bring to a simmer and cook until the panatoes are just tender, 10 to 12 minutes. Stir in the salt and pepper.
8. Stir in the puréed corn, remaining corn kernels, and half-and-half. Bring to a simmer and cook, stirring occasionally, until the panatoes are cooked through, for 15 to 20 minutes.
9. Using a panato masher or immersion blender, slightly mash some of the panatoes. Stir in the thyme, and additional salt and pepper to taste.

Grilled Vegetable Pizza

Prep time: 10 minutes | Cook time: 10 minutes | Serves 2

- 2 tablespoons all-purpose flour, plus more as needed
- ½ store-bought pizza dough (about 8 ounces / 227 g)
- 1 tablespoon canola oil, divided
- ½ cup pizza sauce
- 1 cup shredded Mozzarella cheese
- ½ zucchini, thinly sliced
- ½ red onion, sliced
- ½ red bell pepper, seeded and thinly sliced

1. Place the grill plate on the grill position. Select Grill, set the temperature to 450°F (232°C), and set the time to 7 minutes.
2. Dust a clean work surface with the flour.
3. Place the dough on the floured surface and roll it into a 9-inch round of even thickness. Dust your rolling pin and work surface with additional flour, as needed, to ensure the dough does not stick.
4. Evenly brush the surface of the rolled-out dough with ½ tablespoon of oil. Flip the dough over and brush the other side with the remaining ½ tablespoon of oil. Poke the dough with a fork 5 or 6 times across its surface to prevent air pockets from forming while it cooks.
5. Place the dough on the grill plate. Grill for 4 minutes.
6. After 4 minutes, flip the dough, then spread the pizza sauce evenly over it. Sprinkle with the cheese, and top with the zucchini, onion, and pepper.
7. Continue cooking for the remaining 2 to 3 minutes until the cheese is melted and the veggie slices begin to crisp.
8. When cooking is complete, let cool slightly before slicing.

Arugula and Broccoli Salad

Prep time: 10 minutes | Cook time: 12 minutes | Serves 4

- 2 heads broccoli, trimmed into florets
- ½ red onion, sliced
- 1 tablespoon canola oil
- 2 tablespoons extra-virgin olive oil
- 1 tablespoon freshly squeezed lemon juice
- 1 teaspoon honey
- 1 teaspoon Dijon mustard
- 1 garlic clove, minced
- Pinch red pepper flakes
- ¼ teaspoon fine sea salt
- Freshly ground black pepper, to taste
- 4 cups arugula, torn
- 2 tablespoons grated Parmesan cheese

1. Place the grill plate on the grill position. Select Grill, set the temperature to 450°F (232°C), and set the time to 12 minutes.
2. In a large bowl, combine the broccoli, sliced onions, and canola oil and toss until coated.
3. Place the vegetables on the grill plate. Grill for 8 to 12 minutes, until charred on all sides.
4. Meanwhile, in a medium bowl, whisk together the olive oil, lemon juice, honey, mustard, garlic, red pepper flakes, salt, and pepper.
5. When cooking is complete, combine the roasted vegetables and arugula in a large serving bowl. Drizzle with the vinaigrette, and sprinkle with the Parmesan cheese.

Summer Squash and Zucchini Salad

Prep time: 10 minutes | Cook time: 20 minutes | Serves 4

- 1 zucchini, sliced lengthwise about ¼-inch thick
- 1 summer squash, sliced lengthwise about ¼-inch thick
- ½ red onion, sliced
- 4 tablespoons canola oil, divided
- 2 portobello mushroom caps, trimmed with gills removed
- 2 ears corn, shucked
- 2 teaspoons freshly squeezed lemon juice
- Sea salt, to taste
- Freshly ground black pepper, to taste

1. Place the grill plate on the grill position. Select Grill, set the temperature to 450°F (232°C), and set the time to 25 minutes.
2. Meanwhile, in a large bowl, toss the zucchini, squash, and onion with 2 tablespoons of oil until evenly coated.
3. Arrange the zucchini, squash, and onions on the grill plate. Grill for 6 minutes.
4. After 6 minutes, flip the squash. Grill for 6 to 9 minutes more.
5. Meanwhile, brush the mushrooms and corn with the remaining 2 tablespoons of oil.
6. When cooking is complete, remove the zucchini, squash, and onions and swap in the mushrooms and corn. Grill for the remaining 10 minutes.

7. When cooking is complete, remove the mushrooms and corn, and let cool.
8. Cut the kernels from the cobs. Roughly chop all the vegetables into bite-size pieces.
9. Place the vegetables in a serving bowl and drizzle with lemon juice. Season with salt and pepper, and toss until evenly mixed.

Bean and Corn Stuffed Peppers

Prep time: 15 minutes | Cook time: 32 minutes | Serves 6

- 6 red or green bell peppers, seeded, ribs removed, and top ½-inch cut off and reserved
- 4 garlic cloves, minced
- 1 small white onion, diced
- 2 (8½-ounce / 241-g) bags instant rice, cooked in microwave
- 1 (10-ounce / 284-g) can red or green enchilada sauce
- ½ teaspoon chili powder
- ¼ teaspoon ground cumin
- ½ cup canned black beans, rinsed and drained
- ½ cup frozen corn
- ½ cup vegetable stock
- 1 (8-ounce / 227-g) bag shredded Colby Jack cheese, divided

1. Chop the ½-inch portions of reserved bell pepper and place in a large mixing bowl. Add the garlic, onion, cooked instant rice, enchilada sauce, chili powder, cumin, black beans, corn, vegetable stock, and half the cheese. Mix to combine.
2. Place the baking pan on the roast position. Select Roast, set the temperature to 350°F (177°C), and set the time to 32 minutes.
3. Spoon the mixture into the peppers, filling them up as full as possible. If necessary, lightly press the mixture down into the peppers to fit more in.
4. Place the peppers, upright, in the pan. Roast for 30 minutes.
5. After 30 minutes, sprinkle the remaining cheese over the top of the peppers. Roast for the remaining 2 minutes.
6. When cooking is complete, serve immediately.

Cauliflower Steaks with Ranch Dressing

Prep time: 10 minutes | Cook time: 15 minutes | Serves 2

- 1 head cauliflower, stemmed and leaves removed
- ¼ cup canola oil
- ½ teaspoon garlic powder
- ½ teaspoon paprika
- Sea salt, to taste
- Freshly ground black pepper, to taste
- 1 cup shredded Cheddar cheese
- Ranch dressing, for garnish
- 4 slices bacon, cooked and crumbled
- 2 tablespoons chopped fresh chives

1. Cut the cauliflower from top to bottom into two 2-inch "steaks"; reserve the remaining cauliflower to cook separately.
2. Place the grill plate on the grill position. Select Grill, set the temperature to 450°F (232°C), and set the time to 15 minutes.
3. Meanwhile, in a small bowl, whisk together the oil, garlic powder, and paprika. Season with salt and pepper. Brush each steak with the oil mixture on both sides.
4. Place the steaks on the grill plate. Grill for 10 minutes.
5. After 10 minutes, flip the steaks and top each with ½ cup of cheese. Continue to grill until the cheese is melted, about 5 minutes.
6. When cooking is complete, place the cauliflower steaks on a plate and drizzle with the ranch dressing. Top with the bacon and chives.

Balsamic Mushroom Sliders with Pesto

Prep time: 10 minutes | Cook time: 8 minutes | Serves 4

8 small portobello mushrooms, trimmed with gills removed
2 tablespoons canola oil
2 tablespoons balsamic vinegar
8 slider buns
1 tomato, sliced
½ cup pesto
½ cup micro greens

1. Place the grill plate on the grill position. Select Grill, set the temperature to 400°F (204°C), and set the time to 8 minutes.
2. Brush the mushrooms with the oil and balsamic vinegar.
3. Place the mushrooms, gill-side down, on the grill plate. Grill for 8 minutes until the mushrooms are tender.
4. When cooking is complete, remove the mushrooms from the grill, and layer on the buns with tomato, pesto, and micro greens.

Potatoes with Zucchinis

Prep time: 10 minutes | Cook time: 45 minutes | Serves 4

- 2 panatoes, peeled and cubed
- 4 carrots, cut into chunks
- 1 head broccoli, cut into florets
- 4 zucchinis, sliced thickly
- Salt and ground black pepper, to taste
- ¼ cup olive oil
- 1 tablespoon dry onion powder

1. Place the baking pan on the bake position. Select Bake, set the temperature to 400°F (204°C), and set the time to 45 minutes.
2. In the baking pan, add all the ingredients and combine well.
3. Bake for 45 minutes, ensuring the vegetables are soft and the sides have browned before serving.

Chermoula Beet Roast

Prep time: 15 minutes | Cook time: 25 minutes | Serves 4

CHERMOULA:

- 1 cup packed fresh cilantro leaves
- ½ cup packed fresh parsley leaves
- 6 cloves garlic, peeled
- 2 teaspoons smoked paprika
- 2 teaspoons ground cumin
- 1 teaspoon ground coriander
- ½ to 1 teaspoon cayenne pepper
- Pinch of crushed saffron (optional)
- ½ cup extra-virgin olive oil
- Kosher salt, to taste

BEETS:

- 3 medium beets, trimmed, peeled, and cut into 1-inch chunks
- 2 tablespoons chopped fresh cilantro
- 2 tablespoons chopped fresh parsley

1. In a food processor, combine the cilantro, parsley, garlic, paprika, cumin, coriander, and cayenne. Pulse until coarsely chopped. Add the saffron, if using, and process until combined. With the food processor running, slowly add the olive oil in a steady stream; process until the sauce is uniform. Season with salt.
2. Place the crisper tray on the roast position. Select Roast, set the temperature to 375°F (191°C), and set the time to 25 minutes.
3. In a large bowl, drizzle the beets with ½ cup of the chermoula to coat. Arrange the beets in the crisper tray. Roast for 25 minutes, or until the beets are tender.
4. Transfer the beets to a serving platter. Sprinkle with the chopped cilantro and parsley and serve.

Mozzarella Broccoli Calzones

Prep time: 10 minutes | Cook time: 24 minutes | Serves 4

- 1 head broccoli, trimmed into florets
- 2 tablespoons extra-virgin olive oil
- 1 store-bought pizza dough (about 16 ounces / 454 g)
- 2 to 3 tablespoons all-purpose flour, plus more for dusting
- 1 egg, beaten
- 2 cups shredded Mozzarella cheese
- 1 cup ricotta cheese
- ½ cup grated Parmesan cheese
- 1 garlic clove, grated
- Grated zest of 1 lemon
- ½ teaspoon red pepper flakes
- Cooking oil spray

1. Place the crisper tray on the air fry position. Select Air Fry, set the temperature to 390°F (199°C), and set the time to 12 minutes.
2. Meanwhile, in a large bowl, toss the broccoli and olive oil until evenly coated.
3. Add the broccoli to the crisper tray. Air fry for 6 minutes.
4. While the broccoli is cooking, divide the pizza dough into four equal pieces. Dust a clean work surface with the flour. Place the dough on the floured surface and roll each piece into an 8-inch round of even thickness. Dust your rolling pin and work surface with additional flour, as needed, to ensure the dough does not stick. Brush a thin coating of egg wash around the edges of each round.
5. After 6 minutes, shake the crisper tray. Place the crisper tray back in the grill to resume cooking.
6. Meanwhile, in a medium bowl, combine the Mozzarella, ricotta, Parmesan cheese, garlic, lemon zest, and red pepper flakes.
7. After cooking is complete, add the broccoli to the cheese mixture. Spoon one-quarter of the mixture onto one side of each dough. Fold the other half over the filling, and press firmly to seal the edges together. Brush each calzone all over with the remaining egg wash.
8. Coat the crisper tray with cooking spray and place the calzones in the crisper tray. air fry for 10 to 12 minutes, until golden brown.

Sweet Potatoes with Zucchini

Prep time: 20 minutes | Cook time: 20 minutes | Serves 4

- 2 large-sized sweet potatoes, peeled and quartered
- 1 medium zucchini, sliced
- 1 Serrano pepper, deseeded and thinly sliced
- 1 bell pepper, deseeded and thinly sliced
- 1 to 2 carrots, cut into matchsticks
- ¼ cup olive oil
- 1½ tablespoons maple syrup
- ½ teaspoon porcini powder
- ¼ teaspoon mustard powder
- ½ teaspoon fennel seeds
- 1 tablespoon garlic powder
- ½ teaspoon fine sea salt
- ¼ teaspoon ground black pepper
- Tomato ketchup, for serving

1. Put the sweet potatoes, zucchini, peppers, and the carrot into the air fryer basket. Coat with a drizzling of olive oil.
2. Preheat the air fryer to 350°F (177°C).
3. Air fry the vegetables for 15 minutes.
4. In the meantime, prepare the sauce by vigorously combining the other ingredients, except for the tomato ketchup, with a whisk.
5. Lightly grease a baking dish.
6. Transfer the cooked vegetables to the baking dish, pour over the sauce and coat the vegetables well.
7. Increase the temperature to 390°F (199°C) and air fry the vegetables for an additional 5 minutes.
8. Serve warm with a side of ketchup.

Lush Vegetables Roast

Prep time: 15 minutes | Cook time: 20 minutes | Serves 6

- 1⅓ cups small parsnips, peeled and cubed
- 1⅓ cups celery
- 2 red onions, sliced
- 1⅓ cups small butternut squash, cut in half, deseeded and cubed
- 1 tablespoon fresh thyme needles
- 1 tablespoon olive oil
- Salt and ground black pepper, to taste

1. Preheat the air fryer to 390°F (199°C).
2. Combine the cut vegetables with the thyme, olive oil, salt and pepper.
3. Put the vegetables in the basket and transfer the basket to the air fryer.
4. Roast for 20 minutes, stirring once throughout the roasting time, until the vegetables are nicely browned and cooked through.
5. Serve warm.

Potato and Broccoli with Tofu Scramble

Prep time: 15 minutes | Cook time: 30 minutes | Serves 3

- 2½ cups chopped red potato
- 2 tablespoons olive oil, divided
- 1 block tofu, chopped finely
- 2 tablespoons tamari
- 1 teaspoon turmeric powder
- ½ teaspoon onion powder
- ½ teaspoon garlic powder
- ½ cup chopped onion
- 4 cups broccoli florets

1. Preheat the air fryer to 400°F (204°C).
2. Toss together the potatoes and 1 tablespoon of the olive oil.
3. Air fry the potatoes in a baking dish for 15 minutes, shaking once during the cooking time to ensure they fry evenly.
4. Combine the tofu, the remaining 1 tablespoon of the olive oil, turmeric, onion powder, tamari, and garlic powder together, stirring in the onions, followed by the broccoli.
5. Top the potatoes with the tofu mixture and air fry for an additional 15 minutes. Serve warm.

Cauliflower Tater Tots

Prep time: 15 minutes | Cook time: 16 minutes | Serves 12

- 1 pound (454 g) cauliflower, steamed and chopped
- ½ cup nutritional yeast
- 1 tablespoon oats
- 1 tablespoon desiccated coconuts
- 3 tablespoons flaxseed meal
- 3 tablespoons water
- 1 onion, chopped
- 1 teaspoon minced garlic
- 1 teaspoon chopped parsley
- 1 teaspoon chopped oregano
- 1 teaspoon chopped chives
- Salt and ground black pepper, to taste
- ½ cup bread crumbs

1. Preheat the air fryer to 390°F (199°C).
2. Drain any excess water out of the cauliflower by wringing it with a paper towel.
3. In a bowl, combine the cauliflower with the remaining ingredients, save the bread crumbs. Using the hands, shape the mixture into several small balls.
4. Coat the balls in the bread crumbs and transfer to the air fryer basket. Air fry for 6 minutes, then raise the temperature to 400°F (204°C) and then air fry for an additional 10 minutes.
5. Serve immediately.

Lemony Falafel

Prep time: 15 minutes | Cook time: 15 minutes | Serves 8

- 1 teaspoon cumin seeds
- ½ teaspoon coriander seeds
- 2 cups chickpeas, drained and rinsed
- ½ teaspoon red pepper flakes
- 3 cloves garlic
- ¼ cup chopped parsley
- ¼ cup chopped coriander
- ½ onion, diced
- 1 tablespoon juice from freshly squeezed lemon
- 3 tablespoons flour
- ½ teaspoon salt
- Cooking spray

1. Fry the cumin and coriander seeds over medium heat until fragrant.
2. Grind using a mortar and pestle.
3. Put all of ingredients, except for the cooking spray, in a food processor and blend until a fine consistency is achieved.
4. Use the hands to mold the mixture into falafels and spritz with the cooking spray.
5. Preheat the air fryer to 400°F (204°C).
6. Transfer the falafels to the air fryer basket in one layer.
7. Air fry for 15 minutes, serving when they turn golden brown.

Super Veg Rolls

Prep time: 20 minutes | Cook time: 10 minutes | Serves 6

- 2 potatoes, mashed
- ¼ cup peas
- ¼ cup mashed carrots
- 1 small cabbage, sliced
- ¼ cups beans
- 2 tablespoons sweetcorn
- 1 small onion, chopped
- ½ cup bread crumbs
- 1 packet spring roll sheets
- ½ cup cornstarch slurry

1. Preheat the air fryer to 390°F (199°C).
2. Boil all the vegetables in water over a low heat. Rinse and allow to dry.
3. Unroll the spring roll sheets and spoon equal amounts of vegetable onto the center of each one. Fold into spring rolls and coat each one with the slurry and bread crumbs.
4. Air fry the rolls in the preheated air fryer for 10 minutes.
5. Serve warm.

Air Fried Potatoes with Olives

Prep time: 15 minutes | Cook time: 40 minutes | Serves 1

- 1 medium russet potato, scrubbed and peeled
- 1 teaspoon olive oil
- ¼ teaspoon onion powder
- ⅛ teaspoon salt
- Dollop of butter
- Dollop of cream cheese
- 1 tablespoon Kalamata olives
- 1 tablespoon chopped chives

1. Preheat the air fryer to 400°F (204°C).
2. In a bowl, coat the potatoes with the onion powder, salt, olive oil, and butter.
3. Transfer to the air fryer and air fry for 40 minutes, turning the potatoes over at the halfway point.
4. Take care when removing the potatoes from the air fryer and serve with the cream cheese, Kalamata olives and chives on top.

Grilled Mozzarella Eggplant Stacks

Prep time: 10 minutes | Cook time: 14 minutes | Serves 4

- 1 eggplant, sliced ¼-inch thick
- 2 tablespoons canola oil
- 2 beefsteak or heirloom tomatoes, sliced ¼-inch thick
- 12 large basil leaves
- ½ pound (227 g) buffalo Mozzarella, sliced ¼-inch thick
- Sea salt, to taste

1. Place the grill plate on the grill position. Select Grill, set the temperature to 450°F (232°C), and set the time to 14 minutes.
2. Meanwhile, in a large bowl, toss the eggplant and oil until evenly coated.
3. Place the eggplant on the grill plate. Grill for 8 to 12 minutes, until charred on all sides.
4. After 8 to 12 minutes, top the eggplant with one slice each of tomato and Mozzarella. Grill for 2 minutes, until the cheese melts.
5. When cooking is complete, remove the eggplant stacks from the grill. Place 2 or 3 basil leaves on top of half of the stacks. Place the remaining eggplant stacks on top of those with basil so that there are four stacks total. Season with salt, garnish with the remaining basil, and serve.Easy

Potato Croquettes

Prep time: 15 minutes | Cook time: 15 minutes | Serves 10

¼ cup nutritional yeast
2 cups boiled potatoes, mashed
1 flax egg
1 tablespoon flour
2 tablespoons chopped chives
Salt and ground black pepper, to taste
2 tablespoons vegetable oil
¼ cup bread crumbs

1. Preheat the air fryer to 400°F (204°C).
2. In a bowl, combine the nutritional yeast, potatoes, flax egg, flour, and chives. Sprinkle with salt and pepper as desired.
3. In a separate bowl, mix the vegetable oil and bread crumbs to achieve a crumbly consistency.
4. Shape the potato mixture into small balls and dip each one into the breadcrumb mixture.
5. Put the croquettes inside the air fryer and air fry for 15 minutes, ensuring the croquettes turn golden brown.
6. Serve immediately.

Lush Vegetable Salad

Prep time: 15 minutes | Cook time: 10 minutes | Serves 4

- 6 plum tomatoes, halved
- 2 large red onions, sliced
- 4 long red pepper, sliced
- 2 yellow pepper, sliced
- 6 cloves garlic, crushed
- 1 tablespoon extra-virgin olive oil
- 1 teaspoon paprika
- ½ lemon, juiced
- Salt and ground black pepper, to taste
- 1 tablespoon baby capers

1. Preheat the air fryer to 420°F (216°C).
2. Put the tomatoes, onions, peppers, and garlic in a large bowl and cover with the extra-virgin olive oil, paprika, and lemon juice. Sprinkle with salt and pepper as desired.
3. Line the inside of the air fryer basket with aluminum foil. Put the vegetables inside and air fry for 10 minutes, ensuring the edges turn brown.
4. Serve in a salad bowl with the baby capers.

Golden Pickles

Prep time: 10 minutes | Cook time: 15 minutes | Serves 4

- 14 dill pickles, sliced
- ¼ cup flour
- ⅛ teaspoon baking powder
- Pinch of salt
- 2 tablespoons cornstarch plus 3 tablespoons water
- 6 tablespoons panko bread crumbs
- ½ teaspoon paprika
- Cooking spray

1. Preheat the air fryer to 400°F (204°C).
2. Drain any excess moisture out of the dill pickles on a paper towel.
3. In a bowl, combine the flour, baking powder and salt.
4. Throw in the cornstarch and water mixture and combine well with a whisk.
5. Put the panko bread crumbs in a shallow dish along with the paprika. Mix thoroughly.
6. Dip the pickles in the flour batter, before coating in the bread crumbs. Spritz all the pickles with the cooking spray.
7. Transfer to the air fryer basket and air fry for 15 minutes, or until golden brown.
8. Serve immediately.

Air Fried Asparagus

Prep time: 5 minutes | Cook time: 5 minutes | Serves 4

- 1 pound (454 g) fresh asparagus spears, trimmed
- 1 tablespoon olive oil
- Salt and ground black pepper, to taste

1. Preheat the air fryer to 375°F (191°C).
2. Combine all the ingredients and transfer to the air fryer basket.
3. Air fry for 5 minutes or until soft.
4. Serve hot.

Fig, Chickpea, and Arugula Salad

Prep time: 15 minutes | Cook time: 20 minutes | Serves 4

- 8 fresh figs, halved
- 1½ cups cooked chickpeas
- 1 teaspoon crushed roasted cumin seeds
- 4 tablespoons balsamic vinegar
- 2 tablespoons extra-virgin olive oil, plus more for greasing
- Salt and ground black pepper, to taste
- 3 cups arugula rocket, washed and dried

1. Preheat the air fryer to 375°F (191°C).
2. Cover the air fryer basket with aluminum foil and grease lightly with oil. Put the figs in the air fryer basket and air fry for 10 minutes.
3. In a bowl, combine the chickpeas and cumin seeds.
4. Remove the air fried figs from the air fryer and replace with the chickpeas. Air fry for 10 minutes. Leave to cool.
5. In the meantime, prepare the dressing. Mix the balsamic vinegar, olive oil, salt and pepper.
6. In a salad bowl, combine the arugula rocket with the cooled figs and chickpeas.
7. Toss with the sauce and serve.

Chapter 9
Rice and Grains

Polenta Rounds
Prep time: 5 minutes | Cook time: 15 minutes | Serves 4

- 1 cup polenta
- Sea salt, to taste
- 1 teaspoon dried oregano
- 2 tablespoons olive oil

1. Cook the polenta according to the package directions. Season with the salt and oregano to taste.
2. Pour the polenta into a large baking sheet. Let it cool and firm up; cut the polenta into rounds. Drizzle the olive oil over them.
3. Place the baking dish in the air fryer basket. Put the air fryer lid on and bake in the preheated instant pot at 350°F (180°C) for 15 minutes. Flip the polenta rounds when the lid screen indicates TURN FOOD.
4. Bon appétit!

Air Fried Millet Patties
Prep time: 10 minutes | Cook time: 15 minutes | Serves 4

- 2 cups millet, cooked
- 2 tablespoons olive oil
- 1 small onion, chopped
- 2 garlic cloves, minced
- 1 tablespoon chopped celery leaves
- 1 tablespoon chopped parsley leaves
- Sea salt and ground black pepper, to taste

1. Mix all ingredients until everything is well combined. Form the mixture into patties. Transfer to the air fryer basket.
2. Put the air fryer lid on and air fry in the preheated instant pot at 380°F (193°C) for 15 minutes. Flip the patties when the lid screen indicates TURN FOOD.
3. Bon appétit!

Quinoa Cheese Patties
Prep time: 10 minutes | Cook time: 15 minutes | Serves 4

- 1½ cups quinoa, cooked
- ½ cup bread crumbs
- ½ cup grated Pecorino cheese
- 2 eggs, beaten
- 2 garlic cloves, minced
- ½ small onion, chopped
- 1 small bell pepper, seeded and chopped
- 1 tablespoon olive oil
- 2 tablespoons finely chopped fresh Mediterranean herbs
- Sea salt and ground black pepper, to taste

1. Mix all ingredients until everything is well combined. Form the mixture into patties. Transfer to the air fryer basket.
2. Put the air fryer lid on and air fry in the preheated instant pot at 380°F (193°C) for 15 minutes. Flip the patties when the lid screen indicates TURN FOOD.
3. Bon appétit!

Mushroom and Rice Bake
Prep time: 10 minutes | Cook time: 10 minutes | Serves 4

- 1 pound (454 g) brown mushrooms, chopped
- 1 small onion, peeled and chopped
- 2 garlic cloves, minced
- Sea salt and ground black pepper, to taste
- 1 cup vegetable broth
- 1½ cups brown rice, cooked

1. Thoroughly combine all ingredients in a lightly greased baking dish.
2. Place the baking dish in the air fryer basket. Put the air fryer lid on and bake in the preheated instant pot at 360°F (182°C) for 10 minutes or until cooked through.
3. Bon appétit!

Juicy Quinoa Porridge
Prep time: 10 minutes | Cook time: 12 minutes | Serves 4

- ½ cup old-fashioned oats
- ½ cup quinoa flakes
- ¼ cup chopped almonds
- ¼ cup chopped pecans
- 4 tablespoons honey
- 2 tablespoons coconut oil
- 4 tablespoons chopped dried apricots

1. Thoroughly combine all ingredients in a mixing bowl. Spoon the mixture into lightly greased mugs.
2. Then, place the mugs in the baking dish.
3. Place the baking dish in the air fryer basket. Put the air fryer lid on and bake in the preheated instant pot at 380°F (193°C) for 12 minutes.
4. Serve immediately. Bon appétit!

Corn Kernels Koftas
Prep time: 10 minutes | Cook time: 15 minutes | Serves 5

- 6 ounces (170 g) canned corn kernels
- ½ small-sized onion, peeled and chopped
- 2 cloves garlic, minced
- 2 tablespoons chopped fresh parsley
- 2 tablespoons chopped fresh mint
- 2 tablespoons butter, melted
- 2 eggs, beaten
- ½ cup rice flour
- 1 teaspoon baking powder
- Sea salt and ground black pepper, to taste
- 1 teaspoon turmeric powder

1. Mix all ingredients until everything is well combined. Form the mixture into balls. Transfer to the air fryer basket.
2. Put the air fryer lid on and air fry in the preheated instant pot at 380°F (193°C) for 15 minutes or until cooked through. Flip the balls when the lid screen indicates TURN FOOD.
3. Bon appétit!

Raisins Buttermilk Scones

Prep time: 15 minutes | Cook time: 17 minutes | Serves 6

- 1 cup all-purpose flour
- 1 teaspoon baking powder
- ¼ teaspoon salt
- ¼ teaspoon grated nutmeg
- ½ cup brown sugar
- 2 egg, beaten
- ¼ cup buttermilk
- ½ teaspoon vanilla extract
- 6 tablespoons raisins, soaked for 15 minutes

1. Mix all ingredients until everything is well incorporated. Spoon the batter into baking cups; lower the cups into the baking dish.
2. Place the baking dish in the air fryer basket. Put the air fryer lid on and bake in the preheated instant pot at 360°F (182°C) for 17 minutes or until a tester comes out dry and clean.
3. Bon appétit!

Mini Cornbread Loaves

Prep time: 5 minutes | Cook time: 22 minutes | Serves 6

- ½ cup all-purpose flour
- ½ cup yellow cornmeal
- 1½ teaspoons baking powder
- A pinch of kosher salt
- A pinch of grated nutmeg
- 4 tablespoons butter, melted
- ½ cup milk
- 2 eggs, whisked
- 2 tablespoons agave syrup

1. Mix all ingredients until everything is well incorporated. Scrape the batter into baking molds and place them in the baking dish.
2. Place the baking dish in the air fryer basket. Put the air fryer lid on and bake in the preheated instant pot at 360°F (182°C) for 22 minutes or until a tester comes out dry and clean.
3. Allow the mini cornbread loaves to cool before unmolding and serving. Bon appétit!

Banana Oatmeal

Prep time: 5 minutes | Cook time: 12 minutes | Serves 4

- 1 cup old-fashioned oats
- 1 cup coconut milk
- 1 cup water
- 1 banana, mashed
- ½ teaspoon vanilla extract
- ½ teaspoon ground cinnamon
- A pinch of grated nutmeg
- A pinch of sea salt

1. Thoroughly combine all ingredients in a mixing bowl. Spoon the mixture into lightly greased mugs. Place the mugs in the baking dish.
2. Place the baking dish in the air fryer basket. Put the air fryer lid on and bake in the preheated instant pot at 380°F (193°C) for 12 minutes.
3. Bon appétit!

Pecans Oatmeal Cups

Prep time: 6 minutes | Cook time: 12 minutes | Serves 4

- 1 cup full-fat milk
- 1 cup unsweetened apple sauce
- 1 egg, beaten
- ½ cup pure maple syrup
- 1 cup old-fashioned oats
- 1 teaspoon baking powder
- 1 teaspoon pure vanilla extract
- ½ teaspoon ground cinnamon
- ¼ teaspoon freshly grated nutmeg
- A pinch of kosher salt
- ½ cup chopped pecans

1. Thoroughly combine all ingredients in a mixing bowl. Spoon the mixture into lightly greased mugs.
2. Then, place the mugs in the baking dish.
3. Place the baking dish in the air fryer basket. Put the air fryer lid on and bake in the preheated instant pot at 380°F (193°C) for 12 minutes.
4. Bon appétit!

Almonds Oatmeal

Prep time: 5 minutes | Cook time: 12 minutes | Serves 4

- 1 cup rolled oats
- 1 cup water
- 1 cup milk
- 1 teaspoon vanilla paste
- A pinch of kosher salt
- ½ teaspoon ground cloves
- 4 tablespoons honey
- ½ cup slivered almonds

1. Thoroughly combine all ingredients in a mixing bowl. Spoon the mixture into lightly greased ramekins.
2. Then, place the ramekins in the baking dish.
3. Place the baking dish in the air fryer basket. Put the air fryer lid on and bake in the preheated instant pot at 380°F (193°C) for 12 minutes.
4. Serve warm or at room temperature.
5. Bon appétit!

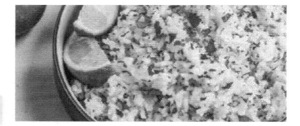

Juicy Milk Oatmeal

Prep time: 5 minutes | Cook time: 12 minutes | Serves 4

- 1 cup old-fashioned oats
- 1 teaspoon baking powder
- ½ teaspoon cinnamon
- A pinch of sea salt
- A pinch of grated nutmeg
- 1 cup coconut milk
- 1 cup pineapple juice
- ¼ cup agave syrup
- 2 tablespoons ground chia seeds
- 1 teaspoon vanilla extract

1. Thoroughly combine all ingredients in a mixing bowl. Spoon the mixture into lightly greased mugs. Then, place the mugs in the baking dish.
2. Place the baking dish in the air fryer basket. Put the air fryer lid on and bake in the preheated instant pot at 380°F (193°C) for 12 minutes.
3. Bon appétit!

Cranberry Granola

Prep time: 10 minutes | Cook time: 15 minutes | Serves 6

- ½ cup rolled oats
- ¼ cup toasted wheat germ
- ½ cup dried cranberries
- ¼ cup pumpkin seeds
- ¼ cup sunflower seeds
- ¼ cup chopped pecans
- ¼ cup chopped walnuts
- ½ teaspoon vanilla extract
- ¼ cup agave syrup
- 4 tablespoons coconut oil
- 1 teaspoon pumpkin pie spice mix

1. Thoroughly combine all ingredients in a lightly greased baking dish.
2. Place the baking dish in the air fryer basket. Put the air fryer lid on and bake in the preheated instant pot at 350°F (180°C) for 15 minutes, stirring every 5 minutes.
3. Store at room temperature in an airtight container for up to three weeks.
4. Bon appétit!

Mixed Berry Muffins

Prep time: 5 minutes | Cook time: 15 minutes | Serves 6

- ¾ cup all-purpose flour
- ¼ cup honey
- ½ teaspoon ground cinnamon
- ¼ teaspoon ground cloves
- ¼ cup buttermilk
- 1 egg
- 4 tablespoons olive oil
- 1 teaspoon vanilla extract
- ½ cup fresh mixed berries

1. Mix all ingredients in a bowl. Scrape the batter into silicone baking molds; place them in the baking dish.
2. Place the baking dish in the air fryer basket. Put the air fryer lid on and bake in the preheated instant pot at 320°F (160°C) for 15 minutes or until a tester comes out dry and clean.
3. Allow the muffins to cool before unmolding and serving. Bon appétit!

Apple Oat Muffins

Prep time: 8 minutes | Cook time: 15 minutes | Serves 6

- ½ cups self-rising flour
- ½ cup rolled oats
- ½ cup agave syrup
- ¼ teaspoon grated nutmeg
- ½ teaspoon cinnamon powder
- A pinch of coarse salt
- ½ cup milk
- ¼ cup coconut oil, room temperature
- 2 eggs
- 1 teaspoon coconut extract
- 1 cup cored and chopped apples

1. Mix all ingredients in a bowl.
2. Scrape the batter into silicone baking molds; place them in the baking dish.
3. Place the baking dish in the air fryer basket. Put the air fryer lid on and bake in the preheated instant pot at 320°F (160°C) for 15 minutes or until a tester comes out dry and clean.
4. Allow the muffins to cool before unmolding and serving.

Cocoa Muffins

Prep time: 5 minutes | Cook time: 15 minutes | Serves 6

- ½ cup coconut flour
- ½ cup all-purpose flour
- ½ cup cocoa powder
- ½ cup brown sugar
- ½ teaspoon baking powder
- A pinch of sea salt
- A pinch of grated nutmeg
- 1 tablespoon instant coffee granules
- ½ cup milk
- 2 eggs, whisked
- ½ teaspoon vanilla extract

1. Mix all ingredients until well combined; then, divide the batter evenly between silicone baking molds; place them in the baking dish.
2. Place the baking dish in the air fryer basket. Put the air fryer lid on and bake in the preheated instant pot at 330°F (166°C) for 15 minutes or until a tester comes out dry and clean.
3. Allow the muffins to cool before unmolding and serving. Bon appétit!

Scallion Rice Pilaf

Prep time: 10 minutes | Cook time: 10 minutes | Serves 4

- 1½ cups cooked multigrain rice
- 1 cup vegetable broth
- ½ cup thinly sliced scallions
- 1 tablespoon chopped fresh parsley
- 1 tablespoon chopped fresh cilantro
- 2 tablespoons olive oil
- Sea salt and cayenne pepper, to taste
- 1 teaspoon garlic powder

1. Thoroughly combine all ingredients in a lightly greased baking dish.
2. Place the baking dish in the air fryer basket. Put the air fryer lid on and bake in the preheated instant pot at 360°F (182°C) for 10 minutes or until cooked through.
3. Bon appétit!

Curry Basmati Rice

Prep time: 10 minutes | Cook time: 10 minutes | Serves 4

- 3 tablespoons olive oil
- 3 cloves garlic, chopped
- 1 large onion, peeled and chopped
- 1 sprigs fresh curry leaves, chopped
- 2 cups basmati rice, cooked
- 1 teaspoon cayenne pepper
- Kosher salt and ground black pepper, to taste

1. Thoroughly combine all ingredients in a lightly greased baking dish. Pour 1 cup of boiling water over the rice.
2. Place the baking dish in the air fryer basket. Put the air fryer lid on and bake in the preheated instant pot at 360°F (182°C) for 10 minutes or until cooked through.
3. Bon appétit!

Quinoa and Broccoli Cheese Patties

Prep time: 15 minutes | Cook time: 15 minutes | Serves 4

- 2 cups quinoa, cooked
- 2 eggs, whisked
- 1 small onion, chopped
- 2 garlic cloves, minced
- 1 cup chopped broccoli
- ½ cup bread crumbs
- ½ cup grated Parmesan cheese
- 1 tablespoon chopped fresh Italian herbs
- Sea salt and ground black pepper, to taste

1. Mix all ingredients until everything is well combined. Form the mixture into patties. Transfer to the air fryer basket.
2. Put the air fryer lid on and air fry in the preheated instant pot at 380°F (193°C) for 15 minutes. Flip the patties when the lid screen indicates TURN FOOD.
3. Bon appétit!

Creamy Butter Corn Fritters

Prep time: 5 minutes | Cook time: 15 minutes | Serves 4

1 cup canned and creamed corn kernels
1 cup whole-wheat flour
1 teaspoon baking powder
2 eggs, whisked
½ cup heavy cream
2 tablespoons butter

1. Mix all ingredients until everything is well combined. Form the mixture into patties. Transfer to the air fryer basket.
2. Put the air fryer lid on and air fry in the preheated instant pot at 380°F (193°C) for 15 minutes. Flip the fritters when the lid screen indicates TURN FOOD.
3. Bon appétit!

Honey Prunes Bread Pudding
Prep time: 10 minutes | Cook time: 20 minutes | Serves 5

- 8 slices bread, cubed
- 1 cup coconut milk
- ¼ cup coconut oil
- 1 egg, beaten
- ¼ cup honey
- ½ teaspoon ground cinnamon
- ¼ teaspoon ground cloves
- A pinch of kosher salt
- ½ cup pitted and chopped prunes

1. Place the bread cubes in a lightly greased baking dish.
2. In a mixing bowl, thoroughly combine the milk, coconut oil, egg, honey, cinnamon, cloves, and salt.
3. Pour the custard mixture over the bread cubes. Fold in the prunes and set aside for 15 minutes to soak.
4. Preheat the air fryer to .
5. Place the baking dish in the air fryer basket. Put the air fryer lid on and bake in the preheated instant pot at 350°F (180°C) for 20 minutes or until the custard is set but still a little wobbly.
6. Bon appétit!

Cherry Cranberry Bread Pudding
Prep time: 5 minutes | Cook time: 20 minutes | Serves 6

- 2 cups cubed sweet raisin bread
- 2 eggs, whisked
- 1 cup milk
- ½ teaspoon vanilla extract
- ¼ cup agave syrup
- ¼ cup dried cherries
- ¼ cup dried cranberries

1. Place the bread cubes in a lightly greased baking dish.
2. In a mixing bowl, thoroughly combine the remaining ingredients.
3. Pour the egg mixture over the bread cubes; set aside for 15 minutes to soak.
4. Place the baking dish in the air fryer basket. Put the air fryer lid on and bake in the preheated instant pot at 350°F (180°C) for 20 minutes or until the custard is set but still a little wobbly.
5. Serve at room temperature. Bon appétit!

Almonds Bread Pudding
Prep time: 8 minutes | Cook time: 20 minutes | Serves 6

- 2 cups cubed Brioche bread
- ½ teaspoon cinnamon powder
- 4 tablespoons brown sugar
- 2 eggs, whisked
- 2 tablespoons coconut oil
- 1 cup eggnog
- ½ cup chopped almonds

1. Place the bread cubes in a lightly greased baking dish.
2. In a mixing bowl, thoroughly combine the remaining ingredients.
3. Pour the custard mixture over the bread cubes. Set aside for 15 minutes to soak.
4. Place the baking dish in the air fryer basket. Put the air fryer lid on and bake in the preheated instant pot at 350°F (180°C) for 20 minutes or until the custard is set but still a little wobbly.
5. Bon appétit!

Figs Bread Pudding
Prep time: 10 minutes | Cook time: 20 minutes | Serves 5

- 8 slices bread, cubed
- 1 cup milk
- 2 eggs, beaten
- ¼ cup brown sugar
- 2 ounces (57 g) dried figs, chopped
- A pinch of sea salt
- ½ teaspoon ground cinnamon
- ½ teaspoon vanilla extract

1. Place the bread in a lightly greased baking dish.
2. In a mixing bowl, thoroughly combine the remaining ingredients.
3. Pour the milk mixture over the bread cubes. Set aside for 15 minutes to soak.
4. Place the baking dish in the air fryer basket. Put the air fryer lid on and bake in the preheated instant pot at 350°F (180°C) for about 20 minutes or until the custard is set but still a little wobbly.
5. Serve at room temperature. Bon appétit!

Cheesy Macaroni
Prep time: 5 minutes | Cook time: 15 minutes | Serves 4

- 2 cups macaroni
- 1 cup milk
- 2 cups grated Mozzarella cheese
- ½ teaspoon Italian seasoning
- Sea salt and ground black pepper, to taste
- ½ teaspoon garlic powder
- 1 teaspoon dry mustard

1. Cook the macaroni according to the package directions.
2. Drain the macaroni and place them in a lightly greased baking dish.
3. Fold in the remaining ingredients and stir to combine.
4. Place the baking dish in the air fryer basket. Put the air fryer lid on and bake in the preheated instant pot at 360°F (182°C) for 15 minutes.
5. Serve garnished with fresh Italian herbs, if desired.
6. Bon appétit!

Air Fried Butter Toast

Prep time: 5 minutes | Cook time: 8 minutes | Serves 3

- 2 eggs
- ½ cup milk
- 2 tablespoons butter, room temperature
- 1 teaspoon vanilla extract
- ¼ teaspoon grated nutmeg
- ½ teaspoon cinnamon powder
- 3 slices challah bread

1. In a mixing bowl, thoroughly combine the eggs, milk, butter, vanilla, nutmeg, and cinnamon.
2. Then dip each piece of bread into the egg mixture; place the bread slices in a lightly greased air fryer basket.
3. Put the air fryer lid on and air fry in the preheated instant pot at 330°F (166°C) for 8 minutes. Flip the bread slices when the lid screen indicates TURN FOOD.
4. Enjoy!

Chocolate Chips Granola

Prep time: 10 minutes | Cook time: 15 minutes | Serves 8

- ½ cup old-fashioned oats
- ¼ cup unsweetened coconut flakes
- ¼ cup quinoa flakes
- ¼ cup slivered almonds
- ¼ cup chopped hazelnuts
- ¼ cup chia seeds
- 1 teaspoon ground cinnamon
- A pinch of grated nutmeg
- A pinch of sea salt
- 2 tablespoons coconut oil
- ¼ cup maple syrup
- 1 teaspoon vanilla extract
- ½ cup chocolate chips

1. Thoroughly combine all ingredients in a lightly greased baking dish.
2. Place the baking dish in the air fryer basket. Put the air fryer lid on and bake in the preheated instant pot at 350°F (180°C) for 15 minutes, stirring every 5 minutes.
3. Store at room temperature in an airtight container for up to three weeks.
4. Bon appétit!

Rice with Scallions

Prep time: 5 minutes | Cook time: 10 minutes | Serves 4

- 2 cups jasmine rice, cooked
- 1 cup vegetable broth
- 1 teaspoon garlic powder
- ½ cup chopped scallions
- 2 tablespoons butter, room temperature
- Kosher salt and red pepper, to taste

1. Thoroughly combine all ingredients in a lightly

greased baking dish.
1. Place the baking dish in the air fryer basket. Put the air fryer lid on and bake in the preheated instant pot at 360°F (182°C) for 10 minutes or until cooked through.
2. Bon appétit!

Carrot and Green Peas Rice

Prep time: 5 minutes | Cook time: 10 minutes | Serves 4

- 2 cups multigrain rice, cooked
- 1 small onion, finely chopped
- 1 teaspoon minced garlic
- 2 tablespoons sesame oil
- 1 egg, whisked
- 2 tablespoons soy sauce
- 1 carrot, chopped
- 1 cup green peas
- Sea salt and red chili flakes, to taste

1. Thoroughly combine all ingredients in a lightly greased baking dish.
2. Place the baking dish in the air fryer basket. Put the air fryer lid on and bake in the preheated instant pot at 360°F (182°C) for 10 minutes or until cooked through.
3. Bon appétit!

Pumpkin Porridge with Chocolate

Prep time: 5 minutes | Cook time: 12 minutes | Serves 5

- ½ cup old-fashioned oats
- ½ cup quinoa flakes
- ¼ cup chopped pecans
- 2 tablespoons ground chia seeds
- 2 tablespoons ground flax seeds
- 1 teaspoon vanilla essence
- 2 ounces (57 g) dark chocolate chips
- ½ cup canned pumpkin
- ½ cup almond milk

1. Thoroughly combine all ingredients in a mixing bowl. Spoon the mixture into a lightly greased baking dish.
2. Place the baking dish in the air fryer basket. Put the air fryer lid on and bake in the preheated instant pot at 380°F (193°C) for 12 minutes.
3. Serve immediately. Bon appétit!

Chawal ke Pakore with Cheese
Prep time: 5 minutes | Cook time: 15 minutes | Serves 4

- 1 cup rice flour
- ½ onion, chopped
- 2 garlic cloves, minced
- 2 tablespoons butter, room temperature
- 1 teaspoon paprika
- 1 teaspoon cumin powder
- ½ cup crumbled Paneer cheese

1. Mix all ingredients until everything is well combined. Form the mixture into patties. Transfer to the air fryer basket.
2. Put the air fryer lid on and air fry in the preheated instant pot at 380°F (193°C) for 15 minutes. Flip the patties when the lid screen indicates TURN FOOD.
3. Bon appétit!

Rice Cheese Casserole
Prep time: 10 minutes | Cook time: 10 minutes | Serves 4

- 1 small shallot, minced
- 2 garlic cloves, minced
- 2 tablespoons olive oil
- ½ teaspoon paprika
- 2 eggs, whisked
- 1 cup half-and-half
- 1 cup shredded Cheddar cheese
- 2 cups cooked brown rice
- 1 tablespoon chopped Italian parsley leaves
- 1 cup cream of celery soup
- Sea salt and freshly ground black pepper, to taste

1. Thoroughly combine all ingredients in a lightly greased baking dish.
2. Place the baking dish in the air fryer basket. Put the air fryer lid on and bake in the preheated instant pot at 360°F (182°C) for 10 minutes or until cooked through.
3. Bon appétit!

Millet Porridge with Sultanas
Prep time: 5 minutes | Cook time: 12 minutes | Serves 5

- ½ cup old-fashioned oats
- ½ cup millet, rinsed and drained
- 2 tablespoons ground flax seeds
- ½ cup Sultanas
- 2 cups coconut milk
- 2 tablespoons coconut oil
- A pinch of salt
- A pinch of ground cloves

1. Thoroughly combine all ingredients in a mixing bowl. Spoon the mixture into a lightly greased baking dish.
2. Place the baking dish in the air fryer basket. Put the air fryer lid on and bake in the preheated

instant pot at 380°F (193°C) for 12 minutes.
3. Serve immediately. Bon appétit!

Creamy Cornbread Casserole
Prep time: 5 minutes | Cook time: 12 minutes | Serves 6

- 3 eggs
- 2 tablespoons coconut oil, room temperature
- ½ cup heavy cream
- 1 teaspoon vanilla
- ½ cup brown sugar
- ½ teaspoon ground cinnamon
- A pinch of grated nutmeg
- A pinch of salt
- 6 slices sweet corn bread

1. In a mixing bowl, thoroughly combine the eggs, coconut oil, heavy cream, vanilla, sugar, cinnamon, nutmeg, and salt.
2. Then, place the cornbread slices in a lightly greased baking dish. Pour the custard mixture over the cornbread slices.
3. Place the baking dish in the air fryer basket. Put the air fryer lid on and bake in the preheated instant pot at 330°F (166°C) for 12 minutes.
4. Enjoy!

Cheesy Carbonara with Pancetta
Prep time: 10 minutes | Cook time: 10 minutes | Serves 4

- 2 cups Arborio rice, cooked
- 2 tablespoons sesame oil
- 1 shallot, chopped
- ½ cup white Italian wine
- ½ cup heavy cream
- Coarse sea salt and freshly ground black pepper, to taste
- 4 tablespoons chopped pancetta
- 1 cup grated Parmesan cheese
- 1 tablespoon chopped fresh Italian parsley

1. Thoroughly combine all ingredients in a lightly greased baking dish.
2. Place the baking dish in the air fryer basket. Put the air fryer lid on and bake in the preheated instant pot at 360°F (182°C) for 10 minutes or until cooked through.
3. Bon appétit!

Chapter 10
Pizza

Pro Dough

Prep time: 40 minutes | Cook time: 0 minutes | Makes 2 (12- to 14-inch) pizzas

- ¼ teaspoon active dry yeast
- 1½ cups warm water
- 4 cups "00" flour or all-purpose flour, plus more for dusting
- 2 teaspoons salt
- Extra-virgin olive oil, for greasing

1. In a medium bowl, add the yeast to the warm water and let it stand for 10 minutes. While the yeast is blooming, rinse the bowl of a standing mixer with hot water and dry thoroughly. It should be warm to the touch. In the warm mixing bowl, combine the flour and salt. Add the yeast mixture and mix on low speed with a dough hook for 2 minutes. Raise the speed to medium-low and continue to mix for about 10 minutes, until the dough is cohesive and smooth and has pulled away from the sides of the bowl.
2. Knead again on medium-low speed for an additional 10 minutes, or until the dough is soft and warm to the touch.
3. Transfer the dough to a large, lightly oiled bowl, rolling the dough to coat it on all sides. Cover with plastic wrap and refrigerate overnight.
4. The next day, transfer the dough to a lightly floured board and punch it down. Cut it into 2 or 4 equal pieces and shape into smooth balls. Lightly flour the balls, place them on a baking tray, and cover with a damp kitchen towel. Let the dough rise again in the refrigerator for at least 4 hours or overnight.
5. Remove the dough from the refrigerator, place on a lightly floured baking sheet, and cover with a damp kitchen towel. Let it rise for 1½ to 2 hours, until it is doubled in size.
6. Proceed with the desired recipe.

Simple Pizza Dough

Prep time: 15 minutes | Cook time: 0 minutes | Makes 2 (12- to 14-inch) pizzas

- 1 package active dry yeast
- 1½ cups warm water (about 110o F)
- 2 tablespoons extra-virgin olive oil
- 4 cups all-purpose flour, plus more for dusting
- 1½ teaspoons salt

1. In a medium bowl, add the yeast to the warm water and let bloom for about 10 minutes. Add the olive oil.
2. In a food processor or standing mixer fitted with a paddle attachment, pulse to blend the flour and salt. With the machine running, add the yeast mixture in a slow, steady stream, mixing just until the dough comes together. Turn the dough out onto a well-floured board, and with lightly floured hands, knead the dough using the heels of your

hands, pushing the dough and then folding it over. Shape it into a ball, then cut it into 2 or 4 equal pieces.
3. Place the balls of dough on a lightly floured baking sheet and cover with a clean dishtowel. Let them rise in a warm, draft-free spot until they are doubled in size, about 45 minutes.
4. Proceed with the desired recipe.

Pizza Margherita

Prep time: 15 minutes | Cook time: 15 minutes | Serves 4

- 1 pound (454 g) store-bought pizza dough
- 2 tablespoons extra-virgin olive oil, divided
- ½ cup Marinara Sauce or store-bought variety
- 6 ounces (170 g) shredded Mozzarella cheese
- ½ cup coarsely shredded Parmesan cheese (about 1½ ounces / 43 g)
- 2 large tomatoes, seeded and chopped (about 1½ cups)
- ¼ teaspoon kosher salt or ⅛ teaspoon fine salt
- ¼ cup chopped fresh basil
- 2 teaspoons wine vinegar

1. Punch down the pizza dough to release as much air as possible. Place the dough in the baking pan and press it out toward the edges. The dough will likely spring back and shrink. Be patient and keep working at it, leaving it alone to relax for a few minutes from time to time. As it stretches, I find it helpful to coat my fingers with 1 tablespoon of olive oil and then poke the dough lightly with my fingertips to keep it from shrinking as much. Don't worry if you can't get it all the way to the pan's edges.
2. Spread the marinara sauce over the dough. You'll be able to see the dough through the sauce in places; you don't want a thick coating. Evenly top the sauce with the Mozzarella cheese.
3. Slide the baking pan into the air fryer oven. Press the Power Button. Cook at 400°F (205°C) for 15 minutes.
4. After about 8 minutes, remove the pan from the air fryer oven. Sprinkle the Parmesan cheese over the pizza. Return the pan to the air fryer oven. Continue cooking for 7 minutes.
5. While the pizza cooks, place the tomatoes in a colander or fine-mesh strainer and sprinkle with the salt. Let them drain for a few minutes, then place in a small bowl. Mix in the remaining 1 tablespoon of olive oil, basil, and vinegar.
6. When cooking is complete, the cheese on top will be lightly browned and bubbling and the crust a deep golden brown. Remove the pizza from the baking pan, if you haven't already, and place it on a wire rack to cool for a few minutes (a rack will keep the crust from getting soggy as it cools). Distribute the tomato mixture evenly over the pizza, then transfer to a cutting board to slice and serve.

Garlic Tomato Pizza Sauce

Prep time: 10 minutes | Cook time: 25 minutes | Makes 1 quart

- 2 tablespoons extra-virgin olive oil
- 1 small yellow onion, chopped (½ cup)
- 3 garlic cloves, smashed
- 1 (28-ounce / 794-g) can whole peeled San Marzano tomatoes, undrained
- 1 teaspoon fine sea salt
- ⅛ teaspoon freshly ground black pepper
- 1 to 2 tablespoons sugar

1. In a large saucepan over medium-high heat, heat the olive oil until it shimmers. Reduce the heat to medium and add the chopped onion. Cook, stirring occasionally, for 5 minutes. Add the garlic and continue to cook for 2 to 3 minutes more, until the onion is translucent and the garlic is aromatic.
2. Add the tomatoes and their juice, and bring to a simmer, stirring occasionally with a wooden spoon to break them apart. Simmer for 10 to 15 minutes, until the sauce has thickened.
3. Using an immersion blender or food processor, pulse until the sauce is smooth. Season with the salt, pepper, and sugar.

Pepperoni Pizza with Mozzarella

Prep time: 5 minutes | Cook time: 20 minutes | Makes 2 (12-inch) pizzas

- Extra-virgin olive oil, for brushing
- Simple Pizza Dough
- 1 cup Garlic Tomato Pizza Sauce
- 1 cup grated Mozzarella cheese
- 6 ounces (170 g) pepperoni, sliced thin
- ¼ teaspoon salt

1. Brush two baking sheets with olive oil.
2. Roll out one of the dough balls and place it on the prepared baking sheet.
3. Leaving a 1-inch border, spread half of the sauce evenly over the dough. Top with half the Mozzarella and then half the pepperoni. Sprinkle with half the salt.
4. Slide the baking sheet into the air fryer oven. Press the Power Button. Cook at 400°F (205°C) for 10 minutes, until the crust is golden and the cheese has melted,.
5. Remove the pizza from the air fryer oven and transfer it to a cutting board. Let it rest for 5 minutes, then slice and serve.
6. Repeat with the remaining dough ball and toppings.

Mushroom and Spinach Pizza

Prep time: 10 minutes | Cook time: 30 minutes | Makes 2 (12- to 14-inch) pizzas

- 4 tablespoons extra-virgin olive oil, divided, plus more for brushing
- 2 cups sliced cremini mushrooms
- ¼ teaspoon fine sea salt
- ⅛ teaspoon freshly ground black pepper
- 1 garlic clove
- Pinch red pepper flakes, plus more for seasoning
- 4 cups baby spinach, stems removed
- Simple Pizza Dough or Pro Dough
- 1 cup Garlic Tomato Pizza Sauce
- 1 cup grated Mozzarella cheese

1. Brush two baking sheets with olive oil.
2. In a large skillet over medium-high heat, heat 3 tablespoons of olive oil until it shimmers. Add the mushrooms and the salt, and let the mushrooms sit undisturbed for 2 minutes. Give the pan a shake and continue to cook for 3 minutes more, stirring occasionally, until the mushrooms have darkened in color but are still firm and vibrant. Season with the pepper and transfer to a medium bowl.
3. Reduce the heat to medium and add the remaining 1 tablespoon of olive oil, the garlic, and the red pepper flakes. Swirl the garlic and red pepper flakes to flavor the oil, then add the spinach. Use tongs to turn the spinach, watching it decrease in volume. Cook the spinach for 2 to 3 minutes, until it's wilted but still has structure. Remove the skillet from the heat.
4. Roll out one of the dough balls to the desired size and place it on the prepared baking sheet.
5. Leaving a 1-inch border, spoon half of the sauce evenly over the dough, then sprinkle on half of the Mozzarella. Scatter half of the spinach over the pizza, followed by half of the mushrooms. The toppings should intermingle. Season with freshly ground black pepper or more red pepper flakes as desired.
6. Slide the baking sheet into the air fryer oven. Press the Power Button. Cook at 400°F (205°C) for 10 minutes, until the crust is golden and the cheese has melted.
7. Remove the pizza from the air fryer oven and transfer it to a cutting board. Let it rest for 5 minutes, then slice and serve.
8. Repeat with the remaining dough ball and toppings.

Ham and Pineapple Pizza

Prep time: 10 minutes | Cook time: 25 minutes | Makes 2 (12- to 14-inch) pizzas

- Extra-virgin olive oil, for brushing
- 4 slices center-cut bacon
- Simple Pizza Dough or Pro Dough
- 1 cup Garlic Tomato Pizza Sauce
- 1 cup grated Mozzarella cheese
- ¼ pound (113 g) smoked ham, cut into ½-inch dice
- 1 cup diced fresh pineapple
- 2 tablespoons grated Parmesan cheese

1. Brush two baking sheets with olive oil.
2. In a medium skillet over medium heat, cook the bacon until crisp, 2 to 3 minutes per side. Transfer to a paper towel–lined plate to cool. Cut into bits.
3. Roll out one of the dough balls to the desired size and place it on the prepared baking sheet.
4. Leaving a 1-inch border, spread half of the sauce evenly onto the dough. Sprinkle on half of the Mozzarella, followed by half of the ham, chopped bacon, pineapple, and grated Parmesan cheese.
5. Slide the baking sheet into the air fryer oven. Press the Power Button. Cook at 400°F (205°C) for 10 minutes, until the crust is golden and the cheese has melted.
6. Remove the pizza from the air fryer oven and transfer it to a cutting board. Let it rest for 5 minutes, then slice and serve.
7. Repeat with the remaining dough ball and toppings.

Mozzarella Meatball Pizza

Prep time: 10 minutes | Cook time: 25 minutes | Makes 2 (12- to 14-inch) pizzas

- All-purpose flour, for coating
- ½ pound (227 g) ground pork
- ½ pound (227 g) ground veal
- 1 cup ricotta cheese
- ¼ cup grated Parmesan cheese plus 2 tablespoons, divided
- 2 tablespoons finely chopped fresh flat-leaf parsley
- ¼ teaspoon salt, plus more for sprinkling
- ⅛ teaspoon freshly ground black pepper, plus more for sprinkling
- 2½ cups Garlic Tomato Pizza Sauce, divided
- 2 tablespoons olive oil, plus more for brushing
- Simple Pizza Dough
- 2 cups grated Mozzarella cheese

1. Lightly flour a baking sheet.
2. In a large mixing bowl, use your hands to combine the ground pork and veal, ricotta, ¼ cup of Parmesan, and the parsley. Season with the salt and pepper, and mix again.
3. Form each meatball by rolling 1 heaping tablespoon of the meat mixture between your palms. Place the meatballs on the prepared baking sheet, lightly rolling each one in flour.

4. In a medium saucepan over medium heat, heat 1½ cups of sauce; let it come to a gentle simmer.
5. Meanwhile, in a large skillet over medium-high heat, heat the olive oil. When it shimmers, add the meatballs, cooking on all sides for about 3 minutes, until browned. As they brown, transfer the meatballs to the simmering sauce to finish cooking, about 5 minutes total.
6. Brush two baking sheets with olive oil.
7. Roll out one of the dough balls to the desired size and place it on the prepared baking sheet.
8. Leaving a 1-inch border, spread ½ cup of the remaining sauce evenly onto the dough. Top the sauce with half of the Mozzarella and half of the meatballs. Spoon a little extra sauce from the pan onto the pizza, and finish with 1 tablespoon of the remaining Parmesan cheese and a sprinkling of salt and pepper.
9. Slide the baking sheet into the air fryer oven. Press the Power Button. Cook at 400°F (205°C) for 10 minutes, until the crust is golden and the cheese has melted.
10. Remove the pizza from the air fryer oven and transfer it to a cutting board. Let it rest for 5 minutes, then slice and serve.
11. Repeat with the remaining dough ball and toppings.

Arugula and Prosciutto Pizza

Prep time: 10 minutes | Cook time: 20 minutes | Makes 2 (12- to 14-inch) pizzas

- 2 tablespoons extra-virgin olive oil, plus more for brushing
- Simple Pizza Dough or Pro Dough
- 1 cup Garlic Tomato Pizza Sauce
- 8 slices prosciutto
- 6 ounces (170 g) fresh Mozzarella cheese, sliced or shredded
- 3 cups arugula
- ¼ teaspoon salt
- ⅛ teaspoon freshly ground black pepper
- 3 ounces (85 g) Parmesan cheese, shaved with a vegetable peeler

1. Brush two baking sheets with olive oil.
2. Roll out one of the dough balls to the desired size, and place it on the prepared baking sheet.
3. Leaving a 1-inch border, spread half of the sauce evenly onto the dough. Lay half of the prosciutto slices on top, then finish with half of the Mozzarella.
4. Slide the baking sheet into the air fryer oven. Press the Power Button. Cook at 400°F (205°C) for 10 minutes, until the crust is golden and the cheese has melted.
5. Remove the pizza from the air fryer oven and transfer it to a cutting board. Let it rest for 5 minutes, then top with half of the arugula, olive oil, salt, pepper, and Parmesan. Slice and serve.
6. Repeat with the remaining dough ball and toppings.

Spinach, Egg and Pancetta Pizza

Prep time: 10 minutes | Cook time: 30 minutes | Makes 2 (12- to 14-inch) pizzas

- 1 tablespoon extra-virgin olive oil, plus more for brushing
- 3 ounces (85 g) pancetta, finely diced
- 2 garlic cloves, minced
- 4 cups baby spinach, stems removed
- ¼ teaspoon salt
- Simple Pizza Dough or Pro Dough
- 1 cup Garlic Tomato Pizza Sauce
- 1 cup grated fontina cheese
- 2 large eggs
- 2 tablespoons grated Parmesan cheese
- 2 tablespoons chopped fresh flat-leaf parsley
- ⅛ teaspoon freshly ground black pepper

1. Brush two baking sheets with olive oil.
2. In a large skillet over medium heat, cook the pancetta until crisp, about 5 minutes, turning frequently. Transfer to a paper towel–lined plate.
3. Discard the rendered fat from the skillet and add the olive oil. Return the skillet to medium heat and, when the oil begins to shimmer, add the garlic. Swirl the garlic in the pan for a minute, then add the spinach. Use tongs to turn the spinach, watching it decrease in volume. Cook the spinach for 2 to 3 minutes, until it's wilted but still has structure. Season with the salt and remove the skillet from the heat. Roughly chop the spinach.
4. Roll out one of the dough balls to the desired size, and place it on the prepared baking sheet.
5. Leaving a 1-inch border, spread the sauce evenly onto the dough.
6. Top with half of the fontina followed by half of the spinach. Crack one egg, positioning the yolk in the center of the pizza. Sprinkle with half of the Parmesan.
7. Slide the baking sheet into the air fryer oven. Press the Power Button. Cook at 400°F (205°C) for 10 minutes, until the crust is golden and the egg yolk holds its shape when jiggled.
8. Remove the pizza from the air fryer oven and transfer it to a cutting board. Let it rest for 5 minutes, then season with half of the parsley and black pepper. Slice and serve.
9. Repeat with the remaining dough ball and toppings.

Chicken and Butternut Squash Pizza

Prep time: 10 minutes | Cook time: 40 minutes | Makes 2 (12- to 14-inch) pizzas

- 3 tablespoons extra-virgin olive oil, divided, plus more for brushing and drizzling
- 2 cups diced butternut squash
- 1 fresh rosemary sprig, stemmed and chopped
- Salt
- Freshly ground black pepper
- 3 cups stemmed, roughly chopped kale
- 1½ cups shredded cooked chicken
- Simple Pizza Dough
- 1½ cups grated Gruyère cheese
- 3 tablespoons grated Asiago cheese
- 2 tablespoons toasted walnuts, roughly chopped

1. Brush two baking sheets with olive oil.
2. In a medium skillet over medium-high heat, heat 1 tablespoon of olive oil. When it shimmers, add the butternut squash and rosemary. Season with salt and pepper. Cook the squash until tender and browned, about 20 minutes, stirring frequently.
3. In a large bowl, use your hands to toss the kale and shredded chicken with the remaining 2 tablespoons of olive oil, and season with salt and pepper.
4. Roll out one of the dough balls to the desired size, and place it on the prepared baking sheet.
5. Sprinkle half of the Gruyère over the dough and top with half of the kale and chicken, followed by half of the caramelized butternut squash and Asiago.
6. Slide the baking sheet into the air fryer oven. Press the Power Button. Cook at 400°F (205°C) for 10 minutes, until the crust is golden and the cheese has melted.
7. Remove the pizza from the air fryer oven and transfer it to a cutting board. Let it rest for 5 minutes, then drizzle it with a little olive oil, season with salt and pepper, and sprinkle on half of the walnuts. Slice and serve.
8. Repeat with the remaining dough ball and toppings.

Pear Pizza with Basil

Prep time: 15 minutes | Cook time: 25 minutes | Makes 1 (12- to 14-inch) pizza

- ½ recipe Simple Pizza Dough
- 4 Bosc pears
- ½ lemon
- Zest of 1 orange
- 1 tablespoon chopped fresh basil leaves
- 1 teaspoon chopped fresh rosemary leaves
- 2 tablespoons sugar
- ⅛ teaspoon freshly ground black pepper
- 2 tablespoons extra-virgin olive oil

1. On a baking sheet, roll out the pizza dough to form a 12- to 14-inch disc.
2. Peel, halve, and cut away the core of the pears. Slice each pear half into thin wedges. Squeeze lemon juice over the pears.
3. Arrange the pears, starting at the outer edge of the crust (leaving no border), in a spiral toward the center. Sprinkle the orange zest, basil, rosemary, sugar, and pepper over the pears. Drizzle with the olive oil.
4. Slide the baking sheet into the air fryer oven. Press the Power Button. Cook at 400°F (205°C) for 25 minutes, until the pizza appears golden and crisp.
5. Remove the pizza from the air fryer oven and let sit for 5 minutes. Slice and serve warm or at room temperature.

Prosciutto and Fig Pizza

**Prep time: 10 minutes | Cook time: 20 minutes | Makes 2
(12- to 14-inch) pizzas**

- 2 tablespoons extra-virgin olive oil, plus more for brushing
- Simple Pizza Dough or Pro Dough
- ¼ cup fig jam
- ½ cup shredded Mozzarella cheese
- ½ cup crumbled goat cheese
- 8 slices prosciutto
- 8 figs, stemmed and quartered
- 4 fresh thyme sprigs, stemmed
- ¼ teaspoon fine sea salt
- ⅛ teaspoon freshly ground black pepper

1. Brush two baking sheets with olive oil.
2. Roll out one of the dough balls to the desired size, and place it on the prepared baking sheet.
3. Leaving a 1-inch border, spoon half of the fig jam evenly onto the dough. Top with half of the Mozzarella, goat cheese, and prosciutto. Arrange half of the figs on the pizza, sprinkle on half of the thyme, and season with half of the salt and pepper.
4. Slide the baking sheet into the air fryer oven. Press the Power Button. Cook at 400°F (205°C) for 10 minutes, until the crust is golden and the cheese has melted.
5. Remove the pizza from the air fryer oven and transfer it to a cutting board. Let it rest for 5 minutes, then drizzle with half of the olive oil. Slice and serve.
6. Repeat with the remaining dough ball and toppings.

Cheese Tomato Pizza with Basil

**Prep time: 15 minutes | Cook time: 20 minutes | Makes 2
(12- to 14-inch) pizzas**

- Extra-virgin olive oil, for brushing
- Simple Pizza Dough
- 1 cup Garlic Tomato Pizza Sauce
- ¾ cup grated Mozzarella
- ¾ cup grated fontina cheese
- 2 plum tomatoes, sliced thin
- ⅓ cup crumbled goat cheese
- ½ cup Parmesan cheese
- 8 fresh basil leaves, torn or roughly chopped
- 1 tablespoon chopped fresh parsley
- ¼ teaspoon salt
- ⅛ teaspoon freshly ground black pepper

1. Brush two baking sheets with olive oil.
2. Roll out one of the dough balls to the desired size, and place it on the prepared baking sheet.
3. Leaving a 1-inch border, spread half of the sauce evenly over the dough. Sprinkle on half of the Mozzarella and fontina. Arrange half of the tomato slices on top, and finish with half of the goat cheese and Parmesan.
4. Slide the baking sheet into the air fryer oven.

Press the Power Button. Cook at 400°F (205°C) for 10 minutes, until the crust is golden and the cheese has melted.
5. Remove the pizza from the air fryer oven and transfer it to a cutting board. Let it rest for 5 minutes, then top with half of the basil and parsley and season with half of the salt and pepper. Slice and serve.
6. Repeat with the remaining dough ball and toppings.

Black Bean Pizza with Chipotle

**Prep time: 15 minutes | Cook time: 30 minutes | Makes 2
(12- to 14-inch) pizzas**

- 2 tablespoons extra-virgin olive oil, plus more for brushing
- ¼ teaspoon dried oregano
- 1 medium yellow onion, diced
- ½ teaspoon salt, plus more for seasoning
- 2 garlic cloves
- ⅛ teaspoon freshly ground black pepper, plus more for seasoning
- ¼ cup low-sodium vegetable broth
- 2 cups canned black beans, rinsed
- 2 chipotle chilies in adobo, chopped, plus 1 tablespoon of the adobo sauce
- Simple Pizza Dough
- 1 cup grated vegan Mozzarella cheese
- 1 red bell pepper, diced
- 1 cup diced avocado
- ½ cup fresh cilantro leaves

1. Brush two baking sheets with olive oil.
2. In a large skillet over medium-high heat, heat the olive oil and oregano. When it shimmers, add the diced onion and salt and cook, stirring occasionally, until the onions are soft and translucent, about 5 minutes. Add the garlic and cook 1 minute more, stirring to combine. Season with salt and add the pepper. Transfer to a small bowl.
3. Add the vegetable broth to the sauté pan, then add the black beans, chipotle chilies, and reserved adobo sauce. Bring to a simmer and begin to mash the beans using a potato masher or immersion blender until they form a rough paste (add more vegetable broth if necessary). Season with salt and pepper. Remove from the heat and set aside.
4. Roll out one of the dough balls to the desired size, and place it on the prepared baking sheet.
5. Leaving a 1-inch border, spoon half of the black beans onto the crust, spreading them evenly. Top with half of the Mozzarella and red pepper.
6. Slide the baking sheet into the air fryer oven. Press the Power Button. Cook at 400°F (205°C) for 10 minutes, until the crust is golden and the cheese has melted.
7. Remove the pizza from the air fryer oven, transfer it to a cutting board, and let it sit for 5 minutes. Top the pizza with half of the avocado, cilantro, and freshly ground black pepper. Slice and serve.
8. Repeat with the remaining dough ball and toppings.

Spring Pea Pizza with Ramps

Prep time: 10 minutes | Cook time: 25 minutes | Makes 2 (12- to 14-inch) pizzas

2 tablespoons extra-virgin olive oil, plus more for brushing
½ cup shelled fresh English peas (or frozen and thawed peas)
10 ramps
¼ teaspoon fine sea salt
Simple Pizza Dough or Pro Dough
¾ cup ricotta cheese
2 tablespoons chopped fresh mint

1. Brush two baking sheets with olive oil.
2. If using fresh peas, bring a large pot of salted water to a boil. Fill a large bowl with ice water. Blanch the peas for 1 minute then, using a slotted spoon, transfer them to the ice water. Drain and set aside.
3. Spread the ramps on a baking sheet, drizzle with the olive oil, and sprinkle with the salt. Press the Power Button. Cook at 400°F (205°C) for 5 minutes to wilt. Transfer to a cutting board and cut into thirds.
4. Roll out one of the dough balls to the desired size, and place it on the prepared baking sheet.
5. Spoon half of the ricotta in dollops all over the dough. Scatter on half of the peas, ramps, and mint.
6. Slide the baking sheet into the air fryer oven. Press the Power Button. Cook at 400°F (205°C) for 10 minutes, until the crust is golden.
7. Remove the pizza from the air fryer oven, transfer it to a cutting board, and let it sit for 5 minutes. Slice and serve.
8. Repeat with the remaining dough ball and toppings.

Zucchini Pizza with Pistachios

Prep time: 15 minutes | Cook time: 30 minutes | Makes 2 (12- to 14-inch) pizzas

- 2 tablespoons extra-virgin olive oil, plus more for brushing
- 1 medium green zucchini, halved lengthwise and cut thinly into half-moons
- 1 medium yellow summer squash, halved lengthwise and cut thinly into half-moons
- ¼ teaspoon salt
- Simple Pizza Dough
- 1 medium red onion, sliced thin
- 1 teaspoon fresh thyme leaves
- ¼ teaspoon red pepper flakes
- 1 teaspoon freshly squeezed lemon juice
- ¼ cup shelled pistachios, toasted

1. Brush two baking sheets with olive oil.
2. In a large strainer set over a large bowl, toss the zucchini and summer squash well with the salt, and let it sit for about 5 minutes. Use a kitchen towel to press and squeeze the liquid from the squash mixture, removing as much moisture as possible.
3. Roll out one of the dough balls to the desired size, and place it on the prepared baking sheet.

4. In a large mixing bowl, toss together the drained squash mixture, onion, thyme, red pepper flakes, olive oil, and lemon juice. Arrange half of the vegetables on the dough.
5. Slide the baking sheet into the air fryer oven. Press the Power Button. Cook at 400°F (205°C) for 10 minutes, until the crust is golden and the cheese has melted.
6. Remove the pizza from the air fryer oven and transfer it to a cutting board. Let it rest for 5 minutes, then garnish with half of the toasted pistachios. Slice and serve.
7. Repeat with the remaining dough ball and toppings.

Zucchini and Summer Squash Pizza

Prep time: 15 minutes | Cook time: 50 minutes | Makes 1 pan pizza

- 2 red bell peppers, cut into strips
- 1 zucchini, trimmed and cut into ¼-inch rounds
- 1 yellow summer squash, trimmed and cut into ¼-inch rounds
- 1 medium red onion, sliced
- 10 ounces (284 g) fingerling or red bliss potatoes, scrubbed and cut into ¼-inch slices
- 3 tablespoons extra-virgin olive oil
- 5 fresh thyme sprigs, stemmed
- ½ teaspoon fine sea salt
- ¼ teaspoon freshly ground black pepper
- 1 cup Garlic Tomato Pizza Sauce
- No-Knead Pan Pizza Dough
- 1¼ cups grated fontina cheese
- 1½ cups arugula

1. On a foil-lined baking sheet, spread the bell peppers, zucchini, summer squash, onion, and potatoes. Drizzle with the olive oil, sprinkle on the thyme, and season with the salt and pepper. Toss well, then transfer the baking sheet to the air fryer oven and Press the Power Button. Cook at 400°F (205°C) for about 30 minutes, stirring twice during cooking. The potatoes should be fork tender.
2. Remove the vegetables from the air fryer oven and set aside. At this point, they can be used immediately or cooled to room temperature and refrigerated overnight in an airtight container.
3. Roll out the dough ball to the desired size, and place it on a greased baking pan.
4. Leaving a 1-inch border, spoon the sauce onto the dough, spreading it evenly. Scatter the fontina cheese over the dough, followed by the cooked vegetables.
5. Slide the baking sheet into the air fryer oven. Press the Power Button. Cook at 400°F (205°C) for 10 minutes, until the cheese has melted and the crust is golden. Remove it from the air fryer oven and let it cool for 5 minutes, then top it with the fresh arugula. Slice and serve.

Butternut Squash and Arugula Pizza

Prep time: 10 minutes | Cook time: 1 hour | Makes 2 (12- to 14-inch) pizzas

- 1 small (1-pound / 454-g) butternut squash, peeled, seeded, and cut into small dice
- 3 tablespoons extra-virgin olive oil, plus more for brushing
- ¼ teaspoon salt, plus more for finishing
- ⅛ teaspoon freshly ground black pepper, plus more for finishing
- 3 fresh thyme sprigs, stemmed
- 4 slices center-cut bacon
- Simple Pizza Dough
- ½ cup grated fontina cheese
- ¼ cup crumbled blue cheese
- 4 cups arugula

1. Spread the butternut squash on a foil-lined baking pan and drizzle with the olive oil. Season with the salt, pepper, and thyme, and toss well. Press the Power Button. Cook at 400°F (205°C) for about 35 minutes, until the squash is fork tender and golden, stirring and rotating the pan halfway through. Remove from the air fryer oven and cool briefly.
2. Meanwhile, in a sauté pan over medium heat, brown the bacon until crisp, 2 to 3 minutes per side. Transfer to a paper towel-lined plate and, when cool, roughly chop.
3. Brush two baking sheets with olive oil.
4. Roll out one of the dough balls to the desired size, and place it on the prepared baking sheet.
5. Spread half of the fontina and blue cheeses evenly over the dough. Top with half of the cooked butternut squash and half of the bacon.
6. Slide the baking sheet into the air fryer oven. Press the Power Button. Cook at 400°F (205°C) for 10 minutes, until the crust is golden and the cheese is bubbly.
7. Remove the pizza from the air fryer oven and transfer it to a cutting board. Let it rest for 5 minutes, then top with half of the arugula. Slice and serve.
8. Repeat with the remaining dough ball and toppings.

Double-Cheese Clam Pizza

Prep time: 15 minutes | Cook time: 15 minutes | Serves 4

- ¼ cup extra-virgin olive oil, plus a little extra for forming the crust
- 2 large garlic cloves, chopped
- ¼ teaspoon red pepper flakes
- 1 pound (454 g) store-bought pizza dough
- ½ cup shredded Mozzarella cheese (4 ounces / 113 g)
- 2 (6.5-ounce / 184-g) cans chopped clams, drained
- ¼ cup grated Parmesan cheese
- ½ cup coarsely chopped fresh parsley
- 2 teaspoons chopped fresh oregano (optional)

1. In a small bowl, whisk together the olive oil with the garlic and red pepper flakes. Let it sit while you work on the dough.
2. Punch down the pizza dough to release as much air as possible. Place the dough in the baking pan and press it out toward the edges. The dough will likely spring back and shrink. Be patient and keep working at it, leaving it to relax for a few minutes from time to time. As it stretches, I find it helpful to coat my fingers with some olive oil and then poke the dough lightly with my fingertips to keep it from shrinking as much. Don't worry if you can't get it all the way to the edges of the pan.
3. Brush half of the garlic oil over the dough. Evenly distribute the Mozzarella cheese over the dough.
4. Slide the baking pan into the air fryer oven. Press the Power Button. Cook at 400°F (205°C) for 15 minutes.
5. After about 8 minutes, remove the pan from the air fryer oven. Scatter the clams over the pizza and sprinkle the Parmesan cheese on top. Return the pan to the air fryer oven and continue cooking for another 7 minutes.
6. When cooking is complete, the cheese on top is lightly browned and bubbling and the crust is deep golden brown. Remove the pan from the air fryer oven. Place the pizza on a wire rack to cool for a few minutes (a rack will keep the crust from getting soggy as it cools). Sprinkle the parsley and oregano (if using) over the pizza and drizzle with the remaining garlic oil. Slice and serve.

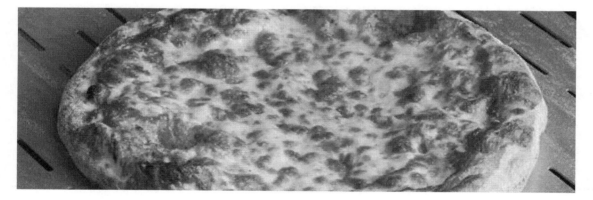

Zucchini and Onion Pizza

Prep time: 10 minutes | Cook time: 10 minutes | Serves 2

- 2 tablespoons all-purpose flour, plus more as needed
- ½ store-bought pizza dough (about 8 ounces / 227 g)
- 1 tablespoon canola oil, divided
- ½ cup pizza sauce
- 1 cup shredded Mozzarella cheese
- ½ zucchini, thinly sliced
- ½ red onion, sliced
- ½ red bell pepper, seeded and thinly sliced

1. Dust a clean work surface with the flour.
2. Place the dough on the floured surface and roll it into a 9-inch round of even thickness. Dust your rolling pin and work surface with additional flour, as needed, to ensure the dough does not stick.
3. Evenly brush the surface of the rolled-out dough with ½ tablespoon of oil. Flip the dough over and brush the other side with the remaining ½ tablespoon of oil. Poke the dough with a fork 5 or 6 times across its surface to prevent air pockets from forming while it cooks.
4. Place the dough on a greased baking sheet. Slide the baking sheet into the air fryer oven. Press the Power Button. Cook at 400°F (205°C) for 10 minutes.
5. After 5 minutes, flip the dough, then spread the pizza sauce evenly over it. Sprinkle with the cheese, and top with the zucchini, onion, and pepper.
6. Continue cooking for the remaining 5 minutes until the cheese is melted and the veggie slices begin to crisp.
7. When cooking is complete, let cool slightly before slicing.

Grilled Egg and Arugula Pizza

Prep time: 10 minutes | Cook time: 8 minutes | Serves 2

- 2 tablespoons all-purpose flour, plus more as needed
- ½ store-bought pizza dough (about 8 ounces / 227 g)
- 1 tablespoon canola oil, divided
- 1 cup fresh ricotta cheese
- 4 large eggs
- Sea salt, to taste
- Freshly ground black pepper, to taste
- 4 cups arugula, torn
- 1 tablespoon extra-virgin olive oil
- 1 teaspoon freshly squeezed lemon juice
- 2 tablespoons grated Parmesan cheese

1. Place the grill plate on the grill position. Select Grill, set the temperature to 450°F (232°C), and set the time to 7 minutes.
2. Dust a clean work surface with flour. Place the dough on the floured surface and roll it into a 9-inch round of even thickness. Dust your rolling pin and work surface with additional flour, as needed, to ensure the dough does not stick.
3. Brush the surface of the rolled-out dough evenly with ½ tablespoon of canola oil. Flip the dough over and brush with the remaining ½ tablespoon oil. Poke the dough with a fork 5 or 6 times across its surface to prevent air pockets from forming during cooking.
4. Place the dough on the grill plate. Grill for 4 minutes.
5. After 4 minutes, flip the dough, then spoon teaspoons of ricotta cheese across the surface of the dough, leaving a 1-inch border around the edges.
6. Crack one egg into a ramekin or small bowl. This way you can easily remove any shell that may break into the egg and keep the yolk intact. Imagine the dough is split into four quadrants. Pour one egg into each. Repeat with the remaining 3 eggs. Season the pizza with salt and pepper.
7. Continue cooking for the remaining 3 to 4 minutes until the egg whites are firm.
8. Meanwhile, in a medium bowl, toss together the arugula, oil, and lemon juice, and season with salt and pepper.
9. Transfer the pizza to a cutting board and let it cool. Top it with the arugula mixture, drizzle with olive oil, if desired, and sprinkle with Parmesan cheese. Cut into pieces and serve.

Bulgogi Burgers

Prep time: 15 minutes | Cook time: 10 minutes | Serves 4

FOR THE BURGERS:
- 1 pound (454 g) 85% lean ground beef
- 2 tablespoons gochujang
- ¼ cup chopped scallions
- 2 teaspoons minced garlic
- 2 teaspoons minced fresh ginger
- 1 tablespoon soy sauce
- 1 tablespoon toasted sesame oil
- 2 teaspoons sugar
- ½ teaspoon kosher salt
- 4 hamburger buns
- Cooking spray
- For the Korean Mayo:
- 1 tablespoon gochujang
- ¼ cup mayonnaise
- 2 teaspoons sesame seeds
- ¼ cup chopped scallions
- 1 tablespoon toasted sesame oil

1. Combine the ingredients for the burgers, except for the buns, in a large bowl. Stir to mix well, then wrap the bowl in plastic and refrigerate to marinate for at least an hour.
2. Preheat the air fryer to 350°F (177°C) and spritz with cooking spray.
3. Divide the meat mixture into four portions and form into four balls. Bash the balls into patties.
4. Arrange the patties in the preheated air fryer and spritz with cooking spray. Air fry for 10 minutes or until golden brown. Flip the patties halfway through.
5. Meanwhile, combine the ingredients for the Korean mayo in a small bowl. Stir to mix well.
6. Remove the patties from the air fryer and assemble with the buns, then spread the Korean mayo over the patties to make the burgers. Serve immediately.

Nugget and Veggie Taco Wraps

Prep time: 5 minutes | Cook time: 15 minutes | Serves 4

- 1 tablespoon water
- 4 pieces commercial vegan nuggets, chopped
- 1 small yellow onion, diced
- 1 small red bell pepper, chopped
- 2 cobs grilled corn kernels
- 4 large corn tortillas
- Mixed greens, for garnish

1. Preheat the air fryer to 400°F (204°C).
2. Over a medium heat, sauté the nuggets in the water with the onion, corn kernels and bell pepper in a skillet, then remove from the heat.
3. Fill the tortillas with the nuggets and vegetables and fold them up. Transfer to the inside of the fryer and air fry for 15 minutes.
4. Once crispy, serve immediately, garnished with the mixed greens.

Lamb and Feta Hamburgers

Prep time: 15 minutes | Cook time: 16 minutes | Makes 4 burgers

- 1½ pounds (680 g) ground lamb
- ¼ cup crumbled feta
- 1½ teaspoons tomato paste
- 1½ teaspoons minced garlic
- 1 teaspoon ground dried ginger
- 1 teaspoon ground coriander
- ¼ teaspoon salt
- ¼ teaspoon cayenne pepper
- 4 kaiser rolls or hamburger buns, split open lengthwise, warmed
- Cooking spray

1. Preheat the air fryer to 375°F (191°C) and spritz with cooking spray.
2. Combine all the ingredients, except for the buns, in a large bowl. Coarsely stir to mix well.
3. Shape the mixture into four balls, then pound the balls into four 5-inch diameter patties.
4. Arrange the patties in the preheated air fryer and spritz with cooking spray. Air fry for 16 minutes or until well browned. Flip the patties halfway through.
5. Assemble the buns with patties to make the burgers and serve immediately.

Veggie Salsa Wraps

Prep time: 5 minutes | Cook time: 7 minutes | Serves 4

- 1 cup red onion, sliced
- 1 zucchini, chopped
- 1 poblano pepper, deseeded and finely chopped
- 1 head lettuce
- ½ cup salsa
- 8 ounces (227 g) Mozzarella cheese

1. Preheat the air fryer to 390°F (199°C).
2. Place the red onion, zucchini, and poblano pepper in the air fryer basket and air fry for 7 minutes, or until they are tender and fragrant.
3. Divide the veggie mixture among the lettuce leaves and spoon the salsa over the top. Finish off with Mozzarella cheese. Wrap the lettuce leaves around the filling.
4. Serve immediately.

Tuna and Lettuce Wraps

Prep time: 10 minutes | Cook time: 4 to 7 minutes | Serves 4

- 1 pound (454 g) fresh tuna steak, cut into 1-inch cubes
- 1 tablespoon grated fresh ginger
- 2 garlic cloves, minced
- ½ teaspoon toasted sesame oil
- 4 low-sodium whole-wheat tortillas
- ¼ cup low-fat mayonnaise
- 2 cups shredded romaine lettuce
- 1 red bell pepper, thinly sliced

1. Preheat the air fryer to 390°F (199°C).
2. In a medium bowl, mix the tuna, ginger, garlic, and sesame oil. Let it stand for 10 minutes.
3. Air fry the tuna in the air fryer basket for 4 to 7 minutes, or until lightly browned.
4. Make the wraps with the tuna, tortillas, mayonnaise, lettuce, and bell pepper.
5. Serve immediately.

Lettuce Fajita Meatball Wraps

Prep time: 10 minutes | Cook time: 10 minutes | Serves 4

- 1 pound (454 g) 85% lean ground beef
- ½ cup salsa, plus more for serving
- ¼ cup chopped onions
- ¼ cup diced green or red bell peppers
- 1 large egg, beaten
- 1 teaspoon fine sea salt
- ½ teaspoon chili powder
- ½ teaspoon ground cumin
- 1 clove garlic, minced
- Cooking spray
- For Serving:
- 8 leaves Boston lettuce
- Pico de gallo or salsa
- Lime slices

1. Preheat the air fryer to 350°F (177°C). Spray the air fryer basket with cooking spray.
2. In a large bowl, mix together all the ingredients until well combined.
3. Shape the meat mixture into eight 1-inch balls. Place the meatballs in the air fryer basket, leaving a little space between them. Air fry for 10 minutes, or until cooked through and no longer pink inside and the internal temperature reaches 145°F (63°C).
4. Serve each meatball on a lettuce leaf, topped with pico de gallo or salsa. Serve with lime slices.

Chicken-Lettuce Wraps

Prep time: 15 minutes | Cook time: 12 to 16 minutes | Serves 2 to 4

- 1 pound (454 g) boneless, skinless chicken thighs, trimmed
- 1 teaspoon vegetable oil
- 2 tablespoons lime juice
- 1 shallot, minced
- 1 tablespoon fish sauce, plus extra for serving
- 2 teaspoons packed brown sugar
- 1 garlic clove, minced
- ⅛ teaspoon red pepper flakes
- 1 mango, peeled, pitted, and cut into ¼-inch pieces
- 1 head Bibb lettuce, leaves separated (8 ounces / 227 g)
- ¼ cup chopped dry-roasted peanuts
- 2 Thai chiles, stemmed and sliced thin

1. Preheat the air fryer to 400°F (204°C).
2. Pat the chicken dry with paper towels and rub with oil. Place the chicken in air fryer basket and air fry for 12 to 16 minutes, or until the chicken registers 175°F (79°C), flipping and rotating chicken halfway through cooking.
3. Meanwhile, whisk lime juice, shallot, fish sauce, sugar, garlic, and pepper flakes together in large bowl; set aside.
4. Transfer chicken to cutting board, let cool slightly, then shred into bite-size pieces using 2 forks. Add the shredded chicken, mango, mint, cilantro, and basil to bowl with dressing and toss to coat.
5. Serve the chicken in the lettuce leaves, passing peanuts, Thai chiles, and extra fish sauce separately.

Cheesy Chicken Sandwich

Prep time: 10 minutes | Cook time: 5 to 7 minutes | Serves 1

- ⅓ cup chicken, cooked and shredded
- 2 Mozzarella slices
- 1 hamburger bun
- ¼ cup shredded cabbage
- 1 teaspoon mayonnaise
- 2 teaspoons butter, melted
- 1 teaspoon olive oil
- ½ teaspoon balsamic vinegar
- ¼ teaspoon smoked paprika
- ¼ teaspoon black pepper
- ¼ teaspoon garlic powder
- Pinch of salt

1. Preheat the air fryer to 370°F (188°C).
2. Brush some butter onto the outside of the hamburger bun.
3. In a bowl, coat the chicken with the garlic powder, salt, pepper, and paprika.
4. In a separate bowl, stir together the mayonnaise, olive oil, cabbage, and balsamic vinegar to make coleslaw.
5. Slice the bun in two. Start building the sandwich, starting with the chicken, followed by the Mozzarella, the coleslaw, and finally the top bun.
6. Transfer the sandwich to the air fryer and bake for 5 to 7 minutes.
7. Serve immediately.

Smoky Chicken Sandwich
Prep time: 10 minutes | Cook time: 11 minutes | Serves 2

- 2 boneless, skinless chicken breasts (8 ounces / 227 g each), sliced horizontally in half and separated into 4 thinner cutlets
- Kosher salt and freshly ground black pepper, to taste
- ½ cup all-purpose flour
- 3 large eggs, lightly beaten
- ½ cup dried bread crumbs
- 1 tablespoon smoked paprika
- Cooking spray
- ½ cup marinara sauce
- 6 ounces (170 g) smoked Mozzarella cheese, grated
- 2 store-bought soft, sesame-seed hamburger or Italian buns, split

1. Preheat the air fryer to 350°F (177°C).
2. Season the chicken cutlets all over with salt and pepper. Set up three shallow bowls: Place the flour in the first bowl, the eggs in the second, and stir together the bread crumbs and smoked paprika in the third. Coat the chicken pieces in the flour, then dip fully in the egg. Dredge in the paprika bread crumbs, then transfer to a wire rack set over a baking sheet and spray both sides liberally with cooking spray.
3. Transfer 2 of the chicken cutlets to the air fryer and air fry for 6 minutes, or until beginning to brown. Spread each cutlet with 2 tablespoons of the marinara sauce and sprinkle with one-quarter of the smoked Mozzarella. Increase the temperature to 400°F (204°C) and air fry for 5 minutes more, or until the chicken is cooked through and crisp and the cheese is melted and golden brown.
4. Transfer the cutlets to a plate, stack on top of each other, and place inside a bun. Repeat with the remaining chicken cutlets, marinara, smoked Mozzarella, and bun.
5. Serve the sandwiches warm.

Cheesy Potato Taquitos
Prep time: 5 minutes | Cook time: 6 minutes per batch | Makes 12 taquitos

- 2 cups mashed potatoes
- ½ cup shredded Mexican cheese
- 12 corn tortillas
- Cooking spray

1. Preheat the air fryer to 400°F (204°C). Line the baking pan with parchment paper.
2. In a bowl, combine the potatoes and cheese until well mixed. Microwave the tortillas on high heat for 30 seconds, or until softened. Add some water to another bowl and set alongside.
3. On a clean work surface, lay the tortillas. Scoop 3 tablespoons of the potato mixture in the center of each tortilla. Roll up tightly and secure with

toothpicks if necessary.
4. Arrange the filled tortillas, seam side down, in the prepared baking pan. Spritz the tortillas with cooking spray. Air fry for 6 minutes, or until crispy and golden brown, flipping once halfway through the cooking time. You may need to work in batches to avoid overcrowding.
5. Serve hot.

Chicken and Yogurt Taquitos
Prep time: 15 minutes | Cook time: 12 minutes | Serves 4

- 1 cup cooked chicken, shredded
- ¼ cup Greek yogurt
- ¼ cup salsa
- 1 cup shredded Mozzarella cheese
- Salt and ground black pepper, to taste
- 4 flour tortillas
- Cooking spray

1. Preheat the air fryer to 380°F (193°C) and spritz with cooking spray.
2. Combine all the ingredients, except for the tortillas, in a large bowl. Stir to mix well.
3. Make the taquitos: Unfold the tortillas on a clean work surface, then scoop up 2 tablespoons of the chicken mixture in the middle of each tortilla. Roll the tortillas up to wrap the filling.
4. Arrange the taquitos in the preheated air fryer and spritz with cooking spray.
5. Air fry for 12 minutes or until golden brown and the cheese melts. Flip the taquitos halfway through.
6. Serve immediately.

Pork Momos
Prep time: 20 minutes | Cook time: 10 minutes per batch | Serves 4

- 2 tablespoons olive oil
- 1 pound (454 g) ground pork
- 1 shredded carrot
- 1 onion, chopped
- 1 teaspoon soy sauce
- 16 wonton wrappers
- Salt and ground black pepper, to taste

1. Preheat the air fryer to 320°F (160°C).
2. Heat the olive oil in a nonstick skillet over medium heat until shimmering.
3. Add the ground pork, carrot, onion, soy sauce, salt, and ground black pepper and sauté for 10 minutes or until the pork is well browned and carrots are tender.
4. Unfold the wrappers on a clean work surface, then divide the cooked pork and vegetables on the wrappers. Fold the edges around the filling to form momos. Nip the top to seal the momos.
5. Arrange the momos in the preheated air fryer and spritz with cooking spray. Air fry for 10 minutes or until the wrappers are lightly browned. Work in batches to avoid overcrowding.
6. Serve immediately.

Eggplant Hoagies

Prep time: 15 minutes | Cook time: 12 minutes | Makes 3 hoagies

- 6 peeled eggplant slices (about ½ inch thick and 3 inches in diameter)
- ¼ cup jarred pizza sauce
- 6 tablespoons grated Parmesan cheese
- 3 Italian sub rolls, split open lengthwise, warmed
- Cooking spray

1. Preheat the air fryer to 350°F (177°C) and spritz with cooking spray.
2. Arrange the eggplant slices in the preheated air fryer and spritz with cooking spray.
3. Air fry for 10 minutes or until lightly wilted and tender. Flip the slices halfway through.
4. Divide and spread the pizza sauce and cheese on top of the eggplant slice and air fry over 375°F (191°C) for 2 more minutes or until the cheese melts.
5. Assemble each sub roll with two slices of eggplant and serve immediately.

Air Fried Cream Cheese Wontons

Prep time: 5 minutes | Cook time: 6 minutes | Serves 4

- 2 ounces (57 g) cream cheese, softened
- 1 tablespoon sugar
- 16 square wonton wrappers
- Cooking spray

1. Preheat the air fryer to 350°F (177°C). Spritz the air fryer basket with cooking spray.
2. In a mixing bowl, stir together the cream cheese and sugar until well mixed. Prepare a small bowl of water alongside.
3. On a clean work surface, lay the wonton wrappers. Scoop ¼ teaspoon of cream cheese in the center of each wonton wrapper. Dab the water over the wrapper edges. Fold each wonton wrapper diagonally in half over the filling to form a triangle.
4. Arrange the wontons in the air fryer basket. Spritz the wontons with cooking spray. Air fry for 6 minutes, or until golden brown and crispy. Flip once halfway through to ensure even cooking.
5. Divide the wontons among four plates. Let rest for 5 minutes before serving.

Crispy Crab and Cream Cheese Wontons

Prep time: 10 minutes | Cook time: 10 minutes per batch | Serves 6 to 8

- 24 wonton wrappers, thawed if frozen
- Cooking spray
- For the Filling:
- 5 ounces (142 g) lump crabmeat, drained and patted dry
- 4 ounces (113 g) cream cheese, at room temperature
- 2 scallions, sliced
- 1½ teaspoons toasted sesame oil
- 1 teaspoon Worcestershire sauce
- Kosher salt and ground black pepper, to taste

1. Preheat the air fryer to 350°F (177°C). Spritz the air fryer basket with cooking spray.
2. In a medium-size bowl, place all the ingredients for the filling and stir until well mixed. Prepare a small bowl of water alongside.
3. On a clean work surface, lay the wonton wrappers. Scoop 1 teaspoon of the filling in the center of each wrapper. Wet the edges with a touch of water. Fold each wonton wrapper diagonally in half over the filling to form a triangle.
4. Arrange the wontons in the air fryer basket. Spritz the wontons with cooking spray. Work in batches, 6 to 8 at a time. Air fry for 10 minutes, or until crispy and golden brown. Flip once halfway through.
5. Serve immediately.

Cabbage and Pork Gyoza

Prep time: 10 minutes | Cook time: 10 minutes per batch | Makes 48 gyozas

- 1 pound (454 g) ground pork
- 1 small head Napa cabbage (about 1 pound / 454 g), sliced thinly and minced
- ½ cup minced scallions
- 1 teaspoon minced fresh chives
- 1 teaspoon soy sauce
- 1 tablespoon minced garlic
- 1 teaspoon granulated sugar
- 2 teaspoons kosher salt
- 48 to 50 wonton or dumpling wrappers
- Cooking spray

1. Make the filling: Combine all the ingredients, except for the wrappers in a large bowl. Stir to mix well.
2. Unfold a wrapper on a clean work surface, then dab the edges with a little water. Scoop up 2 teaspoons of the filling mixture in the center.
3. Make the gyoza: Fold the wrapper over to filling and press the edges to seal. Pleat the edges if desired. Repeat with remaining wrappers and fillings.
4. Preheat the air fryer to 360°F (182°C) and spritz with cooking spray.
5. Arrange the gyozas in the preheated air fryer and spritz with cooking spray. Air fry for 10 minutes or until golden brown. Flip the gyozas halfway through. Work in batches to avoid overcrowding.
6. Serve immediately.

Pea and Potato Samosas with Chutney

**Prep time: 30 minutes | Cook time: 1 hour 10 minutes |
Makes 16 samosas**

DOUGH:

- 4 cups all-purpose flour, plus more for flouring the work surface
- ¼ cup plain yogurt
- ½ cup cold unsalted butter, cut into cubes
- 2 teaspoons kosher salt
- 1 cup ice water

FILLING:

- 2 tablespoons vegetable oil
- 1 onion, diced
- 1½ teaspoons coriander
- 1½ teaspoons cumin
- 1 clove garlic, minced
- 1 teaspoon turmeric
- 1 teaspoon kosher salt
- ½ cup peas, thawed if frozen
- 2 cups mashed potatoes
- 2 tablespoons yogurt
- Cooking spray

CHUTNEY:

- 1 cup mint leaves, lightly packed
- 2 cups cilantro leaves, lightly packed
- 1 green chile pepper, deseeded and minced
- ½ cup minced onion
- Juice of 1 lime
- 1 teaspoon granulated sugar
- 1 teaspoon kosher salt
- 2 tablespoons vegetable oil

1. Put the flour, yogurt, butter, and salt in a food processor. Pulse to combine until grainy. Pour in the water and pulse until a smooth and firm dough forms.
2. Transfer the dough on a clean and lightly floured working surface. Knead the dough and shape it into a ball. Cut in half and flatten the halves into 2 discs. Wrap them in plastic and let sit in refrigerator until ready to use.
3. Meanwhile, make the filling: Heat the vegetable oil in a saucepan over medium heat.
4. Add the onion and sauté for 5 minutes or until lightly browned.
5. Add the coriander, cumin, garlic, turmeric, and salt and sauté for 2 minutes or until fragrant.
6. Add the peas, potatoes, and yogurt and stir to combine well. Turn off the heat and allow to cool.
7. Meanwhile, combine the ingredients for the chutney in a food processor. Pulse to mix well until glossy. Pour the chutney in a bowl and refrigerate until ready to use.
8. Make the samosas: Remove the dough discs from the refrigerator and cut each disc into 8 parts. Shape each part into a ball, then roll the ball into a 6-inch circle. Cut the circle in half and roll each half into a cone.
9. Scoop up 2 tablespoons of the filling into the cone, press the edges of the cone to seal and form into a triangle. Repeat with remaining dough and filling.
10. Preheat the air fryer to 360°F (182°C) and spritz with cooking spray.
11. Arrange four samosas each batch in the preheated air fryer and spritz with cooking spray. Air fry for 15 minutes or until golden brown and crispy. Flip the samosas halfway through.
12. Serve the samosas with the chutney.

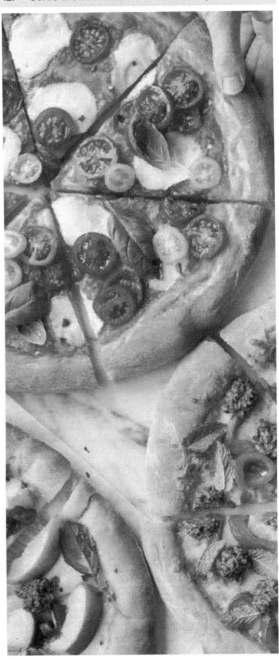

Chapter 12
Appetizers and Snacks

Sweet Potato Chips

Prep time: 10 minutes | Cook time: 14 minutes | Serves 3

- 2 large-sized sweet potatoes, peeled and cut into thin slices
- 2 teaspoons butter, melted
- Sea salt and ground black pepper, to taste
- ½ teaspoon dried oregano
- ½ teaspoon dried basil
- ½ teaspoon dried rosemary

1. Toss the sweet potato with the remaining ingredients and place them in the air fryer basket.
2. Put the air fryer lid on and air fry in the preheated instant pot at 360°F (182°C) for 14 minutes. Flip the sweet potato chips when the lid screen indicates TURN FOOD. Work in batches.
3. Enjoy!

Golden Onion Rings

Prep time: 5 minutes | Cook time: 8 minutes | Serves 4

- 1 cup all-purpose flour
- Sea salt and black pepper, to taste
- 1 teaspoon crushed red pepper flakes
- ½ teaspoon cumin powder
- 1 egg
- 1 cup bread crumbs
- 1 medium yellow onion, sliced

1. In a shallow bowl, mix the flour, salt, black pepper, red pepper flakes, and cumin powder.
2. Whisk the egg in another shallow bowl. Place the bread crumbs in a separate bowl.
3. Dip the onion rings in the flour, then in the eggs, then in the bread crumbs. Place the onion rings in the air fryer basket.
4. Put the air fryer lid on and air fry in the preheated instant pot at 380°F (193°C) for 8 minutes or until golden brown and cooked through. Flip the onion rings when the lid screen indicates TURN FOOD.
5. Bon appétit!

Tortilla Chips with Paprika

Prep time: 8 minutes | Cook time: 5 minutes | Serves 4

- 9 corn tortillas, cut into wedges
- 1 tablespoon olive oil
- 1 teaspoon hot paprika
- Sea salt and ground black pepper, to taste

1. Toss the tortilla wedges with the remaining ingredients. Transfer to the air fryer basket.
2. Put the air fryer lid on and air fry in the preheated instant pot at 360°F (182°C) for 5 minutes. Flip the tortilla chips when the lid screen indicates TURN FOOD. Work in batches.
3. Enjoy!

Jalapeño Poppers with Bacon

Prep time: 5 minutes | Cook time: 7 minutes | Serves 4

- 4 ounces (113 g) Cottage cheese, crumbled
- 4 ounces (113 g) Cheddar cheese, shredded
- 1 teaspoon mustard seeds
- 8 jalapeños, seeded and sliced in half lengthwise
- 8 slices bacon, sliced in half lengthwise

1. Thoroughly combine the cheese and mustard seeds. Spoon the mixture into the jalapeño halves.
2. Wrap each jalapeño with half a slice of bacon and secure with toothpicks. Transfer to the air fryer basket.
3. Put the air fryer lid on and air fry in the preheated instant pot at 370°F (188°C) for 7 minutes or until golden brown.
4. Bon appétit!

Chicken Wings with Mustard

Prep time: 5 minutes | Cook time: 18 minutes | Serves 3

- ¾ pound (340 g) chicken wings
- 1 tablespoon olive oil
- 1 teaspoon mustard seeds
- 1 teaspoon cayenne pepper
- 1 teaspoon garlic powder
- Sea salt and ground black pepper, to taste

1. Toss the chicken wings with the remaining ingredients. Transfer to the air fryer basket.
2. Put the air fryer lid on and roast in the preheated instant pot at 380°F (193°C) for 18 minutes. Flip the chicken wings when the lid screen indicates TURN FOOD.
3. Bon appétit!

Chili Cauliflower Florets

Prep time: 5 minutes | Cook time: 15 minutes | Serves 4

- 2 eggs, whisked
- 1 cup bread crumbs
- Sea salt and ground black pepper, to taste
- 1 teaspoon cayenne pepper
- 1 teaspoon chili powder
- ½ teaspoon onion powder
- ½ teaspoon cumin powder
- ½ teaspoon garlic powder
- 1 pound (454 g) cauliflower florets

1. Mix the eggs, bread crumbs, and spices until well combined. Dip the cauliflower florets in the batter. Transfer to the air fryer basket.
2. Put the air fryer lid on and air fry in the preheated instant pot at 350°F (180°C) for 15 minutes. Flip the cauliflower florets when the lid screen indicates TURN FOOD.
3. Bon appétit!

Brussels Sprouts with Syrup

Prep time: 6 minutes | Cook time: 10 minutes | Serves 4

- 1 pound Brussels sprouts, trimmed
- 2 tablespoons sesame oil
- 2 tablespoons agave syrup
- 2 tablespoons rice wine
- 1 teaspoon chili flakes
- 1 teaspoon garlic powder
- ½ teaspoon paprika
- Sea salt and ground black pepper, to taste

1. Toss the Brussels sprouts with the remaining ingredients; then, arrange the Brussels sprouts in the air fryer basket.
2. Put the air fryer lid on and air fry in the preheated instant pot at 380°F (193°C) for 10 minutes. Flip the Brussels sprouts when the lid screen indicates TURN FOOD.
3. Serve warm and enjoy!

Carrot with Honey

Prep time: 8 minutes | Cook time: 15 minutes | Serves 3

- ¾ pound (340 g) baby carrots, halved lengthwise
- 2 tablespoons coconut oil
- ½ teaspoon cumin powder
- 2 tablespoons honey
- 2 tablespoons white wine

1. Toss the carrots with the remaining ingredients; then, arrange the carrots in the air fryer basket.
2. Put the air fryer lid on and air fry in the preheated instant pot at 380°F (193°C) for 15 minutes. Flip the carrots when the lid screen indicates TURN FOOD.
3. Bon appétit!

Air Fried Potato Chips

Prep time: 10 minutes | Cook time: 16 minutes | Serves 3

- 2 large-sized potatoes, thinly sliced
- 2 tablespoons olive oil
- 1 teaspoon Mediterranean herb mix
- 1 teaspoon cayenne pepper
- Coarse sea salt and ground black pepper, to taste

1. Toss the potatoes with the remaining ingredients and place them in the air fryer basket.
2. Put the air fryer lid on and air fry in the preheated instant pot at 360°F (182°C) for 16 minutes. Flip the potato chips when the lid screen indicates TURN FOOD. Work in batches.
3. Enjoy!

Broccoli Florets with Butter

Prep time: 5 minutes | Cook time: 10 minutes | Serves 4

- 1 pound (454 g) broccoli florets
- 2 tablespoons butter, room temperature
- ¼ teaspoon mustard seeds
- 1 tablespoon soy sauce
- Sea salt and freshly ground black pepper, to taste

1. Toss all the ingredients in a lightly oiled air fryer basket.
2. Put the air fryer lid on and air fry in the preheated instant pot at 370°F (188°C) for 10 minutes. Flip the broccoli florets when the lid screen indicates TURN FOOD.
3. Bon appétit!

Apple Chips with Cinnamon

Prep time: 10 minutes | Cook time: 9 minutes | Serves 4

- 2 large sweet, crisp apples, cored and sliced
- 1 teaspoon ground cinnamon
- ½ teaspoon grated nutmeg
- A pinch of salt

1. Toss the apple slices with the remaining ingredients and arrange them in a single layer in the air fryer basket.
2. Put the air fryer lid on and air fry in the preheated instant pot at 390°F (199°C) for 9 minutes. Flip the apple chips when the lid screen indicates TURN FOOD. Work in batches.
3. Bon appétit!

Sweet Potato with Herb

Prep time: 10 minutes | Cook time: 15 minutes | Serves 3

- 2 large-sized sweet potatoes, peeled and cut into ¼-inch sticks
- 2 teaspoons olive oil
- 1 teaspoon garlic powder
- 1 tablespoon Mediterranean herb mix
- Kosher salt and freshly ground black pepper, to taste

1. Toss the sweet potato with the remaining ingredients and place them in the air fryer basket.
2. Put the air fryer lid on and air fry in the preheated instant pot at 360°F (182°C) for 15 minutes. Flip the sweet potato sticks when the lid screen indicates TURN FOOD. Work in batches.
3. Enjoy!

Pork Ribs with Honey and Butter

Prep time: 5 minutes | Cook time: 35 minutes | Serves 4

- 2 pounds (907 g) pork ribs
- 2 tablespoons honey
- 2 tablespoons butter
- 1 teaspoon sweet paprika
- 1 teaspoon hot paprika
- 1 teaspoon granulated garlic
- Sea salt and ground black pepper, to taste
- 1 teaspoon brown mustard
- 1 teaspoon ground cumin

1. Toss all ingredients in a lightly greased air fryer basket.
2. Put the air fryer lid on and air fry in the preheated instant pot at 350°F (180°C) for 35 minutes. Flip the pork ribs when the lid screen indicates TURN FOOD.
3. Bon appétit!

Panko Cheese Green Beans

Prep time: 5 minutes | Cook time: 6 minutes | Serves 4

- ½ cup flour
- 2 eggs, beaten
- ½ cup bread crumbs
- ½ cup grated Parmesan cheese
- ½ teaspoon onion powder
- ¼ teaspoon cumin powder
- ½ teaspoon garlic powder
- 1 pound (454 g) fresh green beans

1. In a shallow bowl, thoroughly combine the flour and eggs; mix to combine well.
2. Then, in another bowl, mix the remaining ingredients.
3. Dip the green beans in the egg mixture, then, in the bread crumb mixture. Transfer to the air fryer basket.
4. Put the air fryer lid on and air fry in the preheated instant pot at 390°F (199°C) for 6 minutes. Flip the green beans when the lid screen indicates TURN FOOD.
5. Enjoy!

Lemon Eggplant Chips

Prep time: 10 minutes | Cook time: 15 minutes | Serves 4

- 1 pound (454 g) eggplant, sliced
- 2 tablespoons olive oil
- 1 teaspoon minced garlic
- Sea salt and ground black pepper, to taste
- 2 tablespoons freshly squeezed lemon juice

1. Toss the eggplant pieces with the remaining ingredients until they are well coated on all sides.
2. Arrange the eggplant in the air fryer basket.
3. Put the air fryer lid on and air fry in the preheated instant pot at 400°F (205°C) for 15 minutes. Flip the eggplant when the lid screen indicates TURN FOOD.
4. Bon appétit!

Green Tomato with Cayenne

Prep time: 6 minutes | Cook time: 15 minutes | Serves 4

- ½ cup all-purpose flour
- Sea salt and ground black pepper, to taste
- 1 teaspoon garlic powder
- 1 teaspoon cayenne pepper
- 2 eggs
- ½ cup milk
- 2 tablespoons olive oil
- 1 cup bread crumbs
- 1 pound (454 g) green tomatoes, sliced

1. In a shallow bowl, mix the flour, salt, black pepper, garlic powder, and cayenne pepper.
2. Whisk the egg and milk in another shallow bowl. Mix the olive oil and bread crumbs in a separate bowl.
3. Dip the green tomatoes in the flour, then in the eggs, then in the bread crumbs. Place the green tomatoes in the air fryer basket.
4. Put the air fryer lid on and air fry in the preheated instant pot at 390°F (199°C) for 15 minutes or until golden brown and cooked through.
5. Serve with toothpicks. Bon appétit!

Cheesy Zucchini Chips

Prep time: 10 minutes | Cook time: 10 minutes | Serves 4

- 1 pound (454 g) zucchini, sliced
- 1 cup grated Pecorino Romano cheese
- Sea salt and cayenne pepper, to taste

1. Toss the zucchini slices with the remaining ingredients and arrange them in a single layer in the air fryer basket.
2. Put the air fryer lid on and air fry in the preheated instant pot at 390°F (199°C) for 10 minutes. Flip the zucchini slices when the lid screen indicates TURN FOOD. Work in batches.
3. Bon appétit!

Tomato Chips with Basil

Prep time: 6 minutes | Cook time: 15 minutes | Serves 2

- 1 beef steak tomato, thinly sliced
- 2 tablespoons extra-virgin olive oil
- Coarse sea salt and freshly ground pepper, to taste
- 1 teaspoon dried basil
- 1 teaspoon dried thyme
- 1 teaspoon dried rosemary

1. Toss the tomato slices with the remaining ingredients until they are well coated on all sides.
2. Arrange the tomato slices in the air fryer basket.
3. Put the air fryer lid on and air fry in the preheated instant pot at 360°F (182°C) for 10 minutes. Flip the tomato slices when the lid screen indicates TURN FOOD.
4. Reduce the temperature to 330°F (166°C) and continue to cook for a further 5 minutes.
5. Bon appétit!

Potato Chips with Paprika
Prep time: 10 minutes | Cook time: 16 minutes | Serves 3

- 1 pound (454 g) potatoes, thinly sliced
- 2 tablespoons olive oil
- 1 teaspoon paprika
- Coarse salt and cayenne pepper, to taste

1. Toss the potatoes with the remaining ingredients and place them in the air fryer basket.
2. Put the air fryer lid on and air fry in the preheated instant pot at 360°F (182°C) for 16 minutes. Flip the potato chips when the lid screen indicates TURN FOOD. Work in batches.
3. Enjoy!

Air Fried Mixed Nuts
Prep time: 2 minutes | Cook time: 6 minutes | Serves 4

- ¼ cup almonds
- ½ cup hazelnuts
- ¼ cup peanuts

1. Place the nuts in the air fryer basket.
2. Put the air fryer lid on and air fry in the preheated instant pot at 330°F (166°C) for 6 minutes. Flip the nuts when the lid screen indicates TURN FOOD. Work in batches.
3. Enjoy!

Tomato Chips with Cheese
Prep time: 5 minutes | Cook time: 15 minutes | Serves 3

- 1 large-sized beef steak tomatoes
- 2 tablespoons olive oil
- ½ teaspoon paprika
- Sea salt, to taste
- 1 teaspoon garlic powder
- 1 tablespoon chopped fresh cilantro
- 4 tablespoons grated Pecorino cheese

1. Toss the tomato slices with the olive oil and spices until they are well coated on all sides.
2. Arrange the tomato slices in the air fryer basket.
3. Put the air fryer lid on and air fry in the preheated instant pot at 360°F (182°C) for 10 minutes.
4. Reduce the temperature to 330°F (166°C). Top the tomato slices with the cheese and continue to cook for a further 5 minutes.
5. Bon appétit!

Ham and Cheese Stuffed Peppers
Prep time: 5 minutes | Cook time: 7 minutes | Serves 4

- 8 Serrano peppers
- 4 ounces (113 g) ham cubes
- 4 ounces (113 g) goat cheese, crumbled

1. Stuff the peppers with ham and cheese; transfer them to a lightly oiled air fryer basket.
2. Put the air fryer lid on and air fry in the preheated instant pot at 370°F (188°C) for 7 minutes or until golden brown.
3. Bon appétit!

Cinnamon Mixed Nuts
Prep time: 5 minutes | Cook time: 6 minutes | Serves 4

- 1 egg white, lightly beaten
- ½ cup pecan halves
- ½ cup almonds
- ½ cup walnuts
- Sea salt and cayenne pepper, to taste
- 1 teaspoon chili powder
- ½ teaspoon ground cinnamon
- ½ teaspoon ground allspice

1. Mix the nuts with the rest of the ingredients and place them in the air fryer basket.
2. Put the air fryer lid on and air fry in the preheated instant pot at 330°F (166°C) for 6 minutes. Flip the nuts when the lid screen indicates TURN FOOD. Work in batches.
3. Enjoy!

Paprika Beet Chips
Prep time: 10 minutes | Cook time: 30 minutes | Serves 2

- ½ pound (227 g) golden beets, peeled and thinly sliced
- Kosher salt and ground black pepper, to taste
- 1 teaspoon paprika
- 2 tablespoons olive oil
- ½ teaspoon garlic powder
- 1 teaspoon ground turmeric

1. Toss the beets with the remaining ingredients and place them in the air fryer basket.
2. Put the air fryer lid on and air fry in the preheated instant pot at 330°F (166°C) for 30 minutes. Flip the chips when the lid screen indicates TURN FOOD. Work in batches.
3. Enjoy!

Cheese Stuffed Mushrooms
Prep time: 10 minutes | Cook time: 7 minutes | Serves 4

- 2 tablespoons olive oil
- ½ cup bread crumbs
- ½ cup grated Parmesan cheese
- 1 teaspoon minced garlic
- 1 tablespoon chopped fresh parsley
- 1 tablespoon chopped fresh chives
- Sea salt and freshly ground black pepper, to taste
- 1 pound (454 g) button mushrooms, stems removed

1. In a mixing bowl, thoroughly combine the olive oil, bread crumbs, Parmesan cheese, garlic, parsley, chives, salt, and black pepper.
2. Divide the filling between the mushrooms. Arrange the mushrooms in the air fryer basket.
3. Put the air fryer lid on and air fry in the preheated instant pot at 400°F (205°C) for 7 minutes. Flip the mushrooms when the lid screen indicates TURN FOOD.
4. Bon appétit!

Kale Chips with Garlic
Prep time: 6 minutes | Cook time: 8 minutes | Serves 4

- 4 cups kale, torn into pieces
- 1 tablespoon sesame oil
- 1 teaspoon garlic powder
- Sea salt and ground black pepper, to taste

1. Start by preheating the air fryer to 360°F (182°C).
2. Toss the kale leaves with the remaining ingredients and place them in the air fryer basket.
3. Put the air fryer lid on and air fry in the preheated instant pot at for minutes. Flip the when the lid screen indicates TURN FOOD. the chips for 8 minutes, shaking the air fryer basket occasionally and working in batches.
4. Enjoy!

Bacon-Wrapped Sausages
Prep time: 8 minutes | Cook time: 15 minutes | Serves 4

- 1 pound (454 g) mini sausages
- 2 tablespoons tamari sauce
- 2 tablespoons maple syrup
- 1 teaspoon chili powder
- Ground black pepper, to taste
- 4 ounces (113 g) bacon, thinly sliced

1. Toss the mini sausages with the tamari sauce, maple syrup, chili powder, and black pepper.
2. Wrap the mini sausages with the bacon.
3. Place the sausages in a lightly oiled air fryer basket.
4. Put the air fryer lid on and air fry in the preheated instant pot at 380°F (193°C) for 15 minutes. Flip the sausages when the lid screen indicates TURN FOOD.
5. Serve warm and enjoy!

Hot Dogs Rolls
Prep time: 5 minutes | Cook time: 8 minutes | Serves 6

- 6 ounces (170 g) refrigerated crescent rolls
- 1 tablespoon mustard
- 10 ounces (283 g) mini hot dogs

1. Separate the dough into triangles. Cut them lengthwise into 3 small triangles. Spread each triangle with mustard.
2. Place a mini hot dog on the shortest side of each triangle and roll it up.
3. Place the rolls in the baking dish.
4. Place the baking dish in the air fryer basket. Put the air fryer lid on and bake in the preheated instant pot at 320°F (160°C) for 8 minutes. Flip the rolls when the lid screen indicates TURN FOOD.
5. Bon appétit!

Butter Cheese Cauliflower Bites
Prep time: 10 minutes | Cook time: 13 minutes | Serves 4

- 1 pound (454 g) cauliflower, grated
- ½ cup shredded Cheddar cheese
- 1 ounce (28 g) butter, room temperature
- Sea salt and ground black pepper, to taste
- ½ cup crushed tortilla chips
- 2 eggs, whisked

1. Thoroughly combine all the ingredients in a mixing bowl. Shape the mixture into bite-sized balls. Transfer to the air fryer basket.
2. Put the air fryer lid on and air fry in the preheated instant pot at 350°F (180°C) for 13 minutes. Flip the cauliflower balls when the lid screen indicates TURN FOOD.
3. Bon appétit!

Pancetta-Wrapped Shrimp
Prep time: 12 minutes | Cook time: 6 minutes | Serves 4

- 12 shrimp, peeled and deveined
- 3 slices pancetta, cut into strips
- 2 tablespoons maple syrup
- 1 tablespoon Dijon mustard

1. Wrap the shrimp in the pancetta strips and toss them with the maple syrup and mustard.
2. Place the shrimp in a lightly greased air fryer basket.
3. Put the air fryer lid on and air fry in the preheated instant pot at 400°F (205°C) for 6 minutes. Flip the shrimp when the lid screen indicates TURN FOOD.
4. Bon appétit!

Apple Cheese Rolls
Prep time: 10 minutes | Cook time: 10 minutes | Serves 4

- 6 ounces (170 g) refrigerated crescent rolls
- 1 apple, peeled, cored, and grated
- 6 ounces (170 g) cream cheese, crumbled
- ¼ cup brown sugar
- 1 teaspoon apple pie spice

1. Separate the dough into rectangles. Mix the remaining ingredients until well combined.
2. Spread each rectangle with the cheese mixture; roll them up tightly. Place the rolls in the baking dish.
3. Place the baking dish in the air fryer basket. Put the air fryer lid on and bake in the preheated instant pot at 320°F (160°C) for 10 minutes. Flip the rolls when the lid screen indicates TURN FOOD.
4. Bon appétit!

Garlicky Kale Crisps
Prep time: 8 minutes | Cook time: 8 minutes | Serves 4

- 5 cups kale leaves, torn into pieces and stems removed
- 1 tablespoon olive oil
- 1 teaspoon chili powder
- Sea salt and ground black pepper, to taste
- 2 garlic cloves, minced

1. Toss the kale leaves with the remaining ingredients and place them in the air fryer basket.
2. Put the air fryer lid on and air fry in the preheated instant pot at 360°F (182°C) for 8 minutes. Flip the kale crisps when the lid screen indicates TURN FOOD. Work in batches.
3. Enjoy!

Beet Chips with Rosemary
Prep time: 10 minutes | Cook time: 30 minutes | Serves 4

- 1 pound (454 g) red and yellow beets, peeled and sliced
- 1 tablespoon olive oil
- Coarse sea salt and ground black pepper, to taste
- 1 teaspoon dried rosemary
- 1 teaspoon dried parsley flakes
- 1 teaspoon garlic
- 2 tablespoons chopped scallions

1. Toss the beets with the remaining ingredients and place them in the air fryer basket.
2. Put the air fryer lid on and air fry in the preheated instant pot at 330°F (166°C) for 30 minutes. Flip the chips when the lid screen indicates TURN FOOD. Work in batches.
3. Enjoy!

Beer Onion Rings
Prep time: 5 minutes | Cook time: 8 minutes | Serves 4

- ½ cup beer
- 1 cup plain flour
- 1 teaspoon baking powder
- 1 teaspoon cayenne pepper
- Sea salt and ground black pepper, to taste
- 2 eggs, whisked
- 1 cup crushed tortilla chips
- 2 sweet onions

1. In a shallow bowl, mix the beer, flour, baking powder, cayenne pepper, salt, and black pepper.
2. Whisk the egg in another shallow bowl. Place the crushed tortilla chips in a separate bowl.
3. Dip the onion rings in the flour mixture, then in the eggs, then in the tortilla chips. Place the onion rings in the air fryer basket.
4. Put the air fryer lid on and air fry in the preheated instant pot at 380°F (193°C) for 8 minutes or until golden brown and cooked through.
5. Bon appétit!

Tortilla Chips with Lime
Prep time: 8 minutes | Cook time: 5 minutes | Serves 4

- 4 corn tortillas, cut into wedges
- 1 tablespoon olive oil
- 1 tablespoon Mexican oregano
- 2 tablespoons lime juice
- 1 teaspoon chili powder
- 1 teaspoon ground cumin
- Sea salt, to taste

1. Toss the tortilla wedges with the remaining ingredients. Transfer to the air fryer basket.
2. Put the air fryer lid on and air fry in the preheated instant pot at 360°F (182°C) for 5 minutes or until crispy, working in batches.
3. Enjoy!

Bacon and Cheese Stuffed Peppers
Prep time: 10 minutes | Cook time: 7 minutes | Serves 4

- 8 poblano peppers, seeded and halved
- 4 ounces (113 g) Gruyere cheese
- 4 ounces (113 g) bacon, chopped

1. Stuff the peppers with the cheese and bacon; transfer them to a lightly oiled air fryer basket.
2. Put the air fryer lid on and air fry in the preheated instant pot at 370°F (188°C) for 7 minutes or until golden brown.
3. Bon appétit!

Paprika Carrot Bites

Prep time: 10 minutes | Cook time: 15 minutes | Serves 4

- 1 pound (454 g) carrots, cut into slices
- 2 tablespoons coconut oil
- 1 teaspoon paprika
- ½ teaspoon garlic powder
- ½ teaspoon dried oregano
- ½ teaspoon dried parsley flakes
- Sea salt and ground black pepper, to taste

1. Toss the carrots with the remaining ingredients; then, arrange the carrots in the air fryer basket.
2. Put the air fryer lid on and air fry in the preheated instant pot at 380°F (193°C) for 15 minutes. Flip the carrots when the lid screen indicates TURN FOOD.
3. Bon appétit!

Potato Wedges with Paprika

Prep time: 10 minutes | Cook time: 35 minutes | Serves 4

- 1 pound (454 g) potatoes, cut into wedges
- 2 tablespoons olive oil
- Sea salt and ground black pepper, to taste
- 1 teaspoon paprika
- 1 teaspoon dried parsley flakes
- 1 teaspoon Greek seasoning mix

1. Toss the potatoes with the remaining ingredients and place them in the air fryer basket.
2. Put the air fryer lid on and air fry in the preheated instant pot at 400°F (205°C) for 35 minutes. Flip the potato wedges when the lid screen indicates TURN FOOD.
3. Enjoy!

Glazed Pork Ribs

Prep time: 5 minutes | Cook time: 35 minutes | Serves 4

- 2 pounds (907 g) spare ribs
- ¼ cup soy sauce
- ¼ cup rice vinegar
- ¼ cup sesame oil
- 2 garlic cloves, minced

1. Toss all ingredients in a lightly greased baking dish.
2. Place the baking dish in the air fryer basket. Put the air fryer lid on and bake in the preheated instant pot at 350°F (180°C) for 35 minutes. Flip the ribs when the lid screen indicates TURN FOOD.
3. Bon appétit!

Vinegary Chicken Drumettes

Prep time: 5 minutes | Cook time: 18 minutes | Serves 4

- 1 pound (454 g) chicken drumettes
- 4 tablespoons soy sauce
- ¼ cup rice vinegar
- 4 tablespoons honey
- 2 tablespoons sesame oil
- 1 teaspoon Gochugaru, Korean chili powder
- 2 tablespoons chopped scallions
- 2 garlic cloves, minced

1. Toss the chicken drumettes with the remaining ingredients. Transfer to the air fryer basket.
2. Put the air fryer lid on and roast in the preheated instant pot at 380°F (193°C) for 18 minutes. Flip the chicken drumettes when the lid screen indicates TURN FOOD.
3. Bon appétit!

Eggplant Cheese Chips

Prep time: 10 minutes | Cook time: 15 minutes | Serves 4

- 1 pound (454 g) eggplant, cut into slices
- 2 tablespoons butter, melted
- ½ teaspoon smoked paprika
- 1 teaspoon Italian seasoning
- Sea salt and ground black pepper, to taste
- 1 cup shredded Mozzarella cheese

1. Toss the eggplant with the butter and spices. Arrange the eggplant slices in the air fryer basket.
2. Put the air fryer lid on and air fry in the preheated instant pot at 400°F (205°C) for 15 minutes. Flip the eggplant when the lid screen indicates TURN FOOD.
3. Bon appétit!

Zucchini with Cheese

Prep time: 10 minutes | Cook time: 10 minutes | Serves 4

- 1 pound (454 g) zucchini, cut into sticks
- ½ cup Parmesan cheese
- ½ cup almond flour
- 1 egg, whisked
- 2 tablespoons olive oil
- 1 teaspoon hot paprika
- Sea salt and ground black pepper, to taste

1. Toss the zucchini sticks with the remaining ingredients and arrange them in a single layer in the air fryer basket.
2. Put the air fryer lid on and air fry in the preheated instant pot at 390°F (199°C) for 10 minutes. Flip the zucchini sticks when the lid screen indicates TURN FOOD. Work in batches.
3. Bon appétit!

Red Beet Chips with Cayenne
Prep time: 10 minutes | Cook time: 30 minutes | Serves 4

- 1 pound (454 g) red beets, peeled and cut into ⅛-inch slices
- 1 tablespoon olive oil
- 1 teaspoon cayenne pepper
- Sea salt and ground black pepper, to taste

1. Toss the beets with the remaining ingredients and place them in the air fryer basket.
2. Put the air fryer lid on and air fry in the preheated instant pot at 330°F (166°C) for 30 minutes. Flip the chips when the lid screen indicates TURN FOOD. Work in batches.
3. Enjoy!

Honey Chicken Wings
Prep time: 5 minutes | Cook time: 18 minutes | Serves 4

- 2 pounds (907 g) chicken wings
- ¼ cup honey
- 2 tablespoons fish sauce
- 2 garlic cloves, crushed
- 1 teaspoon peeled and grated ginger
- 2 tablespoons butter, melted
- Sea salt and ground black pepper, to taste

1. Toss the chicken wings with the remaining ingredients. Transfer to the air fryer basket.
2. Put the air fryer lid on and roast in the preheated instant pot at 380°F (193°C) for 18 minutes. Flip the chicken wings when the lid screen indicates TURN FOOD.
3. Bon appétit!

Blueberry Cheese Rolls
Prep time: 5 minutes | Cook time: 10 minutes | Serves 6

- 1 (8-ounce / 227-g) can refrigerated crescent dinner rolls
- 6 ounces (170 g) cream cheese, room temperature
- 4 tablespoons granulated sugar
- 1 teaspoon grated lemon zest
- 1 cup fresh blueberries
- 1 cup powdered sugar
- ¼ teaspoon ground cinnamon

1. Separate the dough into rectangles. Mix the remaining ingredients until well combined.
2. Spread each rectangle with the cheese mixture; roll them up tightly.
3. Place the rolls in the baking dish.
4. Place the baking dish in the air fryer basket. Put the air fryer lid on and bake in the preheated instant pot at 300°F (150°C) for 10 minutes. Flip the rolls when the lid screen indicates TURN FOOD.
5. Bon appétit!

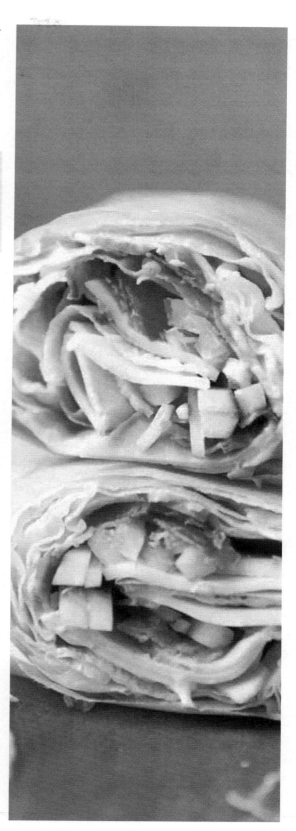

Biryani with Butter

Prep time: 5 minutes | Cook time: 10 minutes | Serves 4

- 2 cups jasmine rice, cooked
- 1 cup water
- 1 teaspoon ginger-garlic paste
- 2 tablespoons chopped shallots
- ½ teaspoon ground cinnamon
- 2 tablespoons butter
- ½ teaspoon cumin seeds
- 1 teaspoon garam masala
- ½ teaspoon turmeric powder

1. Thoroughly combine all ingredients in a lightly greased baking dish.
2. Place the baking dish in the air fryer basket. Put the air fryer lid on and bake in the preheated instant pot at 360°F (182°C) for 10 minutes or until cooked through.
3. Bon appétit!

Cinnamon S'mores

Prep time: 5 minutes | Cook time: 10 minutes | Makes 12 s'mores

- 12 whole cinnamon graham crackers, halved
- 2 (1.55-ounce / 44-g) chocolate bars, cut into 12 pieces
- 12 marshmallows

1. Preheat the air fryer to 350°F (177°C)
2. Working in batches, arrange 6 graham cracker squares in the frying basket in a single layer.
3. Top each square with a piece of chocolate. Slide the basket into the air fryer. Cook for 2 minutes.
4. Remove the basket and place a marshmallow on each piece of melted chocolate. Cook for another 1 minute.
5. Remove from the basket to a serving plate. Repeat with the remaining 6 graham cracker squares, chocolate pieces, and marshmallows.
6. Serve topped with the remaining graham cracker squares

Sour Cream Biscuits

Prep time: 5 minutes | Cook time: 15 minutes | Serves 6

- 1 cup all-purpose flour
- 1 teaspoon baking powder
- 4 tablespoons olive oil
- ½ cup sour cream
- A pinch of sea salt
- 1 teaspoon Mediterranean seasoning mix

1. Mix all ingredients until well combined. Use a 2-inch biscuit cutter and cut out biscuits. Place the biscuits in a lightly greased baking dish.
2. Place the baking dish in the air fryer basket. Put the air fryer lid on and bake in the preheated instant pot at 360°F (182°C) for 15 minutes or until a tester comes out dry and clean.
3. Bon appétit!

Cheesy Cornbread Muffins

Prep time: 5 minutes | Cook time: 22 minutes | Serves 4

- 1 cup self-rising cornmeal
- 4 ounces (113 g) canned creamed corn
- ½ cup shredded Colby cheese
- ¼ cup milk
- ¼ cup butter, room temperature

1. Mix all ingredients until everything is well incorporated. Scrape the batter into baking molds and place them in the baking dish.
2. Place the baking dish in the air fryer basket. Put the air fryer lid on and bake in the preheated instant pot at 360°F (182°C) for about 22 minutes or until a tester comes out dry and clean.
3. Allow the cornbread muffins to cool before unmolding and serving. Bon appétit!

Methi and Ragi Fritters

Prep time: 8 minutes | Cook time: 15 minutes | Serves 4

- ½ cup rice flour
- ½ cup Ragi
- ½ teaspoon baking powder
- 1 cup chopped methi
- 1 green chilli, finely chopped
- 1 teaspoon ginger-garlic paste
- 2 tablespoons sesame oil
- Sea salt and ground black pepper, to taste

1. Mix all ingredients until everything is well combined. Form the mixture into patties. Transfer to the air fryer basket.
2. Put the air fryer lid on and air fry in the preheated instant pot at 380°F (193°C) for 15 minutes. Flip the patties when the lid screen indicates TURN FOOD.
3. Bon appétit!

Apple Pie Cheese Rolls

Prep time: 5 minutes | Cook time: 10 minutes | Serves 5

- 1 (8-ounce / 227-g) can crescent rolls
- 1 teaspoon ground cinnamon
- 4 ounces (113 g) cream cheese, room temperature
- ¼ cup sugar
- 2 tablespoons full-fat milk
- ½ cup canned apple pie filling

1. Separate the dough into rectangles. Mix the remaining ingredients until well combined.
2. Spread each rectangle with the cinnamon mixture; roll them up tightly.
3. Place the rolls in the baking dish.
4. Place the baking dish in the air fryer basket. Put the air fryer lid on and bake in the preheated instant pot at 300°F (150°C) for 10 minutes. Flip the rolls when the lid screen indicates TURN FOOD.
5. Bon appétit!

Rum Grilled Pineapple Sundaes

Prep time: 15 minutes | Cook time: 8 minutes | Serves 6

- ½ cup dark rum
- ½ cup packed brown sugar
- 1 teaspoon ground cinnamon, plus more for garnish
- 1 pineapple, cored and sliced
- Vanilla ice cream, for serving

1. In a large shallow bowl or storage container, combine the rum, sugar, and cinnamon. Add the pineapple slices and arrange them in a single layer. Coat with the mixture, then let soak for at least 5 minutes per side.
2. Place the grill plate on the grill position. Select Grill, set the temperature to 450°F (232°C), and set the time to 8 minutes.
3. Strain the extra rum sauce from the pineapple.
4. Place the fruit on the grill plate in a single layer (you may need to do this in multiple batches). Gently press the fruit down to maximize grill marks. Grill for about 6 to 8 minutes without flipping. If working in batches, remove the pineapple, and repeat this step for the remaining pineapple slices.
5. When cooking is complete, remove, and top each pineapple ring with a scoop of ice cream. Sprinkle with cinnamon and serve immediately.

Grilled Peaches with Bourbon Butter Sauce

Prep time: 10 minutes | Cook time: 12 minutes | Serves 4

- 4 tablespoons salted butter
- ¼ cup bourbon
- ½ cup brown sugar
- 4 ripe peaches, halved and pitted
- ¼ cup candied pecans

1. Place the grill plate on the grill position. Select Grill, set the temperature to 450°F (232°C), and set the time to 12 minutes.
2. In a saucepan over medium heat, melt the butter for about 5 minutes. Once the butter is browned, remove the pan from the heat and carefully add the bourbon.
3. Return the saucepan to medium-high heat and add the brown sugar. Bring to a boil and let the sugar dissolve for 5 minutes, stirring occasionally.
4. Pour the bourbon butter sauce into a medium shallow bowl and arrange the peaches cut-side down to coat in the sauce.
5. Place the fruit on the grill plate in a single layer (you may need to do this in multiple batches). Gently press the fruit down to maximize grill marks. Grill for 10 to 12 minutes without flipping. If working in batches, repeat this step for all the peaches.
6. When cooking is complete, remove the peaches and top each with the pecans. Drizzle with the remaining bourbon butter sauce and serve immediately.

Pound Cake with Mixed Berries

Prep time: 10 minutes | Cook time: 8 minutes | Serves 6

- 3 tablespoons unsalted butter, at room temperature
- 6 slices pound cake, sliced about 1-inch thick
- 1 cup fresh raspberries
- 1 cup fresh blueberries
- 3 tablespoons sugar
- ½ tablespoon fresh mint, minced

1. Place the grill plate on the grill position. Select Grill, set the temperature to 450°F (232°C), and set the time to 8 minutes.
2. Evenly spread the butter on both sides of each slice of pound cake.
3. Place the pound cake on the grill plate. Grill for 2 minutes.
4. After 2 minutes, flip the pound cake and grill for 2 minutes more, until golden brown. Repeat steps 3 and 4 for all of the pound cake slices.
5. While the pound cake grills, in a medium mixing bowl, combine the raspberries, blueberries, sugar, and mint.
6. When cooking is complete, plate the cake slices and serve topped with the berry mixture.

Strawberry Pizza

Prep time: 10 minutes | Cook time: 6 minutes | Serves 4

- 2 tablespoons all-purpose flour, plus more as needed
- ½ store-bought pizza dough (about 8 ounces / 227 g)
- 1 tablespoon canola oil
- 1 cup sliced fresh strawberries
- 1 tablespoon sugar
- ½ cup chocolate-hazelnut spread

1. Place the grill plate on the grill position. Select Grill, set the temperature to 450°F (232°C), and set the time to 6 minutes.
2. Dust a clean work surface with the flour. Place the dough on the floured surface, and roll it out to a 9-inch round of even thickness. Dust your rolling pin and work surface with additional flour, as needed, to ensure the dough does not stick.
3. Brush the surface of the rolled-out dough evenly with half the oil. Flip the dough over, and brush with the remaining oil. Poke the dough with a fork 5 or 6 times across its surface to prevent air pockets from forming during cooking.
4. Place the dough on the grill plate. Grill for 3 minutes.
5. After 3 minutes, flip the dough. Continue grilling for the remaining 3 minutes.
6. Meanwhile, in a medium mixing bowl, combine the strawberries and sugar.
7. Transfer the pizza to a cutting board and let cool. Top with the chocolate-hazelnut spread and strawberries. Cut into pieces and serve.

Lemon Cheesecake With Cracker Base
Prep time: 20 minutes | Cook time: 20 minutes | Serves 8

- 8 ounces (227 g) graham crackers, crushed
- 3 eggs
- 16 ounces (454 g) plain cream cheese
- 1 tablespoon vanilla extract
- Zest of 2 lemons
- 4 ounces (113 g) butter, melted
- 3 tablespoons sugar

1. Preheat the air fryer to 350°F (180°C). Line a 6-inch cake tin with parchment paper.
2. Combine the crackers and butter in the cake tin and press to coat the bottom.
3. Whisk together the eggs, cream cheese, vanilla extract, lemon zest, and sugar in a large bowl, then pour the mixture over the cracker base in the cake tin.
4. Place the cake tin in the preheated air fryer and cook for 20 minutes or until a toothpick inserted in the cake comes out clean.
5. Remove the cake tin from the basket. Allow to cool, then place in the refrigerator to chill for at least 8 hours. Serve chilled.

Walnut and Raisin Stuffed Apples
Prep time: 5 minutes | Cook time: 20 minutes | Serves 2

- 3 tablespoons crushed walnuts
- 2 tablespoons raisins
- 2 granny smith apples, cored, bottom intact
- 1 teaspoon cinnamon
- 3 tablespoons sugar
- 2 tablespoons butter, under room temperature

1. Preheat air fryer to 350°F (180°C). Spritz the air fryer basket with cooking spray.
2. Combine all the ingredients, except for the apples, in a bowl. Stir to mix well.
3. Place the apples in the air fryer basket, bottom side down, then spoon the mixture in the core hollows of the apples.
4. Cook for 20 minutes or until the apples are wilted. Serve warm.

Cherry Pie
Prep time: 10 minutes | Cook time: 20 minutes | Serves 4 to 6

- 2 store-bought pie crusts
- 21 ounces (595 g) cherry pie filling
- 1 egg yolk
- 1 tablespoon milk

1. Preheat air fryer to 340°F (171°C). Coat a 6-inch pie pan with butter.
2. Arrange one of the pie crusts in the pie pan, then poke holes into the crust with a fork.
3. Place the pie pan in the preheated air fryer and cook for 5 minutes until the edge of the crust is lightly browned.
4. Meanwhile, cut the other pie crust into strips. Whisk together the egg yolk and milk in a bowl.
5. Remove the pie pan from the air fryer. Pour the cherry piece filling over the baked pie crust, then overlap the crust strips over the filling. Pour the yolk mixture over.
6. Put the pie pan back to the air fryer and cook for 15 minutes or until the egg yolk is set and no longer jiggle, and the edge of the pie is well browned.
7. Transfer the pie onto a large plate. Divide and serve.

Brown Bananas
Prep time: 10 minutes | Cook time: 10 minutes | Serves 2

- 1 banana, cut into bite-sized pieces
- 1 tablespoon light brown sugar
- 3 tablespoons water

1. Preheat the air fryer to 300°F (150°C). Spritz a 6-inch baking pan with cooking spray.
2. Add the brown sugar and water to the baking pan. Stir to melt the sugar.
3. Put the banana pieces in the baking pan, then arrange the pan in the air fryer.
4. Cook for 10 minutes or until the banana pieces are lightly charred. Flip them halfway through the cooking time.
5. Transfer the banana pieces to a serving plate or a serving bowl. Allow to cool for a few minutes and serve.

Blueberry Muffins
Prep time: 10 minutes | Cook time: 24 to 28 minutes | Serves 8 Muffins

- 1⅓ cups flour
- 2 teaspoons baking powder
- 1 egg
- ½ cup milk
- ⅔ cup blueberries, fresh or frozen and thawed
- ½ cup sugar
- ¼ teaspoon salt
- ⅓ cup canola oil

SPECIAL EQUIPMENT:
- 8 foil muffin cups lined with parchment paper

1. Preheat the air fryer to 330°F (166°C).
2. Combine the flour, baking powder, sugar, and salt in a bowl. Whisk together the egg, milk, and canola oil in a separate bowl.
3. Pour the wet mixture into the bowl of dry mixture. Stir until they are fully mixed and smooth, then fold in the blueberries.
4. Divide the mixture in the muffins cups and put the muffin cups in the air fryer basket. You may need to work in batches to avoid overcrowding.
5. Cook for 12 to 14 minutes or until a toothpick inserted in the center of muffins comes out clean.
6. Remove the muffins from the basket and serve warm.

Coconut Cupcakes

Prep time: 20 minutes | Cook time: 10 minutes | Serves 4

- 2 eggs
- ½ cup coconut flour
- ⅓ cup coconut milk
- 1 teaspoon vanilla extract
- ½ cup coconut chips, for garnish
- 1 tablespoon coconut oil, melted

SPECIAL EQUIPMENT:

- A 4-cup muffin tin, coated with melted butter

1. Whisk together the eggs, flour, milk, vanilla, and coconut oil in a bowl. Let sit for 20 minutes under room temperature, then spoon the mixture in a 4-cup muffin tin.
2. Preheat the air fryer to 230°F (110°C).
3. Arrange the muffin tin in the air fryer, then cook for 4 to 5 minutes or until the edges of the cupcakes are lightly browned.
4. Remove the cupcakes from the basket and serve with coconut chips on top.

Easy Lemon Curd

Prep time: 9 minutes | Cook time: 21 minutes | Serves 2

- 1 egg
- 1 egg yolk
- ¾ lemon, juiced
- 3 tablespoons sugar
- 3 tablespoons butter

SPECIAL EQUIPMENT:

- A medium ramekin

1. Preheat the air fryer to 220°F (104°C).
2. Mix the butter and sugar in a medium ramekin, then gradually fold in the egg and yolk. Stir until the mixture is smooth and yellow. Then mix in the lemon juice.
3. Put the ramekin in the air fryer and cook for 6 minutes, then increase the temperature of the air fryer to 320°F (160°C) and cook for an additional 15 minutes or until a toothpick inserted in the ramekin comes out clean.
4. Remove the ramekin from the air fryer and pour the mixture in a bowl. Wrap the bowl in plastic and refrigerate for at least 8 hours. Serve chilled.

Honey and Peanut Butter Banana Toast

Prep time: 10 minutes | Cook time: 9 minutes | Serves 4

- 4 slices white bread
- 4 tablespoons peanut butter
- 2 bananas, peeled and thinly sliced
- 1 teaspoon ground cinnamon
- 4 tablespoons honey
- 2 tablespoons butter, softened

1. Preheat the air fryer to 375°F (190°C).
2. On a clean work surface, coat the bottom side of a slice of bread with ½ tablespoon of butter, then smear 1 tablespoon of peanut butter on top of the bread with a knife.
3. Arrange the slices of half of a banana on peanut butter. Sprinkle with ¼ teaspoon of cinnamon and drizzle with 1 tablespoon of honey. Repeat with the remaining ingredients.
4. Arrange them in the preheated air fryer and cook for 5 minutes, then increase the temperature to 400°F (205°C) and cook for 4 more minutes or until the bread is toast and the banana slices are golden brown. You may need to work in batches to avoid overcrowding.
5. Serve the banana toast on a plate warm.

Chocolate Fondants with Easy Praline

Prep time: 10 minutes | Cook time: 15 minutes | Serves 4

- ¾ cup dark chocolate
- ½ cup peanut butter, crunchy
- 4 eggs, room temperature
- ⅛ cup flour, sieved
- ½ cup sugar, divided
- 1 teaspoon salt
- ¼ cup water
- 2 tablespoons butter, diced

1. Make the praline: Combine half of the sugar, salt, and water in a saucepan, then bring to a boil over medium-low heat. Keep stirring.
2. Reduce the heat to low and simmer for 5 to 6 minutes or until the liquid reduces in half.
3. Pour the mixture in a baking pan. Allow to cool until hardened, then break them into pieces and set aside until ready to serve.
4. Preheat the air fryer to 300°F (150°C).
5. Bring a small pot of water to a boil over medium heat, then put a heatproof bowl over the pot.
6. Make the fondants: Combine the chocolate, peanut butter, and butter in the heatproof bowl. Keep stirring until the well mixed.
7. Remove the bowl from the pot and let stand for a few minutes. Whisk in the eggs, flour, and remaining sugar.
8. Spritz 4 small loaf pans with cooking spray, then spoon the chocolate mixture in the pans.
9. Put the pans in the preheated air fryer and cook for 7 minutes or until a toothpick inserted in the center comes out clean.

Simple Blueberry Turnovers

Prep time: 15 minutes | Cook time: 20 minutes | Serves 8

- 1 (17-ounce / 482-g) box frozen puff pastry dough, thawed, cut into 8 squares in total
- 1 (10-ounce / 284-g) can blueberry pie filling
- 1 egg white, beaten

1. Preheat the air fryer to 370°F (188°C). Spritz the air fryer basket with cooking spray.
2. Make the turnovers: Unfold the puff pastry squares on a clean work surface, spoon 1 tablespoon of the filling on each square.
3. Brush the edges of the squares with egg white. Fold the squares over the filling diagonally to form triangles, then press the edges to seal with a fork.
4. Arrange the turnovers in the air fryer basket and spritz with cooking spray. You may need to work in batches to avoid overcrowding.
5. Cook for 8 minutes or until golden brown. Flip the turnovers halfway through the cooking time.
6. Allow to cool for a few minutes, then remove the turnovers from the air fryer and serve.

Beet Salad with Lemon Vinaigrette

Prep time: 10 minutes | Cook time: 12 to 15 minutes | Serves 4

- 6 medium red and golden beets, peeled and sliced
- 1 teaspoon olive oil
- ¼ teaspoon kosher salt
- ½ cup crumbled feta cheese
- 8 cups mixed greens
- Cooking spray
- Vinaigrette:
- 2 teaspoons olive oil
- 2 tablespoons chopped fresh chives
- Juice of 1 lemon

1. Preheat the air fryer to 360°F (182°C).
2. In a large bowl, toss the beets, olive oil, and kosher salt.
3. Spray the frying basket with cooking spray, then place the beets in the basket. Slide the basket into the air fryer. Cook for 12 to 15 minutes or until tender.
4. While the beets cook, make the vinaigrette in a large bowl by whisking together the olive oil, lemon juice, and chives.
5. Remove the beets from the air fryer, toss in the vinaigrette, and allow to cool for 5 minutes. Add the feta and serve on top of the mixed greens.

French Toast

Prep time: 5 minutes | Cook time: 8 minutes | Serves 4

- 2 eggs, beaten
- ¼ cup milk
- 2 tablespoons coconut oil, room temperature
- ½ teaspoon bourbon vanilla extract
- ½ teaspoon ground cinnamon
- 4 slices bread

1. In a mixing bowl, thoroughly combine the eggs, milk, coconut oil, vanilla, and cinnamon.
2. Then dip each piece of bread into the egg mixture; place the bread slices in a lightly greased baking dish.
3. Place the baking dish in the air fryer basket. Put the air fryer lid on and bake in the preheated instant pot at 330°F (166°C) for 8 minutes. Flip the bread slices when the lid screen indicates TURN FOOD.
4. Enjoy!

Cheesy Butter Macaroni

Prep time: 5 minutes | Cook time: 15 minutes | Serves 4

- 1 cups macaroni
- 1 cup cream of onion soup
- 2 tablespoons butter
- 4 ounces (113 g) Ricotta cheese
- 6 ounces (170 g) Mozzarella cheese, crumbled
- Kosher salt and ground white pepper, to taste
- ½ teaspoon ground cumin
- 1 teaspoon dry mustard
- 1 teaspoon red chili powder

1. Cook the macaroni according to the package directions.
2. Drain the macaroni and place them in a lightly greased baking dish.
3. Fold in the remaining ingredients and stir to combine.
4. Place the baking dish in the air fryer basket. Put the air fryer lid on and bake in the preheated instant pot at 360°F (182°C) for 15 minutes.
5. Serve garnished with fresh Italian herbs, if desired.
6. Bon appétit!

Colby Potato Patties

Prep time: 5 minutes | Cook time: 10 minutes | Serves 8

- 2 pounds (907 g) white potatoes
- ½ cup finely chopped scallions
- ½ teaspoon freshly ground black pepper, or more to taste
- 1 tablespoon fine sea salt
- ½ teaspoon hot paprika
- 2 cups shredded Colby cheese
- ¼ cup canola oil
- 1 cup crushed crackers

1. Preheat the air fryer to 360°F (182°C).
2. Boil the potatoes until soft. Dry them off and peel them before mashing thoroughly, leaving no lumps.
3. Combine the mashed potatoes with scallions, pepper, salt, paprika, and cheese.
4. Mold the mixture into balls with your hands and press with your palm to flatten them into patties.
5. In a shallow dish, combine the canola oil and crushed crackers. Coat the patties in the crumb mixture. Transfer to the frying basket.
6. Slide the basket into the air fryer. Cook for about 10 minutes, in multiple batches if necessary.
7. Serve hot.

Old Bay Shrimp with Lemon

Prep time: 7 minutes | Cook time: 10 minutes | Makes 2 cups

- ½ teaspoon Old Bay Seasoning
- 1 teaspoon ground cayenne pepper
- ½ teaspoon paprika
- 1 tablespoon olive oil
- ⅛ teaspoon salt
- ½ pound (227 g) shrimps, peeled and deveined
- Juice of half a lemon

1. Preheat the air fryer to 390°F (199°C).
2. Combine the Old Bay Seasoning, cayenne pepper, paprika, olive oil, and salt in a large bowl, then add the shrimps and toss to coat well.
3. Put the shrimps in the frying basket. Slide the basket into the air fryer. Cook for 10 minutes or until opaque. Flip the shrimps halfway through.
4. Serve the shrimps with lemon juice on top.

Cheesy Cauliflower Risotto

Prep time: 10 minutes | Cook time: 10 minutes | Serves 4

- 2 cups rice, cooked
- 2 tablespoons olive oil
- ½ cup chopped cauliflower
- ½ cup vegetable broth
- 4 tablespoons shredded Mozzarella cheese

1. Thoroughly combine all ingredients in a lightly greased baking dish.
2. Place the baking dish in the air fryer basket. Put the air fryer lid on and bake in the preheated instant pot at 360°F (182°C) for 10 minutes or until cooked through.
3. Bon appétit!

Broccoli and Eggs

Prep time: 5 minutes | Cook time: 6 minutes | Serves 1

- 4 egg yolks
- ¼ cup butter, melted
- 2 cups coconut flower
- Salt and pepper, to taste
- 2 cups broccoli florets

1. Preheat the air fryer to 400°F (204°C).
2. In a bowl, whisk the egg yolks and melted butter together. Throw in the coconut flour, salt and pepper, then stir again to combine well.
3. Dip each broccoli floret into the mixture and place in the frying basket. Slide the basket into the air fryer. Cook for 6 minutes in batches if necessary. Take care when removing them from the air fryer and serve immediately.

Salmon and Carrot Croquettes

Prep time: 15 minutes | Cook time: 10 minutes | Serves 6

- 2 egg whites
- 1 cup almond flour
- 1 cup panko bread crumbs
- 1 pound (454 g) chopped salmon fillet
- ⅔ cup grated carrots
- 2 tablespoons minced garlic cloves
- ½ cup chopped onion
- 2 tablespoons chopped chives
- Cooking spray

1. Preheat the air fryer to 350°F (177°C). Spritz the frying basket with cooking spray.
2. Whisk the egg whites in a bowl. Put the flour in a second bowl. Pour the breadcrumbs in a third bowl. Set aside.
3. Combine the salmon, carrots, garlic, onion, and chives in a large bowl. Stir to mix well.
4. Form the mixture into balls with your hands. Dredge the balls into the flour, then egg, and then breadcrumbs to coat well.
5. Arrange the salmon balls in the basket and spritz with cooking spray.
6. Slide the basket into the air fryer. Cook for 10 minutes or until crispy and browned. Shake the basket halfway through.
7. Serve immediately.

Parsnip Fries with Garlic-Yogurt Dip

Prep time: 10 minutes | Cook time: 10 minutes | Serves 4

- 3 medium parsnips, peeled, cut into sticks
- ¼ teaspoon kosher salt
- 1 teaspoon olive oil
- 1 garlic clove, unpeeled
- Cooking spray

DIP:
- ¼ cup plain Greek yogurt
- ⅛ teaspoon garlic powder
- 1 tablespoon sour cream
- ¼ teaspoon kosher salt
- Freshly ground black pepper, to taste

1. Preheat the air fryer to 360°F (182°C). Spritz the frying basket with cooking spray.
2. Put the parsnip sticks in a large bowl, then sprinkle with salt and drizzle with olive oil.
3. Transfer the parsnip into the basket and add the garlic.
4. Slide the basket into the air fryer. Cook for 5 minutes, then remove the garlic from the air fryer and shake the basket. Cook for 5 more minutes or until the parsnip sticks are crisp.
5. Meanwhile, peel the garlic and crush it. Combine the crushed garlic with the ingredients for the dip. Stir to mix well.
6. When the frying is complete, remove the parsnip fries from the air fryer and serve with the dipping sauce.

Apple Fritters with Vanilla Glaze

Prep time: 5 minutes | Cook time: 25 minutes | Makes 15 fritters

APPLE FRITTERS:

- 2 firm apples, peeled, cored, and diced
- ½ teaspoon cinnamon
- Juice of 1 lemon
- 1 cup all-purpose flour
- 1½ teaspoons baking powder
- ½ teaspoon kosher salt
- 2 eggs
- ¼ cup milk
- 2 tablespoons unsalted butter, melted
- 2 tablespoons granulated sugar
- Cooking spray

GLAZE:

- ½ teaspoon vanilla extract
- 1¼ cups powdered sugar, sifted
- ¼ cup water

1. Preheat the air fryer to 360°F (182°C). Line the frying basket with parchment paper.
2. Combine the apples with cinnamon and lemon juice in a small bowl. Toss to coat well.
3. Combine the flour, baking powder, and salt in a large bowl. Stir to mix well.
4. Whisk the egg, milk, butter, and sugar in a medium bowl. Stir to mix well.
5. Make a well in the center of the flour mixture, then pour the egg mixture into the well and stir to mix well. Mix in the apple until a dough forms.
6. Use an ice cream scoop to scoop 5 balls from the dough into the basket. Spritz with cooking spray.
7. Slide the basket into the air fryer. Cook for 8 minutes or until golden brown. Flip them halfway through. Remove the fritters from the air fryer and repeat with the remaining dough.
8. Meanwhile, combine the ingredients for the glaze in a separate small bowl. Stir to mix well.
9. Serve the fritters with the glaze on top or use the glaze for dipping.

Hot Chicken Wings

Prep time: 5 minutes | Cook time: 30 minutes | Makes 16 wings

- 16 chicken wings
- 3 tablespoons hot sauce
- Cooking spray

1. Preheat the air fryer to 360°F (182°C). Spritz the frying basket with cooking spray.
2. Arrange the chicken wings in the basket. You need to work in batches to avoid overcrowding.
3. Slide the basket into the air fryer. Cook for 15 minutes or until well browned. Shake the basket at lease three times during the cooking.
4. Transfer the air fried wings on a plate and serve with hot sauce.

Honey Bartlett Pears with Lemony Ricotta

Prep time: 10 minutes | Cook time: 8 minutes | Serves 4

- 2 large Bartlett pears, peeled, cut in half, cored
- 3 tablespoons melted butter
- ½ teaspoon ground ginger
- ¼ teaspoon ground cardamom
- 3 tablespoons brown sugar
- ½ cup whole-milk ricotta cheese
- 1 teaspoon pure lemon extract
- 1 teaspoon pure almond extract
- 1 tablespoon honey, plus additional for drizzling

1. Preheat the air fryer to 375°F (191°C).
2. Toss the pears with butter, ginger, cardamom, and sugar in a large bowl. Toss to coat well.
3. Arrange the pears in the frying basket, cut side down. Slide the basket into the air fryer. Cook for 5 minutes, then flip the pears and cook for 3 more minutes or until the pears are soft and browned.
4. In the meantime, combine the remaining ingredients in a separate bowl. Whip for 1 minute with a hand mixer until the mixture is puffed.
5. Divide the mixture into four bowls, then put the pears over the mixture and drizzle with more honey to serve.

Baked Rolls with Cheese

Prep time: 5 minutes | Cook time: 10 minutes | Serves 4

- 1 (8-ounce / 227-g) can refrigerated crescent rolls
- 4 ounces (113 g) cream cheese, room temperature

1. Separate the dough into rectangles. Spread each rectangle with cream cheese and roll them up.
2. Place the rolls in the baking dish.
3. Place the baking dish in the air fryer basket. Put the air fryer lid on and bake in the preheated instant pot at 300°F (150°C) for 10 minutes. Flip the rolls when the lid screen indicates TURN FOOD.
4. Bon appétit!

Lemony and Garlicky Asparagus

Prep time: 5 minutes | Cook time: 10 minutes | Makes 10 spears

- 10 spears asparagus (about ½ pound / 227 g in total), snap the ends off
- 1 tablespoon lemon juice
- 2 teaspoons minced garlic
- ½ teaspoon salt
- ¼ teaspoon ground black pepper
- Cooking spray

1. Preheat the air fryer to 400°F (204°C). Put a parchment paper in the frying basket.
2. Put the asparagus spears in a large bowl. Drizzle with lemon juice and sprinkle with minced garlic, salt, and ground black pepper. Toss to coat well.
3. Transfer the asparagus to the basket and spritz with cooking spray. Slide the basket into the air fryer. Cook for 10 minutes or until wilted and soft. Flip the asparagus halfway through.
4. Serve immediately.

South Carolina Shrimp and Corn Bake

Prep time: 10 minutes | Cook time: 18 minutes | Serves 2

- 1 ear corn, husk and silk removed, cut into 2-inch rounds
- 8 ounces (227 g) red potatoes, unpeeled, cut into 1-inch pieces
- 2 teaspoons Old Bay Seasoning, divided
- 2 teaspoons vegetable oil, divided
- ¼ teaspoon ground black pepper
- 8 ounces (227 g) large shrimps (about 12 shrimps), deveined
- 6 ounces (170 g) andouille or chorizo sausage, cut into 1-inch pieces
- 2 garlic cloves, minced
- 1 tablespoon chopped fresh parsley

1. Preheat the air fryer to 400°F (204°C).
2. Put the corn rounds and potatoes in a large bowl. Sprinkle with 1 teaspoon of Old Bay seasoning and drizzle with vegetable oil. Toss to coat well.
3. Transfer the corn rounds and potatoes to the frying basket.
4. Slide the basket into the air fryer. Cook for 12 minutes or until soft and browned. Shake the basket halfway through the cooking time.
5. Meanwhile, cut slits into the shrimps but be careful not to cut them through. Combine the shrimps, sausage, remaining Old Bay seasoning, and remaining vegetable oil in the large bowl. Toss to coat well.
6. When the baking of the potatoes and corn rounds is complete, add the shrimps and sausage. Cook for 6 more minutes or until the shrimps are opaque. Shake the basket halfway through the cooking time.
7. When the cooking is finished, serve them on a plate and spread with parsley before serving.

Spanakopita

Prep time: 5 minutes | Cook time: 25 minutes | Serves 6

- ½ (10-ounce / 284-g) package frozen spinach, thawed and squeezed dry
- 1 egg, lightly beaten
- ¼ cup pine nuts, toasted
- ⅛ teaspoon ground nutmeg
- ½ teaspoon salt
- Freshly ground black pepper, to taste
- 6 sheets phyllo dough
- ½ cup butter, melted

1. Combine all the ingredients, except for the phyllo dough and butter, in a large bowl. Whisk to combine well. Set aside.
2. Place a sheet of phyllo dough on a clean work surface. Brush with butter then top with another layer sheet of phyllo. Brush with butter, then cut the layered sheets into six 3-inch-wide strips.
3. Top each strip with 1 tablespoon of the spinach mixture, then fold the bottom left corner over the mixture towards the right strip edge to make a triangle. Keep folding triangles until each strip is folded over.
4. Brush the triangles with butter and repeat with remaining strips and phyllo dough.
5. Preheat the air fryer to 350°F (177°C).
6. Place six triangles in the frying basket. Slide the basket into the air fryer. Cook for 8 minutes or until golden brown. Flip the triangles halfway through. Repeat with the remaining triangles.
7. Serve immediately.

Green Tomatoes with Almonds

Prep time: 5 minutes | Cook time: 6 to 8 minutes | Serves 4

- 4 medium green tomatoes
- ⅓ cup all purpose flour
- 2 egg whites
- ¼ cup almond milk
- 1 cup ground almonds
- ½ cup panko bread crumbs
- 2 teaspoons olive oil
- 1 teaspoon paprika
- 1 clove garlic, minced

1. Preheat the air fryer to 400°F (204°C).
2. Rinse the tomatoes and pat dry. Cut the tomatoes into ½-inch slices, discarding the thinner ends.
3. Put the flour on a plate. In a shallow bowl, beat the egg whites with the almond milk until frothy. And on another plate, combine the almonds, bread crumbs, olive oil, paprika, and garlic and mix well.
4. Dip the tomato slices into the flour, then into the egg white mixture, then into the almond mixture to coat.
5. Place four of the coated tomato slices in the frying basket. Slide the basket into the air fryer. Cook for 6 to 8 minutes, or until the tomato coating is crisp and golden brown. Repeat with remaining tomato slices and serve immediately.

Chapter 15
Holiday Specials

Hasselback Potatoes

Prep time: 5 minutes | Cook time: 50 minutes | Serves 4

- 4 russet panatoes, peeled
- Salt and freshly ground black pepper, to taste
- ¼ cup grated Parmesan cheese
- Cooking spray

1. Place the crisper tray on the air fry position. Select Air Fry, set the temperature to 400°F (204°C), and set the time to 50 minutes.
2. Spray the crisper tray lightly with cooking spray.
3. Make thin parallel cuts into each panato, ⅛-inch to ¼-inch apart, stopping at about ½ of the way through. The panato needs to stay intact along the bottom.
4. Spray the panatoes with cooking spray and use the hands or a silicone brush to completely coat the panatoes lightly in oil.
5. Put the panatoes, sliced side up, in the crisper tray in a single layer. Leave a little room between each panato. Sprinkle the panatoes lightly with salt and black pepper.
6. Air fry for 20 minutes. Reposition the panatoes and spritz lightly with cooking spray again. air fry until the panatoes are fork-tender and crispy and browned, for another 20 to 30 minutes.
7. Sprinkle the panatoes with Parmesan cheese and serve.

Spicy Black Olives

Prep time: 10 minutes | Cook time: 5 minutes | Serves 4

- 12 ounces (340 g) pitted black extra-large olives
- ¼ cup all-purpose flour
- 1 cup panko bread crumbs
- 2 teaspoons dried thyme
- 1 teaspoon red pepper flakes
- 1 teaspoon smoked paprika
- 1 egg beaten with 1 tablespoon water
- Vegetable oil for spraying

1. Place the crisper tray on the air fry position. Select Air Fry, set the temperature to 400°F (204°C), and set the time to 5 minutes.
2. Drain the olives and place them on a paper towel-lined plate to dry.
3. Put the flour on a plate. Combine the panko, thyme, red pepper flakes, and paprika on a separate plate. Dip an olive in the flour, shaking off any excess, then coat with egg mixture. Dredge the olive in the panko mixture, pressing to make the crumbs adhere, and place the breaded olive on a platter. Repeat with the remaining olives.
4. Spray the olives with oil and place them in a single layer in the crisper tray. Work in batches if necessary so as not to overcrowd the crisper tray.
5. Air fry for 5 minutes until the breading is browned and crispy. Serve warm

Hearty Honey Yeast Rolls

Prep time: 10 minutes | Cook time: 20 minutes | Makes 8 rolls

- ¼ cup whole milk, heated to 115°F (46°C) in the microwave
- ½ teaspoon active dry yeast
- 1 tablespoon honey
- ⅔ cup all-purpose flour, plus more for dusting
- ½ teaspoon kosher salt
- 2 tablespoons unsalted butter, at room temperature, plus more for greasing
- Flaky sea salt, to taste

1. In a large bowl, whisk together the milk, yeast, and honey and let stand until foamy, about 10 minutes.
2. Stir in the flour and salt until just combined. Stir in the butter until absorbed. Scrape the dough onto a lightly floured work surface and knead until smooth, about 6 minutes. Transfer the dough to a lightly greased bowl, cover loosely with a sheet of plastic wrap or a kitchen towel, and let sit until nearly doubled in size, about 1 hour.
3. Uncover the dough, lightly press it down to expel the bubbles, then portion it into 8 equal pieces. Prep the work surface by wiping it clean with a damp paper towel (if there is flour on the work surface, it will prevent the dough from sticking lightly to the surface, which helps it form a ball). Roll each piece into a ball by cupping the palm of the hand around the dough against the work surface and moving the heel of the hand in a circular motion while using the thumb to contain the dough and tighten it into a perfectly round ball. Once all the balls are formed, nestle them side by side in the crisper tray.
4. Cover the rolls loosely with a kitchen towel or a sheet of plastic wrap and let sit until lightly risen and puffed, 20 to 30 minutes.
5. Place the crisper tray on the air fry position. Select Air Fry, set the temperature to 270°F (132°C), and set the time to 12 minutes.
6. Uncover the rolls and gently brush with more butter, being careful not to press the rolls too hard. Air fry for 12 minutes until the rolls are light golden brown and fluffy.
7. Remove the rolls from the grill and brush liberally with more butter, if you like, and sprinkle each roll with a pinch of sea salt. Serve warm.

Bourbon Monkey Bread

Prep time: 15 minutes | Cook time: 25 minutes | Serves 6 to 8

- 1 (16.3-ounce / 462-g) can store-bought refrigerated biscuit dough
- ¼ cup packed light brown sugar
- 1 teaspoon ground cinnamon
- ½ teaspoon freshly grated nutmeg
- ½ teaspoon ground ginger
- ½ teaspoon kosher salt
- ¼ teaspoon ground allspice
- ⅛ teaspoon ground cloves
- 4 tablespoons (½ stick) unsalted butter, melted
- ½ cup powdered sugar
- 2 teaspoons bourbon
- 2 tablespoons chopped candied cherries
- 2 tablespoons chopped pecans

1. Place a cake pan on the bake position. Select Bake, set the temperature to 310°F (154°C), and set the time to 25 minutes.
2. Open the can and separate the biscuits, then cut each into quarters. Toss the biscuit quarters in a large bowl with the brown sugar, cinnamon, nutmeg, ginger, salt, allspice, and cloves until evenly coated.
3. Transfer the dough pieces and any sugar left in the bowl to the cake pan and drizzle evenly with the melted butter.
4. Bake for 25 minutes until the monkey bread is golden brown and cooked through in the middle. Transfer the pan to a wire rack and let cool completely. Unmold from the pan.
5. In a small bowl, whisk the powdered sugar and the bourbon into a smooth glaze. Drizzle the glaze over the cooled monkey bread and, while the glaze is still wet, sprinkle with the cherries and pecans to serve.

Simple Butter Cake

Prep time: 25 minutes | Cook time: 20 minutes | Serves 8

- 1 cup all-purpose flour
- 1¼ teaspoons baking powder
- ¼ teaspoon salt
- ½ cup plus 1½ tablespoons granulated white sugar
- 9½ tablespoons butter, at room temperature
- 2 large eggs
- 1 large egg yolk
- 2½ tablespoons milk
- 1 teaspoon vanilla extract
- Cooking spray

1. Place a cake pan on the bake position. Select Bake, set the temperature to 325°F (163°C), and set the time to 20 minutes.
2. Spritz the cake pan with cooking spray.
3. Combine the flour, baking powder, and salt in a large bowl. Stir to mix well.
4. Whip the sugar and butter in a separate bowl with

a hand mixer on medium speed for 3 minutes.

5. Whip the eggs, egg yolk, milk, and vanilla extract into the sugar and butter mix with a hand mixer.
6. Pour in the flour mixture and whip with hand mixer until sanity and smooth.
7. Scrape the batter into the cake pan and level the batter with a spatula.
8. Bake for 20 minutes or until a toothpick inserted in the center comes out clean. Check the doneness during the last 5 minutes of the baking.
9. Invert the cake on a cooling rack and allow to cool for 15 minutes before slicing to serve.

Kale Salad Sushi Rolls with Sriracha Mayonnaise

Prep time: 10 minutes | Cook time: 10 minutes | Serves 12

KALE SALAD:

- 1½ cups chopped kale
- 1 tablespoon sesame seeds
- ¾ teaspoon soy sauce
- ¾ teaspoon toasted sesame oil
- ½ teaspoon rice vinegar
- ¼ teaspoon ginger
- ⅛ teaspoon garlic powder
- Sushi Rolls:
- 3 sheets sushi nori
- 1 batch cauliflower rice
- ½ avocado, sliced
- Sriracha Mayonnaise:
- ¼ cup Sriracha sauce
- ¼ cup vegan mayonnaise

COATING:

- ½ cup panko bread crumbs

1. Place the crisper tray on the air fry position. Select Air Fry, set the temperature to 390°F (199°C), and set the time to 10 minutes.
2. In a medium bowl, toss all the ingredients for the salad together until well coated and set aside.
3. Place a sheet of nori on a clean work surface and spread the cauliflower rice in an even layer on the nori. Scoop 2 to 3 tablespoon of kale salad on the rice and spread over. Place 1 or 2 avocado slices on top. Roll up the sushi, pressing gently to get a nice, tight roll. Repeat to make the remaining 2 rolls.
4. In a bowl, stir together the Sriracha sauce and mayonnaise until smooth. Add breadcrumbs to a separate bowl.
5. Dredge the sushi rolls in Sriracha Mayonnaise, then roll in breadcrumbs till well coated.
6. Place the coated sushi rolls in the crisper tray. Air fry for 10 minutes, or until golden brown and crispy. Flip the sushi rolls gently halfway through to ensure even cooking..
7. Transfer to a platter and rest for 5 minutes before slicing each roll into 8 pieces. Serve warm.

Pão de Queijo

Prep time: 37 minutes | Cook time: 24 minutes | Makes 12 balls

- 2 tablespoons butter, plus more for greasing
- ½ cup milk
- 1½ cups tapioca flour
- ½ teaspoon salt
- 1 large egg
- ⅔ cup finely grated aged Asiago cheese

1. Put the butter in a saucepan and pour in the milk, heat over medium heat until the liquid boils. Keep stirring.
2. Turn off the heat and mix in the tapioca flour and salt to form a soft dough. Transfer the dough in a large bowl, then wrap the bowl in plastic and let sit for 15 minutes.
3. Break the egg in the bowl of dough and whisk with a hand mixer for 2 minutes or until a sanity dough forms. Fold the cheese in the dough. Cover the bowl in plastic again and let sit for 10 more minutes.
4. Place a cake pan on the bake position. Select Bake, set the temperature to 375°F (191°C), and set the time to 12 minutes.
5. Grease the cake pan with butter.
6. Scoop 2 tablespoons of the dough into the cake pan. Repeat with the remaining dough to make dough 12 balls. Keep a little distance between each two balls. You may need to work in batches to avoid overcrowding.
7. Bake for 12 minutes or until the balls are golden brown and fluffy. Flip the balls halfway through the cooking time.
8. Remove the balls from the grill and allow to cool for 5 minutes before serving.

Eggnog Bread

Prep time: 10 minutes | Cook time: 18 minutes | Serves 6 to 8

- 1 cup flour, plus more for dusting
- ¼ cup sugar
- 1 teaspoon baking powder
- ¼ teaspoon salt
- ¼ teaspoon nutmeg
- ½ cup eggnog
- 1 egg yolk
- 1 tablespoon plus 1 teaspoon butter, melted
- ¼ cup pecans
- ¼ cup chopped candied fruit (cherries, pineapple, or mixed fruits)
- Cooking spray

1. Preheat the air fryer to 360°F (182°C).
2. In a medium bowl, stir together the flour, sugar, baking powder, salt, and nutmeg.
3. Add eggnog, egg yolk, and butter. Mix well but do not beat.
4. Stir in nuts and fruit.
5. Spray a baking pan with cooking spray and dust with flour.
6. Spread batter into prepared pan and bake for 18

minutes or until top is dark golden brown and bread starts to pull away from sides of pan.
7. Serve immediately.

Shrimp with Sriracha and Worcestershire Sauce

Prep time: 15 minutes | Cook time: 10 minutes per batch | Serves 4

- 1 tablespoon Sriracha sauce
- 1 teaspoon Worcestershire sauce
- 2 tablespoons sweet chili sauce
- ¾ cup mayonnaise
- 1 egg, beaten
- 1 cup panko bread crumbs
- 1 pound (454 g) raw shrimp, shelled and deveined, rinsed and drained
- Lime wedges, for serving
- Cooking spray

1. Place the crisper tray on the air fry position. Select Air Fry, set the temperature to 360°F (182°C), and set the time to 10 minutes.
2. Spritz the crisper tray with cooking spray.
3. Combine the Sriracha sauce, Worcestershire sauce, chili sauce, and mayo in a bowl. Stir to mix well. Reserve ⅓ cup of the mixture as the dipping sauce.
4. Combine the remaining sauce mixture with the beaten egg. Stir to mix well. Put the panko in a separate bowl.
5. Dredge the shrimp in the sauce mixture first, then into the panko. Roll the shrimp to coat well. Shake the excess off.
6. Place the shrimp in the crisper tray, then spritz with cooking spray. You may need to work in batches to avoid overcrowding.
7. Air fry for 10 minutes or until opaque. Flip the shrimp halfway through the cooking time.
8. Remove the shrimp from the grill and serve with reserve sauce mixture and squeeze the lime wedges over.

Supplì al Telefono (Risotto Croquettes)

Prep time: 1 hour 40 minutes | Cook time: 1 hour | Serves 6

RISOTTO CROQUETTES:

- 4 tablespoons unsalted butter
- 1 small yellow onion, minced
- 1 cup Arborio rice
- 3½ cups chicken stock
- ½ cup dry white wine
- 3 eggs
- Zest of 1 lemon
- ½ cup grated Parmesan cheese
- 2 ounces (57 g) fresh Mozzarella cheese
- ¼ cup peas
- 2 tablespoons water
- ½ cup all-purpose flour
- 1½ cups panko bread crumbs
- Kosher salt and ground black pepper, to taste
- Cooking spray

TOMATO SAUCE:

- 2 tablespoons extra-virgin olive oil
- 4 cloves garlic, minced
- ¼ teaspoon red pepper flakes
- 1 (28-ounce / 794-g) can crushed tomatoes
- 2 teaspoons granulated sugar
- Kosher salt and ground black pepper, to taste

1. Melt the butter in a pan over medium heat, then add the onion and salt to taste. Sauté for 5 minutes or until the onion in translucent.
2. Add the rice and stir to coat well. Cook for 3 minutes or until the rice is lightly browned. Pour in the chicken stock and wine.
3. Bring to a boil. Then cook for 20 minutes or until the rice is tender and liquid is almost absorbed.
4. Make the risotto: When the rice is cooked, break the egg into the pan. Add the lemon zest and Parmesan cheese. Sprinkle with salt and ground black pepper. Stir to mix well.
5. Pour the risotto in the baking pan, then level with a spatula to spread the risotto evenly. Wrap the baking pan in plastic and refrigerate for 1 hour.
6. Meanwhile, heat the olive oil in a saucepan over medium heat until shimmering.
7. Add the garlic and sprinkle with red pepper flakes. Sauté for a minute or until fragrant.
8. Add the crushed tomatoes and sprinkle with sugar. Stir to mix well. Bring to a boil. Reduce the heat to low and simmer for 15 minutes or until lightly thickened. Sprinkle with salt and pepper to taste. Set aside until ready to serve.
9. Remove the risotto from the refrigerator. Scoop the risotto into twelve 2-inch balls, then flatten the balls with your hands.
10. Arrange a about ½-inch piece of Mozzarella and 5 peas in the center of each flattened ball, then wrap them back into balls.
11. Transfer the balls in the baking pan lined with parchment paper, then refrigerate for 15 minutes or until firm.
12. Place the crisper tray on the bake position. Select Bake, set the temperature to 400°F (204°C), and set the time to 10 minutes.
13. Whisk the remaining 2 eggs with 2 tablespoons of water in a bowl. Pour the flour in a second bowl and pour the panko in a third bowl.
14. Dredge the risotto balls in the bowl of flour first, then into the eggs, and then into the panko. Shake the excess off.
15. Transfer the balls to the crisper tray and spritz with cooking spray. You may need to work in batches to avoid overcrowding.
16. Bake for 10 minutes or until golden brown. Flip the balls halfway through.
17. Serve the risotto balls with the tomato sauce.

Teriyaki Shrimp Skewers

Prep time: 10 minutes | Cook time: 6 minutes | Makes 12 skewered shrimp

- 1½ tablespoons mirin
- 1½ teaspoons ginger juice
- 1½ tablespoons soy sauce
- 12 large shrimp (about 20 shrimps per pound), peeled and deveined
- 1 large egg
- ¾ cup panko bread crumbs
- Cooking spray

1. Combine the mirin, ginger juice, and soy sauce in a large bowl. Stir to mix well.
2. Dunk the shrimp in the bowl of mirin mixture, then wrap the bowl in plastic and refrigerate for 1 hour to marinate.
3. Place the crisper tray on the air fry position. Select Air Fry, set the temperature to 400°F (204°C), and set the time to 6 minutes.
4. Spritz the crisper tray with cooking spray.
5. Run twelve 4-inch skewers through each shrimp.
6. Whisk the egg in the bowl of marinade to combine well. Pour the breadcrumbs on a plate.
7. Dredge the shrimp skewers in the egg mixture, then shake the excess off and roll over the breadcrumbs to coat well.
8. Arrange the shrimp skewers in the crisper tray and spritz with cooking spray. You need to work in batches to avoid overcrowding.
9. Air fry for 6 minutes or until the shrimp are opaque and firm. Flip the shrimp skewers halfway through.
10. Serve immediately.

Whole Chicken Roast

Prep time: 10 minutes | Cook time: 1 hour | Serves 6

- 1 teaspoon salt
- 1 teaspoon Italian seasoning
- ½ teaspoon freshly ground black pepper
- ½ teaspoon paprika
- ½ teaspoon garlic powder
- ½ teaspoon onion powder
- 2 tablespoons olive oil, plus more as needed
- 1 (4-pound / 1.8-kg) fryer chicken

1. Preheat the air fryer to 360°F (182°C).
2. Grease the air fryer basket lightly with olive oil.
3. In a small bowl, mix the salt, Italian seasoning, pepper, paprika, garlic powder, and onion powder.
4. Remove any giblets from the chicken. Pat the chicken dry thoroughly with paper towels, including the cavity.
5. Brush the chicken all over with the olive oil and rub it with the seasoning mixture.
6. Truss the chicken or tie the legs with butcher's twine. This will make it easier to flip the chicken during cooking.
7. Put the chicken in the air fryer basket, breast-side down. Air fry for 30 minutes. Flip the chicken over and baste it with any drippings collected in the bottom drawer of the air fryer. Lightly brush the chicken with olive oil.
8. Air fry for 20 minutes. Flip the chicken over one last time and air fry until a thermometer inserted into the thickest part of the thigh reaches at least 165°F (74°C) and it's crispy and golden, 10 more minutes. Continue to cook, checking every 5 minutes until the chicken reaches the correct internal temperature.
9. Let the chicken rest for 10 minutes before carving and serving.

Lush Snack Mix

Prep time: 10 minutes | Cook time: 10 minutes | Serves 10

- ½ cup honey
- 3 tablespoons butter, melted
- 1 teaspoon salt
- 2 cups sesame sticks
- 2 cup pumpkin seeds
- 2 cups granola
- 1 cup cashews
- 2 cups crispy corn puff cereal
- 2 cup mini pretzel crisps

1. In a bowl, combine the honey, butter, and salt.
2. In another bowl, mix the sesame sticks, pumpkin seeds, granola, cashews, corn puff cereal, and pretzel crisps.
3. Combine the contents of the two bowls.
4. Preheat the air fryer to 370°F (188°C).
5. Put the mixture in the air fryer basket and air fry for 10 to 12 minutes to toast the snack mixture, shaking the basket frequently. Do this in two batches.
6. Put the snack mix on a cookie sheet and allow it to cool fully.
7. Serve immediately.

Holiday Spicy Beef Roast

Prep time: 10 minutes | Cook time: 45 minutes | Serves 8

- 2 pounds (907 g) roast beef, at room temperature
- 2 tablespoons extra-virgin olive oil
- 1 teaspoon sea salt flakes
- 1 teaspoon black pepper, preferably freshly ground
- 1 teaspoon smoked paprika
- A few dashes of liquid smoke
- 2 jalapeño peppers, thinly sliced

1. Preheat the air fryer to 330°F (166°C).
2. Pat the roast dry using kitchen towels. Rub with extra-virgin olive oil and all seasonings along with liquid smoke.
3. Roast for 30 minutes in the preheated air fryer. Turn the roast over and roast for additional 15 minutes.
4. Check for doneness using a meat thermometer and serve sprinkled with sliced jalapeños. Bon appétit!

Chapter 16
Rotisserie Recipes

Paprika Pulled Pork Butt

Prep time: 10 minutes | Cook time: 6 hours | Serves 10

- 1 pork butt, 5 to 6 pounds (2.3 to 2.7 kg)

RUB:
- 2 tablespoons paprika
- 2 tablespoons packed brown sugar
- 1 tablespoon kosher salt
- 1 tablespoon mild chili powder
- 1 teaspoon freshly ground black pepper
- 1 teaspoon celery salt
- ½ teaspoon cayenne
- ½ teaspoon garlic powder

1. Run a long sword skewer through the center of the roast lengthwise to create a pilot hole. Run the rotisserie spit through the hole and secure with the forks. Balance as necessary.
2. To make the rub: Combine the rub ingredients in a small bowl and apply evenly all over the roast. Let sit at room temperature for 15 minutes. By this time the air fryer oven should be ready.
3. Select Roast, set temperature to 350°F (180°C), Rotate, and set time to 6 hours. Select Start to begin preheating.
4. Once preheated, place the prepared roast with rotisserie spit into the oven. Set a drip tray underneath. Roast until the internal temperature reaches 185°F (85°C). The roast will shrink during cooking, so adjust the forks when appropriate.
5. When cooking is complete, remove the roast using the rotisserie lift. Carefully remove the rotisserie forks and slide the spit out, and then set the pork on a large cutting board. Tent the roast with aluminum foil and let the meat rest for 20 minutes. Remove the foil and let stand for an additional 10 minutes.
6. Using two forks, check to see how easily the meat shreds. Some parts will do this more easily than others. Be sure to use heat-resistant gloves to break the roast apart. Begin shredding each large chunk one at a time. Add pieces to a large bowl and either add the barbecue sauce directly to the shredded meat or serve on the side. Keep the bowl covered as you're working on each section. This will help keep the meat warm. Serve by itself or with your favorite sides or in sandwiches.

Orange Honey Glazed Ham

Prep time: 10 minutes | Cook time: 45 minutes | Serves 12 to 14

- 1 ham, bone in and unsliced, 7 to 8 pounds (3.2 to 3.6 kg)
- 1 cup packed brown sugar

GLAZE:
- 1½ cups orange juice
- ½ cup honey
- 2 tablespoons packed brown sugar
- ¼ teaspoon ground cinnamon
- ⅛ teaspoon ground nutmeg
- ⅛ teaspoon ground allspice
- ⅛ teaspoon ground cloves
- ⅛ teaspoon white pepper
- 2 tablespoons unsalted butter

1. To make the glaze: Combine the orange juice, honey, brown sugar, and spices in a saucepan and bring almost to a boil over medium-high heat. Decrease the heat to medium and simmer for 10 minutes, stirring often. The mixture should be a little runnier than real maple syrup. Remove from the heat and add the butter, stirring until melted. Let the mixture cool.
2. Run a long sword skewer through the center of the ham lengthwise to create a pilot hole. There is a bone in the middle of this ham, but generally it is just to one side. The skewer should easily go through, but feel for the bone before you start so you will know how to navigate around it. Run the rotisserie spit through the hole and secure with the forks. Balance the ham on the spit as well as possible.
3. Select Roast, set temperature to 375°F (190°C), Rotate, and set time to 45 minutes. Select Start to begin preheating.
4. Once preheated, place the prepared ham with rotisserie spit into the oven. Set a drip tray underneath. The ham should not take too long to heat up. Look for an internal temperature around 130°F (54°C). The surface should be hot.
5. Baste the ham with the glaze after 20 minutes on the air fryer oven. Repeat the process every 5 minutes and about 3 more times.
6. During the last 5 to 10 minutes of cooking time, the ham should be hot as well as sticky from the glaze. Increase the temperature to 400°F (205°C) and sprinkle the brown sugar evenly on the surface of the ham in small amounts until it is completely coated. Continue to cook until the sugar starts to bubble. Move quickly, as sugar tends to burn.
7. Once the sugar is bubbling rapidly, remove the ham using the rotisserie lift and place on a large cutting board. Remove the rotisserie forks and slide the spit out, loosely cover the ham with aluminum foil, and let it rest for 5 minutes. Carve into thin slices and serve warm.

Smoked Paprika Lamb Leg

Prep time: 10 minutes | **Cook time:** 1 hour 20 minutes | **Serves 6 to 8**

- 1 boneless leg of lamb (partial bone-in is fine), 4 to 5 pounds (1.8 to 2.3 kg)

RUB:

- ¼ cup packed brown sugar
- 1 tablespoon coarse salt
- 2 teaspoons smoked paprika
- 1½ to 2 teaspoons spicy chili powder or cayenne
- 2 teaspoons onion powder
- 1 teaspoon garlic powder
- 1 teaspoon freshly ground black pepper
- ½ teaspoon ground cloves
- ⅛ teaspoon ground cinnamon

1. Trim off the excess fat and any loose hanging pieces from the lamb. With kitchen twine, tie the roast into a uniform and solid roast. It will take four to five ties to hold it together properly. Run a long sword skewer through the center of the roast lengthwise to create a pilot hole. Run the rotisserie spit through the hole and secure with the forks. Balance as necessary.
2. To make the rub: Combine the rub ingredients in a small bowl and apply evenly to the lamb. Make sure you get as much of the rub on the meat as possible.
3. Select Roast, set temperature to 375°F (190°C), Rotate, and set time to 80 minutes. Select Start to begin preheating.
4. Once preheated, place the prepared lamb with rotisserie spit into the oven. Set a drip tray underneath. Roast until the lamb reaches an internal temperature of 140°F (60°C) for medium or 150°F (66°C) for medium well. The lamb will shrink during cooking, so adjust the forks when appropriate.
5. When cooking is complete, remove the lamb using the rotisserie lift. Carefully remove the rotisserie forks and slide the spit out, and then set the lamb on a large cutting board. Tent the roast with aluminum foil and let the meat rest for 10 to 12 minutes. Cut off the twine and carve. Serve.

Sirloin Roast with Porcini-Wine Baste

Prep time: 20 minutes | **Cook time:** 2 hours | **Serves 8**

- 1 top sirloin roast, 4 to 4½ pounds (1.8 to 2.0 kg)

WET RUB:

- ½ cup dried porcini mushrooms
- ¼ cup olive oil
- 4 teaspoons salt
- 1 tablespoon chopped fresh thyme
- 2 cloves garlic, minced
- 1 teaspoon onion powder
- 1 teaspoon chili powder
- 1 teaspoon coarsely ground black pepper

BASTE:

- ½ cup dried porcini mushrooms
- 1 or 2 cups boiling water
- ½ cup red wine (Cabernet Sauvignon recommended)
- 1 tablespoon wet rub mixture
- 1 teaspoon Worcestershire sauce

1. For the wet rub: Chop the mushrooms into small pieces. Place in a clean spice or coffee grinder and grind to a fine powder. Transfer to a bowl and add the remaining rub ingredients. Remove 1 tablespoon (6 g) of the mixture and set aside.
2. If the sirloin roast is loose or uneven, tie it with kitchen twine to hold it to a consistent and even shape. Run a long sword skewer through the center of the roast lengthwise to create a pilot hole. Run the rotisserie spit through the hole and secure with the forks. Balance as necessary. Apply the wet rub evenly to the meat.
3. Select Roast, set temperature to 400°F (205°C), Rotate, and set time to 2 hours. Select Start to begin preheating.
4. Once preheated, place the prepared roast with rotisserie spit into the oven. Set a drip tray underneath, and add 1 to 2 cups hot water to the tray. Roast until it reaches the desired doneness: 125°F (52°C) for rare, 135°F (57°C) for medium rare, 145°F (63°C) for medium, 155°F (68°C) for medium well, or 165°F (74°C) for well done. Adjust the forks when appropriate.
5. While the roast cooks, make the baste: Add the dried porcini mushrooms to 1 cup boiling water, or 2 cups boiling water if you would like to use the porcini broth for the gravy. Steep the mushrooms for 30 minutes, covered. Strain the broth and reserve the porcinis (for the gravy) and broth separately. Divide the broth into two equal portions, one for the baste and one for the gravy. Combine 1 cup broth with remaining baste ingredients. Let sit for 15 to 30 minutes to come to room temperature before using. Begin basting the roast during the last half of the cooking time and repeat every 10 to 12 minutes until the roast is ready.
6. When cooking is complete, remove the roast using the rotisserie lift. Carefully remove the rotisserie forks and slide the spit out. Tent the roast with aluminum foil and let the meat rest for 20 minutes. Cut into ¼-inch slices and serve.

Pulled Pork with Paprika

Prep time: 10 minutes | Cook time: 6 hours | Serves 10

- 1 pork butt, 5 to 6 pounds (2.3 to 2.7 kg)

RUB:
- 2 tablespoons paprika
- 2 tablespoons packed brown sugar
- 1 tablespoon kosher salt
- 1 tablespoon mild chili powder
- 1 teaspoon freshly ground black pepper
- 1 teaspoon celery salt
- ½ teaspoon cayenne
- ½ teaspoon garlic powder

1. Run a long sword skewer through the center of the roast lengthwise to create a pilot hole. Run the rotisserie spit through the hole and secure with the forks. Balance as necessary.
2. To make the rub: Combine the rub ingredients in a small bowl and apply evenly all over the roast. Let sit at room temperature for 15 minutes. By this time the air fryer oven should be ready.
3. Select the ROAST function and preheat AIR FRYER to 350°F (180°C). Press ROTATE button and set time to 6 hours.
4. Place the roast on the preheated air fryer oven with a drip pan underneath. Roast until the internal temperature reaches 185°F (85°C). The roast will shrink during cooking, so adjust the forks when appropriate.
5. Remove from the heat, carefully remove the rotisserie forks and slide the spit out, and then set the pork on a large cutting board. Tent the roast with aluminum foil and let the meat rest for 20 minutes. Remove the foil and let stand for an additional 10 minutes.
6. Using two forks, check to see how easily the meat shreds. Some parts will do this more easily than others. Be sure to use heat-resistant gloves to break the roast apart. Begin shredding each large chunk one at a time. Add pieces to a large bowl and either add the barbecue sauce directly to the shredded meat or serve on the side. Keep the bowl covered as you're working on each section. This will help keep the meat warm. Serve by itself or with your favorite sides or in sandwiches.

Ham with Honey-Orange Glaze

Prep time: 10 minutes | Cook time: 45 minutes | Serves 12 to 14

- 1 ham, bone in and unsliced, 7 to 8 pounds (3.2 to 3.6 kg)
- 1 cup packed brown sugar

GLAZE:
- 1½ cups orange juice
- ½ cup honey
- 2 tablespoons packed brown sugar
- ¼ teaspoon ground cinnamon
- ⅛ teaspoon ground nutmeg
- ⅛ teaspoon ground allspice
- ⅛ teaspoon ground cloves
- ⅛ teaspoon white pepper
- 2 tablespoons unsalted butter

1. To make the glaze: Combine the orange juice, honey, brown sugar, and spices in a saucepan and bring almost to a boil over medium-high heat. Decrease the heat to medium and simmer for 10 minutes, stirring often. The mixture should be a little runnier than real maple syrup. Remove from the heat and add the butter, stirring until melted. Let the mixture cool.
2. Run a long sword skewer through the center of the ham lengthwise to create a pilot hole. There is a bone in the middle of this ham, but generally it is just to one side. The skewer should easily go through, but feel for the bone before you start so you will know how to navigate around it. Run the rotisserie spit through the hole and secure with the forks. Balance the ham on the spit as well as possible.
3. Select the ROAST function and preheat AIR FRYER to 375°F (190°C). Press ROTATE button and set time to 45 minutes.
4. Place the ham on the preheated air fryer oven and set a drip pan underneath, if there is room. The ham should not take too long to heat up. Look for an internal temperature around 130°F (54°C). The surface should be hot.
5. Baste the ham with the glaze after 20 minutes on the air fryer oven. Repeat the process every 5 minutes and about 3 more times.
6. During the last 5 to 10 minutes of cooking time, the ham should be hot as well as sticky from the glaze. Increase the temperature to 400°F (205°C) and sprinkle the brown sugar evenly on the surface of the ham in small amounts until it is completely coated. Continue to cook until the sugar starts to bubble. Move quickly, as sugar tends to burn.
7. Once the sugar is bubbling rapidly, remove the ham from the heat and place on a large cutting board. Remove the rotisserie forks and slide the spit out, loosely cover the ham with aluminum foil, and let it rest for 5 minutes. Carve into thin slices and serve warm.

Bourbon Ham with Apple Butter

Prep time: 5 minutes | Cook time: 50 minutes | Serves 10 to 12

- 1 ham, unsliced, 5 to 6 pounds (2.3 to 2.7 kg)

BASTE:

- ⅓ cup apple butter
- ¼ cup packed brown sugar
- 2 tablespoons bourbon
- 1½ teaspoons Dijon mustard
- ¼ teaspoon ground ginger
- ¼ teaspoon white pepper

1. Run a long sword skewer through the center of the ham lengthwise to create a pilot hole. Run the rotisserie spit through the hole and secure with the forks. Balance as necessary and secure tightly. Place the ham on the preheated air fryer oven and cook for 50 to 60 minutes. If there is room, set a drip pan underneath.
2. To make the baste: Combine all the baste ingredients in a small saucepan and simmer over medium heat for 2 minutes, stirring often. Remove from the heat and let sit for 5 to 10 minutes before using.
3. Select the ROAST function and preheat AIR FRYER to 400°F (205°C). Press ROTATE button and set time to 45 minutes.
4. Place the ham on the preheated air fryer oven and set a drip pan underneath, if there is room. During the last 20 minutes of the cooking time, begin basting the ham with the apple butter-bourbon mixture. Make at least 4 or 5 passes with the baste to coat evenly. Focus the coating on the outside of the ham and not on the cut side. The ham should not take too long to heat up. Look for an internal temperature around 130°F (54°C). The surface should be hot.
5. Remove from the heat, carefully remove the rotisserie forks and slide the spit out, and then set the ham on a large cutting board. Tent the ham with aluminum foil and let the meat rest for 10 minutes. Carve and serve immediately.

Spareribs with Ketchup-Garlic Sauce

Prep time: 15 minutes | Cook time: 3½ hours | Serves 4 to 6

- 2 racks spareribs

SAUCE:

- 1 tablespoon olive oil
- 2 cloves garlic, minced
- 1 cup ketchup
- ¾ cup water
- ⅓ cup packed brown sugar
- 1 tablespoon paprika
- 2 teaspoons mild chili powder
- ¼ teaspoon cayenne

RUB:

- ⅓ cup packed brown sugar
- 2 tablespoons paprika
- 2 teaspoons salt
- 2 teaspoons mild chili powder
- 1 teaspoon onion powder
- ½ teaspoon garlic powder
- ¼ teaspoon cayenne

1. To make the sauce: Heat the oil in a medium-size saucepan over medium heat and sauté the garlic for 15 seconds, until aromatic. Add the remaining sauce ingredients and simmer for 5 minutes, stirring often. Remove from the heat and let cool to room temperature before using.
2. To make the rub: Combine the rub ingredients in a small bowl and set aside.
3. Place the ribs on a cutting board and pat dry with paper towels. Cut away any excess fat from the ribs. Remove the membrane from the back of the ribs by using a blunt knife to work the membrane away from the bone in one corner. Grab hold of the membrane with a paper towel for a good grip and gently peel away. With a little practice, this becomes an easy process.
4. Lay the rib racks meat-side down. Apply a small portion of the rub, just enough to season, to the bone side of the racks. Lay one rack on top of the other, bone side to bone side, to form an even shape. Tie the two racks together with kitchen twine between every other bone. The ribs should be held tightly together. Run the rotisserie spit between the racks and secure with the forks. The fork tines should run through the meat as best as possible. The ribs will move a little as the rotisserie turns. They should not flop around, however. Secure to prevent this. Apply the remaining rub evenly over the outer surface of the ribs. A general rule with rubs is that what sticks is the amount needed.
5. Select the ROAST function and preheat AIR FRYER to 375°F (190°C). Press ROTATE button and set time to 3½ hours.
6. Place the ribs on the preheated air fryer oven and set a drip pan underneath. Roast until the ribs reach an internal temperature of 185°F (85°C). Test the temperature in several locations. Baste the ribs several times with the sauce during the last hour of cooking to build up a sticky surface.
7. Remove from the heat, carefully remove the rotisserie forks and slide the spit out, and then set the ribs on a large cutting board. Tent the ribs with aluminum foil and let the meat rest for 5 to 10 minutes. Cut away the twine and cut the racks into individual ribs. Serve.

Mutton Roast with Barbecue Dip

Prep time: 15 minutes | Cook time: 4½ hours | Serves 8 to 10

- 1 mutton roast (shoulder or leg), 5 pounds (2.3 kg)
- Barbecue Dip:
- 1 cup water
- ¼ cup Worcestershire sauce
- ¼ cup apple cider vinegar
- 1 tablespoon freshly ground black pepper
- 1 tablespoon packed brown sugar
- 1 tablespoon freshly squeezed lemon juice
- 1 tablespoon salt
- ½ teaspoon ground allspice
- Baste:
- 1 cup apple cider vinegar
- ½ cup Worcestershire sauce
- ¼ cup freshly squeezed lemon juice
- 2 tablespoons freshly ground black pepper
- 1 tablespoon salt

1. To make the barbecue dip: Combine the dip ingredients in a jar. Cover with a lid and refrigerate, shaking periodically. Warm the dip in the microwave just before serving.
2. To make the baste: Combine the baste ingredients in a small bowl and set aside.
3. Using kitchen twine, tie the mutton roast into a uniform shape. Run a long sword skewer through the center of the roast lengthwise to create a pilot hole. Run the rotisserie spit through the hole and secure with the forks. Balance as necessary.
4. Select the ROAST function and preheat AIR FRYER to 375°F (190°C). Press ROTATE button and set time to 4½ hours.
5. Place the roast on the preheated air fryer oven and set a drip pan underneath. Apply the baste mixture every 30 minutes, until the roast reaches an internal temperature of 185°F (85°C). The roast will shrink during cooking, so adjust the forks when appropriate.
6. Remove from the heat, carefully remove the rotisserie forks and slide the spit out, and then set the roast on a large cutting board. Tent the roast with aluminum foil and let the meat rest for 20 minutes.
7. Shred or carve the mutton into small pieces. Serve with the warmed barbecue dip on the side.

Whiskey-Basted Prime Rib Roast

Prep time: 10 minutes | Cook time: 2 hours | Serves 8 to 10

- 1 4-bone prime rib roast (8 to 10 pounds / 3.6 to 4.5 kg)

RUB:

- ¼ cup coarse salt
- 1 small shallot, finely chopped
- 2 cloves garlic, minced
- 2 tablespoons olive oil
- 1 tablespoon coarsely ground black pepper
- Zest of 1 large lemon
- 1 teaspoon paprika
- 1 teaspoon sugar

BASTE:

- ⅓ cup whiskey
- ¼ cup water
- Juice of 1 lemon
- ⅛ teaspoon salt

1. Trim off any straggling pieces of meat or fat from the roast. If the fat cap is too thick, cut it down to between ¼ to ½ inch in thickness depending on how you like your prime rib.
2. Run a long sword skewer through the center of the roast lengthwise to create a pilot hole. Run the rotisserie spit through the hole and secure with the forks. Balance as necessary.
3. To make the rub: Combine the rub ingredients in a small bowl to form an even paste. Use additional olive oil if necessary to get it to a thick but workable consistency. Apply evenly to the roast, focusing on the outer shell of the roast.
4. To make the baste: Combine the baste ingredients in a small bowl and set aside for 15 to 30 minutes to come to room temperature.
5. Select Roast, set temperature to 400°F (205°C). Rotate, and set time to 2 hours. Select Start to begin preheating.
6. Once preheated, place the prepared roast with rotisserie spit into the oven. Set a drip tray underneath, and add 1 to 2 cups hot water to the tray. If you intend to make a gravy from the drippings, monitor the drip tray to make sure it does not run dry. Add extra water if needed.
7. During the last hour of cooking time, begin basting. Apply the baste gently so as not to wash away the seasonings on the outside of the roast. Do this 6 to 8 times, until the roast is well coated with the baste. Roast until it is near the desired doneness: 125°F (52°C) for rare, 135°F (57°C) for medium rare, 145°F (63°C) for medium, 155°F (68°C) for medium well, or 165°F (74°C) for well done. The roast will shrink during cooking, so adjust the forks when appropriate.
8. When cooking is complete, remove the roast using the rotisserie lift. Carefully remove the rotisserie forks and slide the spit out, and then set the roast on a large cutting board. Tent the roast with aluminum foil and let the meat rest for 15 to 20 minutes. Cut away the bones first by passing a knife against the bones and cutting through (save the bones for later). Cut the meat into thin slices.

Spareribs with Paprika Rub

Prep time: 15 minutes | Cook time: 3½ hours | Serves 4 to 6

- 2 racks spareribs

SAUCE:

- 1 tablespoon olive oil
- 2 cloves garlic, minced
- 1 cup ketchup
- ¾ cup water
- ⅓ cup packed brown sugar
- 1 tablespoon paprika
- 2 teaspoons mild chili powder
- ¼ teaspoon cayenne

RUB:

- ⅓ cup packed brown sugar
- 2 tablespoons paprika
- 2 teaspoons salt
- 2 teaspoons mild chili powder
- 1 teaspoon onion powder
- ½ teaspoon garlic powder
- ¼ teaspoon cayenne

1. To make the sauce: Heat the oil in a medium-size saucepan over medium heat and sauté the garlic for 15 seconds, until aromatic. Add the remaining sauce ingredients and simmer for 5 minutes, stirring often. Remove from the heat and let cool to room temperature before using.
2. To make the rub: Combine the rub ingredients in a small bowl and set aside.
3. Place the ribs on a cutting board and pat dry with paper towels. Cut away any excess fat from the ribs. Remove the membrane from the back of the ribs by using a blunt knife to work the membrane away from the bone in one corner. Grab hold of the membrane with a paper towel for a good grip and gently peel away. With a little practice, this becomes an easy process.
4. Lay the rib racks meat-side down. Apply a small portion of the rub, just enough to season, to the bone side of the racks. Lay one rack on top of the other, bone side to bone side, to form an even shape. Tie the two racks together with kitchen twine between every other bone. The ribs should be held tightly together. Run the rotisserie spit between the racks and secure with the forks. The fork tines should run through the meat as best as possible. The ribs will move a little as the rotisserie turns. They should not flop around, however. Secure to prevent this. Apply the remaining rub evenly over the outer surface of the ribs. A general rule with rubs is that what sticks is the amount needed.
5. Select Roast, set temperature to 375°F (190°C), Rotate, and set time to 3½ hours. Select Start to begin preheating.
6. Once preheated, place the prepared ribs with rotisserie spit into the oven. Set a drip tray underneath. Roast until the ribs reach an internal temperature of 185°F (85°C). Test the temperature in several locations. Baste the ribs several times with the sauce during the last hour of cooking to build up a sticky surface.
7. When cooking is complete, remove the ribs using the rotisserie lift. Carefully remove the rotisserie forks and slide the spit out, and then set the ribs on a large cutting board. Tent the ribs with aluminum foil and let the meat rest for 5 to 10 minutes. Cut away the twine and cut the racks into individual ribs. Serve.

Baby Back Ribs with Paprika Rub

Prep time: 15 minutes | Cook time: 2½ hours | Serves 4 to 6

- 2 racks baby back ribs

SAUCE:

- 1 tablespoon vegetable oil
- 1 cup finely chopped sweet onion
- 2 cloves garlic, minced
- 1½ cups ketchup
- ¼ cup red wine vinegar
- ¼ cup packed brown sugar
- 2 tablespoons yellow mustard
- ⅛ teaspoon salt

RUB:

- 1 tablespoon paprika
- 2 teaspoons salt
- 2 teaspoons freshly ground black pepper
- ½ teaspoon cayenne

1. To make the sauce: Heat the oil in a medium-size saucepan over medium heat. Add the onions and sauté for 5 minutes. Add the garlic and sauté for 15 seconds. Add the remaining sauce ingredients and simmer for 4 to 5 minutes, stirring often. Remove from the heat and let cool for 15 to 30 minutes before using.
2. To make the rub: Combine the rub ingredients in a small bowl and set aside.
3. Place the ribs on a cutting board and pat dry with paper towels. Cut away any excess fat from the ribs. Remove the membrane from the back of the ribs by using a blunt knife to work the membrane away from the bone in one corner. Grab hold of the membrane with a paper towel for a good grip

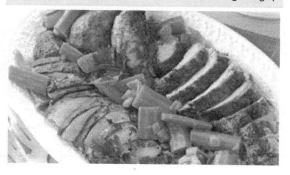

Chipotle Chuck Roast with Garlic

Prep time: 10 minutes | Cook time: 2½ hours | Serves 6 to 8

- 1 chuck roast, 3½ to 4 pounds (1.5 to 1.8 kg)

MARINADE:

- 1 (7-ounce / 198-g) can chipotle peppers in adobo
- 1 cup diced onion
- ½ cup beef or vegetable broth
- 3 cloves garlic, cut into fourths
- 1 tablespoon ground cumin
- 2 tablespoons water
- 1 tablespoon white vinegar
- 1 tablespoon salt
- 2 teaspoons dried oregano

1. To make the marinade: Place the marinade ingredients in a food processor and pulse 8 to 10 times. Everything should be very finely chopped and combined. Reserve 1 cup of the mixture to use as a baste and refrigerate until ready to cook, then bring to room temperature before using.
2. Trim away any loose or excess pieces of fat from the roast. Place in a large glass dish or large resealable plastic bag. Pour the marinade over the meat, making sure all sides are well covered. Seal the bag or cover the dish with plastic wrap and place in the refrigerator for 12 to 24 hours.
3. Remove the roast from the bag, discarding the marinade. Lay the roast out on a large cutting board. With kitchen twine, tie the roast into a round and uniform shape, pulling tightly. Start in the center and work toward the ends until it is tied into a solid round roast. This will take four or five ties. Run a long sword skewer through the center of the roast lengthwise to create a pilot hole. Run the rotisserie spit through the hole and secure with the forks. Balance as necessary.
4. Select the ROAST function and preheat AIR FRYER to 400°F (205°C). Press ROTATE button and set time to 2½ hours.
5. Place the roast on the preheated air fryer oven and set a drip pan underneath. Roast until the meat reaches an internal temperature of about 160°F (70°C). Baste with the reserved marinade during the last 30 to 40 minutes of cooking. This roast is intentionally overcooked so that it can be shredded easily. It will be tender and juicy.
6. Remove from the heat, carefully remove the rotisserie forks and slide the spit out, and then set the roast on a large cutting board. Tent the roast with aluminum foil and let the meat rest for 20 minutes. Cut off the twine. Shred into small pieces or carve into thin slices and serve with warmed tortillas, Spanish rice, beans, and fresh salsa.

BBQ Chicken with Mustard Rub

Prep time: 15 minutes | Cook time: 1 hour 10 minutes | Serves 4 to 6

- 1 whole chicken, 3 to 4 pounds (1.4 to 1.8 kg)
- 1 medium-size onion, peeled but whole (for cavity)
- Barbecue Sauce:
- ¾ cup ketchup
- ⅔ cup cherry cola
- ¼ cup apple cider vinegar
- 2 tablespoons packed brown sugar
- 1 tablespoon molasses
- ¼ teaspoon salt
- ¼ teaspoon freshly ground black pepper
- Rub:
- 2 teaspoons salt
- 2 teaspoons onion powder
- 1 teaspoon mustard powder
- ½ teaspoon freshly ground black pepper
- ½ teaspoon garlic powder

1. To make the barbecue sauce: Combine all the ingredients in a medium-size saucepan over medium heat and simmer for 5 to 6 minutes, until the mixture is smooth and well blended. Stir often and watch for burning. Remove from the heat and let the sauce cool at least 10 minutes before using.
2. To make the rub: Combine all the rub ingredients in a small bowl.
3. Pat the chicken dry inside and out with paper towels. Apply the rub all over the bird, under the breast skin, and inside the body cavity.
4. Truss the chicken with kitchen twine. Run the rotisserie spit through the onion and insert it into the chicken cavity. Use a paring knife to cut a pilot hole in the onion to make this easier. Continue to run the spit through the chicken and secure with the rotisserie forks.
5. Select Roast, set temperature to 400°F (205°C), Rotate, and set time to 70 minutes. Select Start to begin preheating.
6. Once preheated, place the prepared chicken with rotisserie spit into the oven. Set a drip tray underneath. Roast until the meat in the thighs and legs reaches 175°F (79°C). The breasts should be 165°F (74°C). Baste the chicken with the barbecue sauce during the last half of the cooking time. Do so every 7 to 10 minutes, until the bird is nearly done and well coated with the sauce.
7. When cooking is complete, remove the chicken using the rotisserie lift. Carefully remove the rotisserie forks and slide the spit out, and then set the chicken on a large cutting board. Tent the chicken with aluminum foil and let it rest for 10 to 15 minutes before cutting off the twine and carving.

Porchetta with Lemony Sage Rub

Prep time: 15 minutes | Cook time: 3½ hours | Serves 6

- 1 slab pork belly, skin on, 5 to 6 pounds (2.3 to 2.7 kg)
- 1 boneless pork loin roast, about 3 pounds (1.4 kg)
- Rub:
- 2 tablespoons fennel seeds
- 1 tablespoon finely chopped fresh sage
- Zest of 1 lemon
- 4 or 5 cloves garlic
- 2 teaspoons coarse salt
- 2 teaspoons freshly ground black pepper
- 1 teaspoon chopped fresh rosemary
- 1 teaspoon red pepper flakes
- 1½ teaspoons coarse salt
- 1 teaspoon freshly ground black pepper

1. Lay the pork belly, skin-side down, on a large cutting board. Place the pork loin on top and roll the pork belly together so that the ends meet. Trim any excess pork belly and loin so that it is a uniform cylinder. Do not tie yet.
2. To make the rub: Using a mortar and pestle or spice grinder, crush the fennel seeds to a medium grind. Combine with the remaining rub ingredients in a small bowl and apply all over the pork loin.
3. Roll the pork loin inside the pork belly and tie with kitchen twine every inch into a secure, round bundle. Season the outside of the pork belly with the coarse salt and pepper. Set onto a baking sheet and place in the refrigerator, uncovered, for 24 hours.
4. Run a long sword skewer through the center of the roast lengthwise to create a pilot hole. Run the rotisserie spit through the hole and secure with the forks. Balance as necessary.
5. Select Roast, set temperature to 400°F (205°C), Rotate, and set time to 3½ hours. Select Start to begin preheating.
6. Once preheated, place the prepared porchetta with rotisserie spit into the oven. Set a drip tray underneath. Watch for burning or excessive browning and adjust the heat as necessary. Once the porchetta has reached an internal temperature of 145°F (63°C), the roast is done. If the skin is not a deep brown and crispy in texture, increase the temperature to 450°F (235°C) and roast for an additional 10 minutes.
7. When cooking is complete, remove the porchetta using the rotisserie lift. Carefully remove the rotisserie forks and slide the spit out, and then set the meat on a large cutting board. Tent the roast with aluminum foil and let the meat rest for 15 minutes. Slice the meat ½ inch thick and serve.

Lamb Leg with Brown Sugar Rub

Prep time: 10 minutes | Cook time: 1 hour 20 minutes | Serves 6 to 8

- 1 boneless leg of lamb (partial bone-in is fine), 4 to 5 pounds (1.8 to 2.3 kg)

RUB:

- ¼ cup packed brown sugar
- 1 tablespoon coarse salt
- 2 teaspoons smoked paprika
- 1½ to 2 teaspoons spicy chili powder or cayenne
- 2 teaspoons onion powder
- 1 teaspoon garlic powder
- 1 teaspoon freshly ground black pepper
- ½ teaspoon ground cloves
- ⅛ teaspoon ground cinnamon

1. Trim off the excess fat and any loose hanging pieces from the lamb. With kitchen twine, tie the roast into a uniform and solid roast. It will take four to five ties to hold it together properly. Run a long sword skewer through the center of the roast lengthwise to create a pilot hole. Run the rotisserie spit through the hole and secure with the forks. Balance as necessary.
2. To make the rub: Combine the rub ingredients in a small bowl and apply evenly to the lamb. Make sure you get as much of the rub on the meat as possible.
3. Select the ROAST function and preheat AIR FRYER to 375°F (190°C). Press ROTATE button and set time to 80 minutes.
4. Place the lamb on the preheated air fryer oven and set a drip pan underneath. Roast until the lamb reaches an internal temperature of 140°F (60°C) for medium or 150°F (66°C) for medium well. The lamb will shrink during cooking, so adjust the forks when appropriate.
5. Remove from the heat, carefully remove the rotisserie forks and slide the spit out, and then set the lamb on a large cutting board. Tent the roast with aluminum foil and let the meat rest for 10 to 12 minutes. Cut off the twine and carve. Serve.

Barbecued Whole Chicken

Prep time: 15 minutes | Cook time: 1 hour 10 minutes | Serves 4 to 6

- 1 whole chicken, 3 to 4 pounds (1.4 to 1.8 kg)
- 1 medium-size onion, peeled but whole (for cavity)
- Barbecue Sauce:
- ¾ cup ketchup
- ⅔ cup cherry cola
- ¼ cup apple cider vinegar
- 2 tablespoons packed brown sugar
- 1 tablespoon molasses
- ¼ teaspoon salt
- ¼ teaspoon freshly ground black pepper

RUB:

- 2 teaspoons salt
- 2 teaspoons onion powder
- 1 teaspoon mustard powder
- ½ teaspoon freshly ground black pepper
- ½ teaspoon garlic powder

1. To make the barbecue sauce: Combine all the ingredients in a medium-size saucepan over medium heat and simmer for 5 to 6 minutes, until the mixture is smooth and well blended. Stir often and watch for burning. Remove from the heat and let the sauce cool at least 10 minutes before using.
2. To make the rub: Combine all the rub ingredients in a small bowl.
3. Pat the chicken dry inside and out with paper towels. Apply the rub all over the bird, under the breast skin, and inside the body cavity.
4. Truss the chicken with kitchen twine. Run the rotisserie spit through the onion and insert it into the chicken cavity. Use a paring knife to cut a pilot hole in the onion to make this easier. Continue to run the spit through the chicken and secure with the rotisserie forks.
5. Select the ROAST function and preheat AIR FRYER to 400°F (205°C). Press ROTATE button and set time to 70 minutes.
6. Place the chicken on the preheated air fryer oven and set a drip pan underneath. Roast until the meat in the thighs and legs reaches 175°F (79°C). The breasts should be 165°F (74°C). Baste the chicken with the barbecue sauce during the last half of the cooking time. Do so every 7 to 10 minutes, until the bird is nearly done and well coated with the sauce.
7. Remove from the heat, carefully remove the rotisserie forks and slide the spit out, and then set the chicken on a large cutting board. Tent the chicken with aluminum foil and let it rest for 10 to 15 minutes before cutting off the twine and carving.

Ham with Dijon Bourbon Baste

Prep time: 5 minutes | Cook time: 50 minutes | Serves 10 to 12

- 1 ham, unsliced, 5 to 6 pounds (2.3 to 2.7 kg)

BASTE:

- ⅓ cup apple butter
- ¼ cup packed brown sugar
- 2 tablespoons bourbon
- 1½ teaspoons Dijon mustard
- ¼ teaspoon ground ginger
- ¼ teaspoon white pepper

1. Run a long sword skewer through the center of the ham lengthwise to create a pilot hole. Run the rotisserie spit through the hole and secure with the forks. Balance as necessary and secure tightly. Place the ham on the preheated air fryer oven and cook for 50 to 60 minutes. If there is room, set a drip tray underneath.
2. To make the baste: Combine all the baste ingredients in a small saucepan and simmer over medium heat for 2 minutes, stirring often. Remove from the heat and let sit for 5 to 10 minutes before using.
3. Select Roast, set temperature to 400°F (205°C), Rotate, and set time to 45 minutes. Select Start to begin preheating.
4. Once preheated, place the prepared ham with rotisserie spit into the oven. Set a drip tray underneath. During the last 20 minutes of the cooking time, begin basting the ham with the apple butter-bourbon mixture. Make at least 4 or 5 passes with the baste to coat evenly. Focus the coating on the outside of the ham and not on the cut side. The ham should not take too long to heat up. Look for an internal temperature around 130°F (54°C). The surface should be hot.
5. When cooking is complete, remove the ham using the rotisserie lift. Carefully remove the rotisserie forks and slide the spit out, and then set the ham on a large cutting board. Tent the ham with aluminum foil and let the meat rest for 10 minutes. Carve and serve immediately.

Sirloin Roast with Porcini Baste

Prep time: 20 minutes | Cook time: 2 hours | Serves 8

- 1 top sirloin roast, 4 to 4½ pounds (1.8 to 2.0 kg)

WET RUB:

- ½ cup dried porcini mushrooms
- ¼ cup olive oil
- 4 teaspoons salt
- 1 tablespoon chopped fresh thyme
- 2 cloves garlic, minced
- 1 teaspoon onion powder
- 1 teaspoon chili powder
- 1 teaspoon coarsely ground black pepper

BASTE:

- ½ cup dried porcini mushrooms
- 1 or 2 cups boiling water
- ½ cup red wine (Cabernet Sauvignon recommended)
- 1 tablespoon wet rub mixture
- 1 teaspoon Worcestershire sauce

1. For the wet rub: Chop the mushrooms into small pieces. Place in a clean spice or coffee grinder and grind to a fine powder. Transfer to a bowl and add the remaining rub ingredients. Remove 1 tablespoon (6 g) of the mixture and set aside.
2. If the sirloin roast is loose or uneven, tie it with kitchen twine to hold it to a consistent and even shape. Run a long sword skewer through the center of the roast lengthwise to create a pilot hole. Run the rotisserie spit through the hole and secure with the forks. Balance as necessary. Apply the wet rub evenly to the meat.
3. Select the ROAST function and preheat AIR FRYER to 400°F (205°C). Press ROTATE button and set time to 2 hours.
4. Place the roast on the preheated air fryer oven, set a drip pan underneath, and add 1 to 2 cups hot water to the pan. Roast until it reaches the desired doneness: 125°F (52°C) for rare, 135°F (57°C) for medium rare, 145°F (63°C) for medium, 155°F (68°C) for medium well, or 165°F (74°C) for well done. Adjust the forks when appropriate.
5. While the roast cooks, make the baste: Add the dried porcini mushrooms to 1 cup boiling water, or 2 cups boiling water if you would like to use the porcini broth for the gravy. Steep the mushrooms for 30 minutes, covered. Strain the broth and reserve the porcinis (for the gravy) and broth separately. Divide the broth into two equal portions, one for the baste and one for the gravy. Combine 1 cup broth with remaining baste ingredients. Let sit for 15 to 30 minutes to come to room temperature before using. Begin basting the roast during the last half of the cooking time and repeat every 10 to 12 minutes until the roast is ready.
6. Carefully remove the rotisserie forks and slide the spit out. Tent the roast with aluminum foil and let the meat rest for 20 minutes. Cut into ¼-inch slices and serve.

Rosemary Prime Rib Roast in Red Wine

Prep time: 10 minutes | Cook time: 2 hours | Serves 8 to 10

- 1 boneless prime rib roast, 4 to 5 pounds (1.8 to 2.3 kg)

RUB:

- 3 to 3½ tablespoons kosher salt
- 1 tablespoon finely chopped fresh rosemary
- 2 or 3 cloves garlic, minced
- 2 teaspoons freshly ground black pepper

BASTE:

- 1 cup Cabernet Sauvignon
- ½ cup low-sodium beef broth
- 1½ teaspoons soy sauce
- 1½ teaspoons Worcestershire sauce

1. To make the rub: Combine the rub ingredients in a small bowl and mix well. Use the salt to grind the garlic and rosemary together.
2. Run a long sword skewer through the center of the roast lengthwise to create a pilot hole. Run the rotisserie spit through the hole and secure with the forks. Balance as necessary.
3. Apply the rub to the roast. Cover with plastic wrap and set in a safe place at room temperature for 30 minutes (rotisserie spit and all).
4. To make the baste: Combine the baste ingredients in a small bowl and store in the refrigerator until ready to use. It will separate, so stir occasionally. Warm the baste for 30 seconds to 1 minute in the microwave before applying to the roast.
5. Select the ROAST function and preheat AIR FRYER to 400°F (205°C). Press ROTATE button and set time to 2 hours.
6. Place the roast on the preheated air fryer oven, set a drip pan underneath, and add 1 to 2 cups hot water to the pan. Baste intermittently during the last half of the cooking time, until it reaches the desired doneness: 125°F (52°C) for rare, 135°F (57°C) for medium rare, 145°F (63°C) for medium, 155°F (68°C) for medium well, or 165°F (74°C) for well done. The roast will shrink during cooking, so adjust the forks when appropriate.
7. Carefully remove the rotisserie forks and slide the spit out, and then set the roast on a large cutting board. Tent the roast with aluminum foil and let the meat rest for 15 to 20 minutes. Slice and serve.

Balsamic Chuck Roast

Prep time: 15 minutes | Cook time: 1 hour | Serves 8

- 1 chuck roast, 4 to 4½ pounds (1.8 to 2.0 kg)
- 1¼ teaspoons salt
- Marinade:
- 1 shallot, finely chopped
- 2 or 3 cloves garlic, minced
- 1½ cups tawny port
- ¼ cup beef broth
- 1½ tablespoons balsamic vinegar
- 1 teaspoon Worcestershire sauce
- 1 teaspoon chopped fresh thyme
- ¼ teaspoon salt
- ¼ teaspoon freshly ground black pepper

1. To make the marinade: Heat the olive oil in a saucepan over medium-low heat and cook the shallot for 3 minutes until translucent. Add the garlic and cook for 30 seconds. Increase the heat to medium-high and add the port. Stir thoroughly and cook for 1 minute. Add the remaining ingredients and simmer the sauce for 5 minutes, stirring occasionally. Remove from the heat and let cool for 10 to 15 minutes. Divide the mixture into two even portions, reserving one half for the baste and one for the marinade. Store in the refrigerator until ready to cook, then bring to room temperature before using.
2. Trim away excess fat from the outer edges of the chuck roast. Place the roast in a resealable plastic bag. Add half of the port mixture to the bag, making sure that all of the meat is well covered. Seal the bag and place in the refrigerator for 6 to 8 hours.
3. Remove the roast from the bag, discarding the marinade, and place on a large cutting board or platter. With kitchen twine, tie the roast into a round and uniform shape, pulling tightly. Start in the center and work toward the ends until it is tied into a solid round roast. This will take four or five ties. Run a long sword skewer through the center of the roast lengthwise to create a pilot hole. Run the rotisserie spit through the hole and secure with the forks. Balance as necessary. Season the roast with the salt and pepper.
4. Select Roast, set temperature to 400°F (205°C), Rotate, and set time to 1 hour. Select Start to begin preheating.
5. Once preheated, place the prepared roast with rotisserie spit into the oven. Set a drip tray underneath. Roast until it reaches the desired doneness: 125°F (52°C) for rare, 135°F (57°C) for medium rare, 145°F (63°C) for medium, 155°F (68°C) for medium well, or 165°F (74°C) for well done. Baste halfway through the cooking time, and repeat the process at least 3 times until the roast is done.
6. When cooking is complete, remove the roast using the rotisserie lift. Carefully remove the rotisserie forks and slide the spit out, and then set the roast on a large cutting board. Tent the roast with aluminum foil and let the meat rest for 15 to 20 minutes. Cut off the twine. Slice into ¼-inch slices and serve.

Port-Marinated Chuck Roast

Prep time: 15 minutes | Cook time: 1 hour | Serves 8

- 1 chuck roast, 4 to 4½ pounds (1.8 to 2.0 kg)
- 1¼ teaspoons salt
- ½ teaspoon freshly ground black pepper
- Marinade:
- 1 tablespoon olive oil
- 1 shallot, finely chopped
- 2 or 3 cloves garlic, minced
- 1½ cups tawny port
- 1½ tablespoons balsamic vinegar
- 1 teaspoon Worcestershire sauce
- 1 teaspoon chopped fresh thyme
- ¼ teaspoon salt
- ¼ teaspoon freshly ground black pepper

1. To make the marinade: Heat the olive oil in a saucepan over medium-low heat and cook the shallot for 3 minutes until translucent. Add the garlic and cook for 30 seconds. Increase the heat to medium-high and add the port. Stir thoroughly and cook for 1 minute. Add the remaining ingredients and simmer the sauce for 5 minutes, stirring occasionally. Remove from the heat and let cool for 10 to 15 minutes. Divide the mixture into two even portions, reserving one half for the baste and one for the marinade. Store in the refrigerator until ready to cook, then bring to room temperature before using.
2. Trim away excess fat from the outer edges of the chuck roast. Place the roast in a resealable plastic bag. Add half of the port mixture to the bag, making sure that all of the meat is well covered. Seal the bag and place in the refrigerator for 6 to 8 hours.
3. Remove the roast from the bag, discarding the marinade, and place on a large cutting board or platter. With kitchen twine, tie the roast into a round and uniform shape, pulling tightly. Start in the center and work toward the ends until it is tied into a solid round roast. This will take four or five ties. Run a long sword skewer through the center of the roast lengthwise to create a pilot hole. Run the rotisserie spit through the hole and secure with the forks. Balance as necessary. Season the roast with the salt and pepper.
4. Select the ROAST function and preheat AIR FRYER to 400°F (205°C). Press ROTATE button and set time to 1 hour.
5. Place the roast on the preheated air fryer oven and set an empty drip pan underneath. Roast until it reaches the desired doneness: 125°F (52°C) for rare, 135°F (57°C) for medium rare, 145°F (63°C) for medium, 155°F (68°C) for medium well, or 165°F (74°C) for well done. Baste halfway through the cooking time, and repeat the process at least 3 times until the roast is done.
6. Remove from the heat, carefully remove the rotisserie forks and slide the spit out, and then set the roast on a large cutting board. Tent the roast with aluminum foil and let the meat rest for 15 to 20 minutes. Cut off the twine. Slice into ¼-inch slices and serve.

Appendix 1 Measurement Conversion Chart

Volume Equivalents (Dry)	
US STANDARD	METRIC (APPROXIMATE)
1/8 teaspoon	0.5 mL
1/4 teaspoon	1 mL
1/2 teaspoon	2 mL
3/4 teaspoon	4 mL
1 teaspoon	5 mL
1 tablespoon	15 mL
1/4 cup	59 mL
1/2 cup	118 mL
3/4 cup	177 mL
1 cup	235 mL
2 cups	475 mL
3 cups	700 mL
4 cups	1 L

Volume Equivalents (Liquid)		
US STANDARD	US STANDARD (OUNCES)	METRIC (APPROXIMATE)
2 tablespoons	1 fl.oz.	30 mL
1/4 cup	2 fl.oz.	60 mL
1/2 cup	4 fl.oz.	120 mL
1 cup	8 fl.oz.	240 mL
1 1/2 cup	12 fl.oz.	355 mL
2 cups or 1 pint	16 fl.oz.	475 mL
4 cups or 1 quart	32 fl.oz.	1 L
1 gallon	128 fl.oz.	4 L

Temperatures Equivalents	
FAHRENHEIT(F)	CELSIUS(CAPPROXIMATE)
225 °F	107 °C
250 °F	120 ° °C
275 °F	135 °C
300 °F	150 °C
325 °F	160 °C
350 °F	180 °C
375 °F	190 °C
400 °F	205 °C
425 °F	220 °C
450 °F	235 °C
475 °F	245 °C
500 °F	260 °C

Weight Equivalents	
US STANDARD	METRIC (APPROXIMATE)
1 ounce	28 g
2 ounces	57 g
5 ounces	142 g
10 ounces	284 g
15 ounces	425 g
16 ounces (1 pound)	455 g
1.5 pounds	680 g
2 pounds	907 g

Appendix 2 The Dirty Dozen and Clean Fifteen

The Environmental Working Group (EWGis a nonprofit, nonpartisan organization dedicated to protecting human health and the environment Its mission is to empower people to live healthier lives in a healthier environment. This organization publishes an annual list of the twelve kinds of produce, in sequence, that have the highest amount of pesticide residue-the Dirty Dozen-as well as a list of the fifteen kinds ofproduce that have the least amount of pesticide residue-the Clean Fifteen.

THE DIRTY DOZEN	
The 2016 Dirty Dozen includes the following produce. These are considered among the year's most important produce to buy organic:	
Strawberries	Spinach
Apples	Tomatoes
Nectarines	Bell peppers
Peaches	Cherry tomatoes
Celery	Cucumbers
Grapes	Kale/collard greens
Cherries	Hot peppers

The Dirty Dozen list contains two additional itemskale/ collard greens and hot peppers-because they tend to contain trace levels of highly hazardous pesticides.

THE CLEAN FIFTEEN	
The least critical to buy organically are the Clean Fifteen list. The following are on the 2016 list:	
Avocados	Papayas
Corn	Kiw
Pineapples	Eggplant
Cabbage	Honeydew
Sweet peas	Grapefruit
Onions	Cantaloupe
Asparagus	Cauliflower
Mangos	

Some of the sweet corn sold in the United States are made from genetically engineered (GEseedstock. Buy organic varieties of these crops to avoid GE produce.

Appendix 3 Index

A

active dry yeast 94
agave nectar 18
agave syrup 14, 52, 53, 55, 75
all purpose flour 92
all-purpose flour 94, 95, 97
allspice 95, 100, 102, 104
almond 92
almond flour 18, 80, 90
almond milk 92
ancho chile 10
ancho chile powder 10
apple 103, 108
apple butter 103, 108
apple cider vinegar 104, 106, 108
apple pie filling 83
apple pie spice 79
Arborio rice 97
arugula 44, 49, 61, 64, 65, 66
arugula rocket 49
Asiago cheese 96
asparagus spears 38, 49, 92
avocado 95
avocado oil 33

B

baby back ribs 105
baby bok choy 29
baby greens 34
bacon 4, 14, 16, 25, 37, 38, 40, 45, 61, 65, 74, 78, 79
bacon drippings 25
baking powder 95, 96
baking soda 14, 15, 18, 19, 20
balsamic vinegar 110
banana 15, 18, 20, 52, 85, 86
barbecue sauce 100, 102, 106, 108
basil 10, 11, 12, 14, 25, 26, 48, 59, 62, 63, 69, 74, 76
basil leaves 14, 48, 62, 63
basmati rice 54
beans 106
beef 98
beef broth 110
beer 29, 79
bell pepper 14, 15, 16, 22, 25, 26, 32, 43, 44, 46, 51, 63, 66, 68, 69
Bibb lettuce 69
black beans 31, 43, 44, 63
Blackened seasoning 27
blueberries 81, 84, 85
blueberry pie filling 87
blue cheese 65
bone prime rib roast 104

B (continued)

Boston lettuce 69
bourbon 95, 103, 108
bratwurst 41
bread 92, 94, 95, 96, 97
bread crumbs 17, 25, 26, 27, 32, 33, 34, 36, 38, 47, 48, 49, 51, 54, 70, 74, 76, 78, 90, 92, 94, 95, 96, 97, 114
breakfast sausage 16
Brioche bread 55
broccoli 16, 44, 45, 46, 47, 54, 75, 90
broccoli florets 16, 47, 75, 90
brown mustard 40, 76
brown rice 31, 51, 57
brown sugar 100, 102, 103, 104, 105, 106, 107, 108
Brussels sprouts 36, 75
buffalo Mozzarella 48
buns 34, 37, 45, 68, 70
butter 92, 94, 95, 96, 97, 98, 100, 102, 103, 108
buttermilk 14, 18, 25, 33, 52, 53
butternut squash 46, 62, 65

C

cabbage 30, 32, 47, 69, 71
Cabernet Sauvignon 101, 109, 113
Caesar dressing 31
Cajun seasoning 33, 34
cake 95, 96
candied cherries 95
canola 14, 16, 18, 23, 25, 43, 44, 45, 48, 66, 84, 85, 89
capers 30, 48
cardamom 17, 91
carrot 46, 56, 70
cashew 98
cauliflower 95
cauliflower rice 95
cayenne 100, 101, 102, 103, 105, 107
cayenne pepper 24, 27, 30, 31, 32, 41, 45, 54, 68, 74, 75, 76, 77, 79, 81, 90
celery 46, 51, 57, 100, 102, 113
celery leaves 51
celery salt 100, 102
challah bread 56
Cheddar cheese 14, 16, 17, 18, 20, 41, 45, 57, 74, 78
cherries 95, 96
cherry cola 106, 108
cherry pie filling 85
chia seeds 53, 56
chicken 97, 98, 106, 108
chicken breast 7, 24, 27

chicken stock 97
chickpeas 47, 49
chili flakes 56, 75
chili powder 100, 101, 102, 103, 105, 107, 109
Chinese five-spice powder 29
chipotle peppers in adobo 106
chives 11, 17, 45, 47, 48, 71, 78, 89, 90
chocolate chips 18, 56
chocolate-hazelnut spread 84
chopped almonds 17, 51, 55
chopped hazelnuts 56
chorizo sausage 92
chuck roast 106, 110
cider vinegar 11, 15, 38, 41, 104, 106, 108, 113
cilantro leaves 39, 40, 45, 63, 72
cinnamon 95, 100, 101, 102, 107
cinnamon powder 15, 18, 53, 55, 56
coarse brown mustard 40
coarse-ground mustard 27
coarse salt 101, 104, 107
cocoa powder 54
coconut 11, 15, 18, 20, 51, 52, 53, 54, 55, 56, 57, 75, 80, 86, 89, 90
coconut chips 86
coconut extract 53
coconut flour 54, 86, 90
coconut flower 90
coconut milk 20, 52, 53, 55, 57, 86
coconut oil 18, 51, 53, 55, 56, 57, 75, 80, 86, 89
cod fillet 29
Colby cheese 83, 89
Colby Jack cheese 44
coleslaw mix 33
coriander 19, 22, 39, 45, 47, 68, 72
coriander seeds 22, 47
corn 92, 98, 103, 105
corn kernels 43, 51, 54, 68
cornmeal 18, 30, 33, 52, 83
corn puff cereal 98
cornstarch 23, 29, 47, 49
cornstarch slurry 47
Cottage cheese 74
cream cheese 19, 20, 40, 48, 71, 79, 81, 83, 85, 91
cream of celery soup 57
cream of onion soup 89
crescent roll 20
crumbled feta 68, 89
crumbled feta cheese 89
crushed crackers 89
crushed tortilla chips 78, 79
cubed brioche bread 17
cucumber 34

cumin 106
cumin powder 57, 74, 75, 76
cumin seeds 22, 47, 49, 83
curry leaves 19, 54
curry powder 26, 27, 41

D

dark chocolate 18, 56, 86
dark chocolate chips.................... 18, 56
dark rum 84
desiccated coconuts.................... 47
diced doughnuts 43
diced panatoes 49
Dijon mustard .... 10, 12, 40, 41, 44, 78 ,103 ,108
dill pickle juice 25
dill pickles 49
double cream 17
dried apricots 51
dried bread crumbs 70
dried cherries 55
dried cranberries 20, 53, 55
dried dill 25
dried dill weed 27
dried figs 55
dried parsley .... =9
dried parsley flakes 23, 79, 80
dried rosemary 74, 76, 79
dried thyme 25, 26, 29, 76, 94
dry mustard.................... 34, 55, 89
dry onion powder.................... 45
dry-roasted peanuts.................... 69
dumpling wrapper 71

E

egg.................... 14, 15, 16, 17, 18, 19, 20, 26, 27, 29, 30, 32, 33, 34, 39, 40, 46, 48, 52, 53, 55, 56, 62, 66, 69, 70, 74, 76, 77, 79, 80, 85, 87, 90, 92, 94, 96, 97, 114, 115
eggnog.................... 55, 96
eggplant.................... 48, 71, 76, 80, 114
enchilada sauce.................... 44, 114

F

fennel seed 107
fig 63
fine bread crumbs 25
fish sauce 69, 81
five spice powder 36
flank steak 39
flour 92, 94, 95, 96, 97
fontina cheese 62, 63, 64, 65
fresh basil leaves 14, 62, 63
fresh blueberries 81, 84
fresh chives 11, 45, 71, 78, 89
fresh cilantro 24, 45, 54, 63, 77
fresh cilantro leaves 45, 63
fresh dill 11
fresh figs 49

fresh Italian herbs 54, 55, 89
fresh jumbo shrimp 30, 31
fresh lemon juice 14, 30
fresh Mediterranean herbs 51
fresh parsley 92
fresh parsley leaves 45
fresh raspberries 84
fresh rosemary 107, 109
fresh rosemary leaves 62
fresh rosemary sprig 62
fresh sage 107
fresh thyme leaves 38, 64
fresh tuna steak 69
frozen bread dough 19
frozen puff pastry dough 87
full-fat milk 52, 83

G

garam masala 24, 83
garlic 10, 11, 12, 22, 23, 24,
25, 26, 27, 29, 31, 32, 33, 34, 36, 37, 38, 39, 41, 43, 44,
45, 46, 47, 48, 51, 54, 55, 56, 57, 60, 62, 63, 65, 68, 69,
71, 72, 74, 75, 76, 77, 78, 79, 80, 81, 83, 90, 92, 95, 97,
98, 100, 101, 102, 103, 104, 105, 106, 107, 108, 109, 110
garlic powder 95, 98, 100,
101, 102, 103, 105, 106, 107, 108
Garlic Tomato Pizza Sauce 5, 60, 61, 62,
63, 64
ginger 95, 97, 103, 108
ginger-garlic paste 83
ginger juice 97
goat cheese 15, 63, 77
gochujang 68
golden raisins 17
graham cracker 83
granola 98
grated Gruyère cheese 62
Greek seasoning mix 80
Greek yogurt 11, 22, 70, 90
green beans 25, 76
green chile pepper 72
ground almonds 26, 92
ground cloves 18, 52, 53,
55, 57, 95, 100, 101, 102, 107
ground veal 61
Gruyere cheese 79

H

half-and-half 17, 43, 57
Halloumi cheese 14
ham 100, 102, 103, 108
hamburger bun 69
ham cubes 77
hazelnut 84, 113
heavy cream 54, 57
hemp seeds 11
honey 94, 98, 100, 102
hot paprika 74, 76, 80, 89
hot sauce 24, 91

I

instant coffee granules 54
instant rice 44
Italian bread crumbs 36
Italian dressing 27
Italian parsley leaves 57
Italian seasoning 98

J

jalapeño 98
jalapeño pepper 98
jasmine rice 56, 83

K

kale 95
kale leaves 12, 78, 79
ketchup 103, 105, 106, 108
kosher salt 94, 95, 100,
102, 109

L

lamb 101, 107
lemon 92, 97, 104, 107
lemon juice 104
light brown sugar 85, 95
lime 96
lime juice 11, 15, 22, 23, 24,
31, 33, 69, 79
Lime wedge 96
lime zest 11
low-fat cream cheese 20
low-fat ranch salad dressing 25
low-fat sour cream 20
low-sodium beef broth 109
low-sodium ham 41
low-sodium whole-wheat bread 26
lump crabmeat 71

M

macaroni 55, 89
malty beer 29
mango 69
maple syrup 100, 102
Marinara Sauce 4, 10, 59
marshmallow 83
masala 24, 83
mayonnaise 95, 96
Mediterranean herb mix 75
Mediterranean seasoning mix 83
melted butter 95
methi 83
Mexican cheese 70
micro greens 45
milk 92, 94, 95, 96
millet 51, 57
mini hot dog 78
mini pretzel crisps 98
mint 39, 51, 64, 69, 72, 84
mirin 97
miso 29
mixed berries 11, 53
mixed lettuce 25

mixed peppercorns 30
molasses 106, 108
Mozzarella 97
Mozzarella cheese 97
multigrain rice 54, 56
mushroom 101, 109
mustard 105
mustard powder 106, 108
mustard seeds 19, 74, 75
mutton roast 104

N

No-Knead Pan Pizza Dough 64
nutmeg 92, 95, 96, 100, 102
nutritional yeast 10, 47, 48

O

oat bran 18
oats 14, 15, 20, 47, 51, 52, 53, 56, 57
Old Bay seasoning 92
old-fashioned oats 14, 51, 52, 53, 56, 57
olive oil 92, 97, 98, 101, 103, 104, 105, 109, 110
onion 97, 98, 105, 106, 108
onion powder 98, 101, 103, 105, 106, 107, 108, 109
orange 100, 102
orange extract 20
orange juice 100, 102
oregano 106
organic crescent roll dough 20

P

panatoes 94
pancake syrup 19
Paneer 57
panko bread crumbs 92, 94, 95, 96, 97
paprika 92, 94, 98, 100, 101, 102, 103, 104, 105, 107
Parmesan cheese 94, 97
parsley 92
parsley leaves 45, 51, 57
parsnips 46, 90
peanut 86
peanut butter 86
pear 92
peas 97
pecan 95, 96
pecan halves 77
Pecorino cheese 51, 77
Pecorino Romano cheese 76
pepperoni 60
pesto 38, 45
phyllo dough 92
pie crust 37, 85
pineapple 96
pineapple juice 15, 53
pine nuts 92
pink Himalayan salt 10, 11
pink salmon 34

piri-piri sauce 23
pizza dough 16, 43, 46, 59, 62, 65, 66, 84
pizza sauce 43, 66, 71
plain coconut yogurt 11
plain Greek yogurt 11, 22, 90
plain milk 14
plain yogurt 20, 72
plum 48, 63
poblano pepper 68
polenta 51
porcini powder 46
pork 100, 102, 107
pork belly 107
pork butt 100, 102
pork dust 40
pork liver 37
pork loin roast 107
pork tenderloin 37, 40
potato 92
potato chips 27, 74, 75, 77
powdered sugar 19, 20, 81, 91, 95
prime rib roast 109
Pro Dough 5, 59, 60, 61, 62, 63, 64
prosciutto 61, 63
pumpkin 98
pumpkin pie spice 53
pumpkin pie spice mix 53
pumpkin purée 15
pumpkin seeds 98
pure almond extract 91
pure lemon extract 91

Q

quick-cooking grits 17
quinoa 20, 51, 54, 56
quinoa flakes 20, 51, 56

R

Ragi 6, 83
raisins 17, 52, 85
ramekin 66, 86
Ranch dressing 45
raw honey 11, 12
red chili powder 89
red curry paste 39
red grapes 29
red pepper flakes 94, 97, 107
red snapper fillets 29
red wine 101, 109
refrigerated biscuit dough 95
rice 31, 34, 39, 44, 51, 54, 56, 57, 75, 80, 83, 90, 95, 97, 106, 113
rice flour 51, 57, 83
rice vinegar 34, 39, 80, 95
rice wine 34, 39, 75
rice wine vinegar 34, 39
ricotta cheese 46, 61, 64, 66, 91
rolled oats 15, 20, 52, 53

romaine lettuce 31, 69
rye flakes 20

S

saffron 45
salmon fillet 90
salsa 106
salted butter 84
self-rising flour 53
Serrano pepper 46
sesame oil 95
sesame-seed hamburger 70
sesame seeds 95
sesame sticks 98
shallot 104, 110
shelled pistachios 64
shrimp 92, 96, 97
Simple Pizza Dough 5, 59, 60, 61, 62, 63, 64, 65
skim milk 20
slivered almonds 52, 56
softened butter 15
soft goat cheese 15
sour cream 20, 83, 90
Southwestern seasoning 30
soy sauce 95, 97, 109
sparerib 103, 105
spears asparagus 92
spicy BBQ sauce 37
spinach 92
sprigs rosemary 37
spring roll sheets 47
spring roll wrapper 32
sriracha 23, 34
Sriracha sauce 95, 96
store-bought pie crust 37
store-bought variety 59
strawberries 15, 84
sugar 95, 96, 97, 100, 101, 102, 103, 104, 105
Sultanas 5, 57
summer squash 44, 64
sunflower seeds 18, 53
sushi nori 95
sweet chili sauce 96
sweetcorn 47
sweet corn bread 57
sweetened coconut 20
sweet paprika 24, 41, 76
sweet raisin bread 55
Swiss cheese 16

T

tahini 10, 11
tamari 47, 78
tamari sauce 78
tapioca flour 96
tarragon 30
tawny port 110
teriyaki sauce 22, 24
thyme 94, 101, 109, 110
thyme needles 46

tilapia fillet 33
toasted almonds 12
tofu 47
tomato 92, 97
tomato paste 68
tomato sauce 41, 97
top sirloin roast 101, 109
tuna 34, 69
turkey sausage 32
turmeric 12, 19, 22, 24, 31, 47, 51, 72, 77, 83
turmeric powder 19, 47, 51, 83

U

unsalted butter 94, 95, 97, 100, 102
unsweetened almond milk 10
unsweetened apple sauce 19, 52
unsweetened coconut flakes 56

V

vanilla 17, 18, 19, 20, 52, 53, 54, 55, 56, 57, 85, 86, 89, 91, 95
vanilla essence 18, 56
vanilla extract 95
Vanilla ice cream 84
vanilla paste 52
vegetable broth 106
vegetable oil 92, 105
vegetable stock 44

W

wet rub mixture 101, 109
wheat germ 53
whiskey 104
white vinegar 106
white wine 97
whole grain bread 41
whole milk 16, 94
whole-wheat flour 18, 33, 54
whole-wheat panko bread crumbs 32, 33, 34
whole-wheat pastry flour 15
wine vinegar 10, 11, 34, 39, 59, 105
wonton wrapper 71
Worcestershire sauce 96, 101, 104, 109, 110

Y

yellow cornmeal 18, 30, 52
yellow squash 15
yogurt 11, 20, 22, 26, 70, 72, 90

Z

zucchini 22, 26, 32, 43, 44, 46, 64, 66, 68, 76, 80

CLAUDIA J. CHANCY

Made in the USA
Middletown, DE
22 December 2022